TEACHING & LEARNING
in the New Millennium
KAPPA DELTA PI

Kappa Delta Pi Biennial 1998–2000

Teaching and Learning in the New Millennium reflects the Society's commitment to study issues and practices relating to the biennial theme. This volume is among the books that the Society commissions each biennium to explore critical issues in education in ways that develop new knowledge and new understandings.

Kappa Delta Pi, International Honor Society in Education, was founded in 1911 and is dedicated to scholarship and excellence in education. The Society promotes among its intergenerational membership of educators the development and dissemination of worthy educational ideas and practices, enhances the continuous growth and leadership of its diverse membership, fosters inquiry and reflection of significant educational issues, and maintains a high degree of professional fellowship.

The motto of the Society is Knowledge-Duty-Power.

So to teach that our words inspire a will to learn; so to serve that each day may enhance the growth of exploring minds; so to live that we may guide young and old to know the truth and love the right.

TEACHING & LEARNING
in the New Millennium
KAPPA DELTA PI

Edited by **Barbara D. Day**

KAPPA DELTA PI
International Honor Society in Education
Indianapolis, Indiana
1999

Direct all inquiries to the Director of Publications,
Kappa Delta Pi, 3707 Woodview Trace, Indianapolis, Indiana 46268-1158.

Editorial Team: Grant E. Mabie
Juli Knutson
Karen L. Allen
Michael P. Wolfe

Copy Editors: Nicholas Drake
Kenneth T. Henson
Thomas J. Buttery

Editorial Assistant: Nadia Ibrahim

Art Director: Karen L. Klutzke

Library of Congress Cataloging-in-Publication Data
Teaching and learning in the new millennium/Kappa Delta Pi; edited by Barbara D. Day.
    p. cm.
    Includes bibliographical references.
    ISBN 0-912099-36-4
    1. Education—Aims and objectives—United States. 2. Educational change—United
States. 3. Teaching—United States. 4. Learning. I. Title: Teaching and learning in the new
millennium. II. Day, Barbara, 1938– III. Kappa Delta Pi (honor society)

LA217.2 .T43 1999
370 .973—dc21
99-052741

CIP

Printed in the United States of America
99 00 01 02 03 5 4 3 2 1

Contents

Introduction

As the millennium approaches, we are surrounded by messages of apprehension coming from all directions. Whether it is the news media discussing the so-called "Y2K problem" or a millenarian preaching the Apocalypse, most of us have been hit by the millennium bug in one form or other. Though few of us are worried about cataclysms, virtually everyone has concerns over the Year 2000 glitch threatening to turn off our lights, delay our flights, and bring our economy to a halt—at least for a day or two. Many of these messages of impending doom are, of course, more a reflection of *fin de siècle* sentiment than real threats to our way of life. Still, the millennium does pose a deadline, if only an artificial one. The milestone gives us pause to think about where we are today, where we are going tomorrow, and where we will be in the future. Hence the Kappa Delta Pi theme of the 42nd biennium and the name of this new Society publication: *Teaching and Learning in the New Millennium.*

The anxiety surrounding the new millennium may indeed be a social phenomenon spurred by an increasingly media-saturated society. Yet people's fears of change are justified. We live in a rapidly changing society in which what is true today very likely will not be true tomorrow. A poignant example is the increased importance, range, and accessibility of the World Wide Web and the Internet. Five years ago, few of us knew the Internet existed, much less how to surf it. Hypertext Markup Language, otherwise known as HTML, the programming language of the Web, was in its infancy. Today, most of our schools have Internet access, and instructors are struggling to find useful and appropriate applications of the Web for instructional purposes. With the recent introduction of WebTV and the marketing of free computers with the purchase of Internet service, more and more of our students access the Web daily from home for entertainment and, at least occasionally, educational purposes. As educators, if we do not stay abreast of these vast changes, we will not be effective at accomplishing our mission. We must stay ahead of the curve and hone our skills so we can educate good citizens capable of living in and adapting to an ever-evolving world.

In the United States, it has been only ten years since the Charlottesville Education Summit brought national focus to public education. In the wake of that historic meeting in Virginia of U.S. President George Bush, state governors, and prominent educators, we must ask ourselves: Are we better able to prepare our students to meet the challenges of the 21st century? Have we made any progress on the six National Education Goals born from that summit? Looking back, it seems the main outcome of that assemblage was to open debate at national, state, and local levels on how public schools should achieve their mission. For some observers, the debate focused more on what that mission entailed exactly. To date, little consensus has been reached, but new trends and challenges have emerged.

Certainly, education reform remains a key issue throughout the United States and at all levels of government. Much discussion about reform centers on privatization of our public schools—whether through voucher systems, charter schools, or hiring "educational corporations" to run schools. New trends in assessment and account-ability for teachers and schools have resulted in many unforeseeable outcomes. During the 1990s, the push for national standards and national testing of skills gave way to testing at the state level. Yet, today, many educators fear linking student perfor-mance on skills-assessment exams with school funding and accreditation because it reduces teachers' effectiveness: Too much focus is placed on "teaching the exam." Still, new assessment measures of student learning are required to ensure that stu-dents gain the higher-order thinking skills necessary for problem-solving abilities in the new millennium.

The fast-paced change of world technology and our transition to an informa-tion-based society highlights the need for better mathematics, science, and technol-ogy education for children. Furthermore, we need to understand the implications of scientific research on how students are educated. New and evolving computer-assisted learning programs undoubtedly will change the classroom experience. In-deed, some classrooms already have been eliminated. Regardless of whether we maintain traditional classrooms, however, technology holds serious implications for institutional composition, instructional practices, and preparing children to func-tion as adults. The requirements of a high school education 20 years ago are no longer adequate to secure a living wage in today's global economy.

Demographic change under way in the United States indicates an increasingly diverse society in terms of class, ethnicity, and race. Though the economic boon of the 1990s has made individuals in the information industries incredibly rich, it has left behind many inner-city dwellers and blue-collar workers who relied on strength of body rather than strength of mind to earn a living. Surveys on U.S. wealth and poverty suggest that this division in wealth has disproportionately affected minority populations. Beyond the question of class, the rate of immigration to the United States continues to increase. Despite a focus in the media on migration from Latin America, newcomers arrive from all over the world. By the year 2010, demographers say, Span-ish will be the first language of many U.S. citizens. How will our schools handle this transformation? The U.S. education system and the thousands of teachers who serve it loyally *must* find new means to integrate multicultural education.

Teaching and Learning in the New Millennium examines the development of in-creased community involvement in public education and better public-private part-nership in the realm of education. Balancing the tide of commercial interests in U.S.

society, for example, is the need for media literacy among our children. As the fast-est-growing segment of the population with disposable income, children are exposed to incredibly sophisticated marketing. Whereas television and radio moguls have long recognized the benefits of directing commercial messages to young people, adver-tisers are becoming more and more cagey in marketing to them. These trends under-line the challenge for improved citizenship education among our students.

Within the United States, we must return to the early motivations for a public education system: to prepare and educate children to become functional adult citi-zens; to protect the ideals upon which the nation was founded; and to ensure that young people are prepared to participate fully in our democracy. Citizens of other nations must make similar demands of themselves and their schools.

To approach these challenges effectively, improved teacher education and prepa-ration are vital. The respect accorded the teaching profession 50 years ago has de-clined in the face of decreasing teacher salaries and increasing opportunities in other domains for intelligent youth. We must bring about reinvigorated respect—both sym-bolic and financial—to the teaching profession to attract these individuals. Further-more, we need greater teacher education and preparation to maintain the skills of existing educators in the onslaught of technological innovations. Many educators believe that educational partnerships are crucial to maintaining and improving the core skills of teachers.

To bring focus and understanding on these issues and to examine the next cen-tury of education, Kappa Delta Pi commissioned *Teaching and Learning in the New Millennium* to enlighten and provoke all readers—members as well as nonmembers, educators as well as noneducators. We asked outstanding educators to share their insights about our profession and the students who benefit from it, including our successes, failures, and new directions. All of the authors have contributed signifi-cantly to the field of education in a variety of ways, and all are recognized leaders in their areas of expertise.

In Chapter 1, I introduce the foremost trends in U.S. society and their potential impact on our education system. Approaching education through the lens of com-plex systems enables us to understand more fully the areas in which educators can make the most difference. Included in these trends are information-age transitions, public-private partnerships, education reform, governance and management issues, change agents, technology's impact, instructional practices, assessment and account-ability, and teacher education. The book's contributors address many of these topics in greater detail in subsequent chapters.

Michael Fullan explores reform and its impact at the policy level and at local levels of education in Chapter 2. He proposes that education reform is currently in a period of transition and that the next five years will be crucial to shaping the future of teaching and learning. From the policy level, Fullan asserts the need for improved assessment policies and, in particular, underscores teacher education and commu-nity involvement. At the local level, he proposes that schools allow public scrutiny as a means to ensure better accountability and performance. He outlines five external forces necessary for successful education reform: parents and community, technol-ogy, corporate connections, government policy, and the wider teaching profession.

Fullan concludes by asserting the need for simultaneous top-down and bottom-up reform strategies.

In Chapter 3, Bettye Caldwell explains implications of recent scientific research in brain development on how we educate young children. New understandings about brain-development processes focus on the importance of proper practices in early childhood education. She outlines five primary connections:

(1) Behavior provides the clearest window into the brain.

(2) Education about brain development is vital.

(3) Emphasis must be placed on the interconnectedness of development and experience.

(4) Increased creativity in education programming during the first three years of life is crucial.

(5) Individual differences must be respected.

Caldwell concludes by remarking that teachers have been doing things right all along and that, with increased understanding of brain development and emphasis on holistic learning in the early childhood years, education will be even more successful in the future.

In Chapter 4, Charles R. Coble calls for a return to the roots of teacher education, recalling a time earlier in this century when U.S. teacher colleges were an important segment of higher education institutions. He highlights the findings of recent state and national studies that emphasize the need for improved quality in teacher education and preparation. Moreover, he stresses the importance of public education to the economic well-being and civic consciousness of a democratic society. Coble outlines an ambitious program for successful university-school collaboration, including improved partnerships and a dismantling of the status quo in higher education.

James A. Banks challenges the current paradigm of citizenship education in Chapter 5. He asserts that current citizenship education is inadequate for our increasingly multicultural society and a world in which borders are growing more permeable. In addition, he proposes full integration of multiculturalism into our education system as key to forming good citizens. Banks conceptualizes multicultural education as consisting of five dimensions: (1) content integration, (2) knowledge-construction process, (3) prejudice reduction, (4) equity pedagogy, and (5) an empowering school and social structure. He concludes by outlining the consistent goals of multicultural education within the mission of U.S. schools: to develop thoughtful citizens who can function effectively in the world of work and in the civic community.

In Chapter 6, R. Freeman Butts examines the rancorous U.S. political debates over national standards and national testing that threatened to derail educational reform in the early 1990s. He outlines the major trends in the "free market approach to education reform," including parental rights, vouchers, privatization, and charter schools. Especially intriguing, he addresses partisan lines taken by Republicans and Democrats in the U.S. political system. Butts argues against free-market projects in educational reform, instead proposing greater study of civics and government to counteract leanings that threaten the very idea of public education as a foundation of U.S. democracy. He challenges educators to revive civics and government as the most formidable subjects in the curriculum—kindergarten through grade 12.

Assessment of student performance is vital to all great education programs. In Chapter 7, Tracie Y. Hargrove examines assessment and evaluation from an historical perspective to point the way for future practices. She analyzes the successes and failures of comprehensive accountability plans enacted in Kentucky, Tennessee, Texas, and North Carolina, and then outlines dichotomous trends in assessment nationally—constructivist instructional reform (more locally focused) versus measurement/ technical quality (state, district, and nationally focused). Hargrove offers three main characteristics of authentic and meaningful assessments: (1) a wide-ranging scope of sources for making an evaluation, (2) the involvement of many different voices to arrive at the final evaluation, and (3) a focus on the process of evaluation rather than the product. Finally, she puts forth two assessment models with characteristics for success.

In Chapter 8, William S. Palmer and David K. Pugalee note that increased emphasis on interactive processes in teaching English Language Arts necessitates new assessment measures of student learning. These educators provide an overview of current perspectives for language arts assessment, including standardized tests, authentic assessment, performance-based assessment, portfolio assessment, statewide literacy-assessment efforts, and national reading assessment. They then predict future perspectives for assessment. New instruments will attempt to measure a learner's critical-thinking ability, but standardized tests will still be used to document some student achievement. Greater emphasis will be placed on the use of bibliotherapy and narrative inquiry. Performance-based reading assessment will include strategies to measure reading within and across disciplines. Portfolio assessment will include more parental involvement. At state levels, reading assessment will become more extensive. Electronic literacy will be measured as well. Overall, English Language Arts will have to adapt to additional demands, particularly bridging the language gap in the multicultural classroom of the next millennium.

David Elkind focuses on three major obstacles to effective early childhood education in Chapter 9: (1) the futility of using reflective or logical analysis to teach young children, (2) the need to understand the transductive thinking of children, and (3) the fundamental curriculum priorities of young children. He then explores the implications of these obstacles for educating young children in math, science, and technology. The most of important of these are observing young children learning, encouraging young children's imagination and curiosity, and the value of engaging children's spontaneous motivation.

In Chapter 10, Hunter Ballew asserts that attainment of higher-order thinking by young people in math classes is the most critical challenge faced by that branch of the education community in the coming millennium. He calls on educators to go beyond "school math" and begin teaching higher cognitive skills needed for success in our rapidly changing world. Ballew rejects the current paradigm of math education, because it emphasizes procedure rather than concept. U.S. students, he argues, are not taught *how* to think mathematically. Ballew offers two concrete suggestions to remedy this gap: (1) provide favorable conditions for the development of cognitive strategies and (2) orchestrate classroom discourse to promote the investigation and growth of mathematical ideas.

Xue Lan Rong underscores educators' absolute need for technological training in Chapter 11. She believes teachers must develop skills necessary to negotiate the media-focused world. Social studies educators, for example, must teach media literacy so students will not be vulnerable to manipulation. Rong emphasizes electronic media literacy because it easily engages students, remains teachers' weakest skills area, and serves as *the* main source of information about social studies for young people. She then offers characteristics of a good media-literacy program: (1) teaching students to become informed and conscientious consumers; (2) teacher screening of multimedia to identify hidden agendas, discern bias, and examine historical inaccuracies; (3) helping students understand how the media affect their beliefs and values; and (4) involving students in an experiential learning process. Rong concludes by highlighting the role of media literacy in preparing reflective, competent, and concerned citizens living in a global and culturally diverse world.

Chapter 12 looks at the rapidity of technological development and its implications for learning in the new millennium. Dave Moursund presents a futuristic educational scenario from 2012, then shows how it is no mere science fiction but a likely development of information technology. He cites the current instructional uses of information technology in the K–12 curriculum as falling into three categories: (1) computer and information science, (2) problem solving or using computers as tools, and (3) computer-assisted learning or research. The educator showcases the weakness of computer information science in K–12 curricula as well as a lack of computer science knowledge among instructors. He notes that, since the introduction of microcomputers into the classroom more than 20 years ago, the focus has shifted to having students learn to use computers as tools. Moreover, despite rapid technological advancements in calculators and computers, teaching math has remained fundamentally the same. Moursund elaborates on two current goals for information technology education: (1) to make information technology an effective aid to accomplish the "traditional" goals of education and (2) to learn information technology as a method for problem solving. He says new technology standards and computer-literacy assessment tools must be developed. Moursund concludes by outlining three educational goals for the new millennium: (1) provide every student with lifelong opportunities to obtain a good education, (2) implement the best theory-based and practitioner-based ideas developed for improving education, and (3) help students gain effective levels of expertise over a wide range of disciplines.

The Epilogue focuses again on the implications that these many exciting challenges and trends have for educators today. I launch a charge for us to recommit ourselves to the preparation of well-rounded, humane citizens of a global community. *Teaching and Learning in the New Millennium* is Kappa Delta Pi's examination and vision for the future of education. As we embark on the 21st century, educators must seek better ways, develop better skills, and become better teachers for our children's futures. As members of an International Honor Society in Education, we must lead the way.

Barbara D. Day
President, Kappa Delta Pi

1

Participatory Education: A Proactive Approach to U.S. Education in the 21st Century

By *Barbara D. Day*

As society enters the new millennium, perhaps the most elusive and certainly the most debated question in the teaching profession is, "What is the purpose of education?" This question is not new. For at least 3 million years, humans have been engaged in knowledge acquisition in a cultural context. Our ancestors were concerned with teaching one another about hunting-and-gathering techniques, dependable shelter construction, and the development of rituals and customs that created a common bond. Centuries later, Greeks such as Socrates and Plato debated the purpose of education on a philosophical level, suggesting that students have existing knowledge and untold potential that educators should use as building blocks instead of forcing information upon them. By holding this philosophical approach as a guiding torch toward envisioning the future of education, questions about the basic purposes underlying education must be reconsidered. Do we want to make changes that promote diversity and the unique qualities of individuals, or do we want to superimpose control and uniformity of content that extinguishes creativity and ignores individual differences? Do we want an educational system in which teachers point and show the path toward learning or a system in which students are drilled on basic skills for test-taking purposes?

Like many people worldwide, United States citizens sense excitement in anticipation of the approaching millennium. A collective sense exists that those of us experiencing the turn of a century have a special opportunity and a deep responsibility to generate changes that will profoundly impact future generations. What will life look like in the next 100 years—the next 1,000 years? What forces are moving us toward a more global society? Consider these anticipated changes (Oliver 1999):

• The world's population will increase from more than 5 billion people in 1994 to approximately 8 billion people in the year 2020.

• The development of a global culture will include greater privatization and deregulation to meet consumer demands for the same selection of products. Economic bodies, such as the European Union, will dominate political units.

• The world will become even more mobile, with more than one-fifth of the population traveling or migrating annually. Larger numbers of cultures will be dispersed and shared throughout the world, creating the potential for global citizenship.

• Telecommunication and broadcast technologies will continue to connect populations worldwide instantaneously. Though a majority of people will remain close to their birth origins, most will be impacted by the global media.

• Intelligent technologies will continue to replace the need for human workers in machine-related jobs, ranging from factories to farmers to computer-generated products.

Education is no exception to the excitement and speculation of life in the next millennium. Numerous initiatives focused on improving U.S. education have been enacted, ranging from the Goals 2000: Educate America Act (1994) to statewide reform programs. Whether one agrees or disagrees with attempts to create a more effective educational system, they are evidence of our society's sincere concern that public education must be better prepared to meet the changing needs of the next century. The call for change is not new. Since the inception of compensatory education in the United States, there has been a steady clamoring for changes to improve the quality of our educational system. These calls for change are directly related to the purpose of education, which has been altered many times in our history.

There continue to be divergent camps concerning the purpose of education and the types of changes needed to ensure a quality education for each child. Generally, policy makers, parents, educators, and society at large agree that children should learn some basic information that will enable them to participate meaningfully in the world. Yet the percentage of emphasis on "the basics" in contrast to other facets of learning, such as participatory instructional methods and the importance of teaching children how to participate responsibly and cooperatively in society, continue to cause confusion about the purpose of education. Most likely, the needs of people living in the new millennium will change more rapidly than during previous centuries. Therefore, conceptualization of the purpose of education for the 21st century must be flexible, diverse, and adaptable to change. Technological expertise, critical-thinking skills, problem-solving abilities, and the capacity to use and manage technology creatively will be important to successful participation in the emerging global economy and community of the next millennium (Banathy 1991; Reigeluth and Garfinkle 1994; Schlechty 1990; Schlechty and Cole 1991).

THEORETICAL FRAMEWORK

During the past 30 years, scientists have learned that changes are not necessarily linear (Capra 1996). When a change occurs, it may move back and forth between its former state and the state of becoming. Or change may occur unexpectedly. This new understanding of change stems from nonlinear scientific theories, one of which is called complex systems theory. Complex systems theory examines the world as an open, nonlinear system that exchanges information, matter, and energy with its surroundings (Fleener and Pourdavood 1997; Fullan 1993; Gleick 1987; Prigogine and Stengers 1984). In constructivist terms, the open, complex system experiences a continuous and inseparable dialogue with the environment. Likewise, the structural components within this organizational system interact with one another. These processes or interactions are inherently impossible to control and appear unpredictable and chaotic (Kauffman 1995; Fleener and Pourdavood 1997; Gleick 1987; Prigogine and Stengers 1984). For example, if a new teaching strategy is introduced into the educational system, a hundred teachers will use it in a hundred different ways.

Envisioning our educational system as an open, complex system may be more challenging than the linear perspectives of the past but also more realistic, because all systems constantly experience changes in an infinite number of ways. In the past, interpretation of systems in linear, behavioristic terms was an important virtue, because they could generally be taken apart and put together again. To wit, the pieces added up. Nonlinear systems have a way of changing the rules for understanding systems (Gleick 1987). This observation is important in relation to systems change in U.S. education. The more traditional, modern view of educational reform is linear and comfortable. Students attend school, learn the basics, and then are tested on the information taught. If they pass the test, they are considered successful. However, the concept of systems thinking implies a connectedness between relationships and interactions within an overall context not necessarily linear or predictable. From a systems viewpoint, the essential properties are of the whole rather than the independent parts. In other words, organisms, humans, and organizational systems such as U.S. education are defined by their wholeness. If the interactions or relationships of the whole are destroyed, the isolated elements do not maintain the identity of the whole (Capra 1996). This type of systems thinking has caused a revolution in the natural sciences that is slowly making its way into the social sciences.

Those of us preparing for the turn of the century have an extraordinary opportunity to examine the role of change in education through systems thinking, which may impact the purpose and implementation of public education. Indeed, our national and world community may be especially primed for substantial change. During the past 500 years, for example, profound global shifts have occurred near the turn of each century that resulted in changes altering the course of history. The Age of Enlightenment at the turn of the 18th century included Newton's advances in understanding gravity and calculus. The birth of the modern era at the turn of the 20th century came about through the innovative work of people such as Einstein, Freud, Picasso, Stravinsky, and Darwin. We are in a unique position of not only preparing for the dawn of a new century but also the beginning of a new millennium! What current characteristics of our society will cause global shifts? Think about how different the year A.D. 2000 is from the year A.D. 1000. What will it be like to live during A.D. 3000? The possibilities for changes that will occur during the next 100 or 1,000 years are staggering.

STRUCTURAL SYSTEMS

By examining U.S. education through the lens of complex systems, an ecological approach can be taken that recognizes the relationships and interactions of the

people, policies, and structural components that, together, define the basic context and principles of our educational system. Therefore, systems change will be central to this chapter's vision of education in the next century. To accomplish this task, we will build on successful elements of the 20th-century educational system, based on what we know through the results of research and practical application. Several key areas of our educational system will be examined in this discussion, including:
- the foundation shift from the Industrial Age to an information-based society;
- private-public partnerships;
- centralized versus decentralized school system approaches;
- governance and management issues;
- the role of change agents;
- the impact of technology;
- curriculum and the role of assessment;
- arts education; and
- the role of higher education.

Foundation Shift: From the Industrial Age to an Information-Based Society

The shift from the Industrial Age mentality of the 20th century toward the information-based society of the future provides the backdrop for structural changes in U.S. education. The assumed relationship between a successful public education system and the economic well-being of the United States will continue to be a primary catalyst for educational reform. Before discussing this relationship further, however, a caution must be voiced. Economic survival should not be the sole purpose of education. Love of learning and the intrinsic rewards gained through knowledge acquisition are just as important to the overall well-being of any society's populace. Figure 1.1 on page 5 presents a glimpse of some of the changes we are already experiencing in the transition from the Industrial Age society to the information-based society.

Changes should not be expected to happen quickly, especially in the field of education—the factory model has become deeply embedded in the service-delivery structure of education (Carlson 1995). For example, in a recent study on preservice teacher-class interactions, Fry and Fleener (1997) found that models of education based on managerial metaphors focus on control and authoritative, adult-centered approaches to teaching and learning. Though preservice teachers in this study stated that creating caring relationships with students was their primary goal in the classroom community, the results indicated control of students as the dominant factor in teacher-student interactions. This finding represents the deep-seated nature of the factory model in educational practices. Such control-based environments may perpetuate effects detrimental to students and staff members, including discriminatory attitudes toward people with disabilities, minorities, and low socioeconomic groups; dehumanization of students resulting in impersonal, product-oriented classrooms; narrow expectations for curriculum content and student-achievement levels; and a focus on basic skills rather than invention and innovation, wherein the teacher is a facilitator of interaction (Fry and Fleener 1997). Thus, a shift from the Industrial Age

Figure 1.1

Industrial Age Society	Information-Based Society
Family paradigm centered around nuclear family model	Movement toward single-parent families
Linear communication systems	Networking and global communication systems
Family-owned business and later bureaucracies	Megacorporations focused on team planning and implementation
Processes are centered around energy to produce material goods	Processes are centered around intelligent use of technology to produce information
Our physical strengths are extended through machines	Our intellectual abilities are extended through cybernetic technology
Technologies are dominated by manufacturing, engineering, physical inventions	Technologies are focused on organizing and storing information, communicating, and system planning
Societal focus is centered around nationalism	Societal focus is centered on a growing global consciousness

(Adapted from Banathy 1991; Reigeluth and Garfinkle 1994)

model to an information-based model will require less emphasis on control in our education system and greater emphasis on responsive, mutually participatory interactions.

Greater numbers of people prepared to manipulate information and develop new understandings through critical-thinking skills and creative capacities will be a vital part of the shift toward an information-based society (Banathy 1994; Schlechty 1990). Some researchers use the term "knowledge work" to refer to the ability to use ideas and symbols mentally to produce purposeful results (Schlechty 1990), suggesting that the majority of U.S. citizens will need to be capable of knowledge work to maintain current living standards and compete in the future global economy. For example, only 2 percent of U.S. workers currently farm, yet the field of agriculture today produces more than when half the population farmed, due to improved techniques and more sophisticated equipment (Schlechty 1990). This example provides insight about the shift from the machinery and muscle power mentality of the Industrial Age (how to operate a tractor) to an emphasis on the management and use of knowledge of the information-based age (creating strategies to improve the productivity of a tractor).

Businesses and labor leaders already have begun to recognize the important benefits of a workforce prepared to do knowledge work. Roughly 44 percent of the labor force will be service workers during the first part of the new century. They will be responsible for collecting, analyzing, synthesizing, structuring, and retrieving information for companies. The composite of technological knowledge used in the early 1990s will represent only 1 percent of the knowledge available in 2050. Rapid demands for greater quantities of more complex information have precipitated changes in the business world with implications for education (Bell and Graubard 1997; Oliver 1999). A few provocative changes under development include:

  • smart cards, or multifunctional chip cards, in which information can be stored and processed for use as bank cards, health cards, Social Security cards, driver's licenses, and even keys to houses and cars;

  • sensors to mediate the physical world of the customer and electronic devices, such as smart-courier boxes whose "skin" adjusts to changing shipping conditions; and

  • knowbots, or intelligent machines, that will operate without human supervision, including anticipation of needs such as replacing thinning tires on your car.

As corporations move toward a greater emphasis on knowledge work, many have downsized, due in part to technological advances. For example, 94 percent of 2,000 corporate executives from the world's leading industrial nations reported a permanent reduction in their workforce in a 1995 survey (Education Commission of the States 1997). In what ways will the shift from the factory model to an information-based society affect U.S. education? How are the private and public sectors preparing for these shifts? What changes in governance will better enable education to prepare students for the demands of an information-based society?

Private-Public Partnerships

One response to these questions has been increasing involvement in educational reform by business leaders across the United States. One coalition of top corporate executive officers, for instance, made a ten-year commitment to improve education in their respective states after a call for action by the Business Roundtable and federal leaders in the early 1980s. In 1983, President Ronald Reagan established the Private Sector Initiatives program, which provided federal funding in support of school-business partnerships. By the late 1980s, organizations such as the National Association of Partners in Education (NAPE) were established to support partnerships between schools and businesses (Hopkins and Wendel 1997; Sipple, Miskel, Matheney, and Kearney 1997). Such private-public partnerships have the potential to evoke powerful change (Sipple et al. 1997). However, the potential for promoting self-serving interests that are not beneficial for students can be a negative aspect of such partnerships.

Mutual participation can address such concerns about business-school partnerships. Research by Mann (1984; 1987) identified four components of truly reciprocal partnerships: (1) a coordinating structure; (2) multiple purposes; (3) multiple players; and (4) stability. Hopkins and Wendel (1997) stated that only 17 percent of the partnerships examined by Mann had all four of these features—which suggests that people developing schools and educational systems must carefully delineate roles and responsibilities to ensure mutually beneficial relationships. More recent studies reveal an increased integration of these four components in successful business-school partnerships. Studies conducted in the 1990s have estimated that at least 65 percent of U.S. public schools have partnerships with the business community and that 33 states have affiliates with NAPE (Hopkins and Wendel 1997).

Examples of successful business-school partnerships currently being implemented include (Hopkins and Wendel 1997):

• reverse apprenticeships in which students take innovative ideas to businesses or businesses bring problems to students to solve (computer technology supports this interactive partnership);

• training on similar thinking strategies to help teachers, students, and community members learn ways to solve common problems through combined resources;

• corporate grants to individual schools or the creation of corporate education divisions within companies such as the IBM Educational Systems Division;

• school-partnership councils with multiple partners that collaborate through monthly meetings;

• curriculum models in which partnerships are organized around the expertise or the interest of the business and match objectives according to subject areas, curriculum departments, or grade levels; and

• coalition-based models in which a group of educators and business partners meet and develop a specific project that will meet a community need.

Centralized versus Decentralized School Systems

The Education Commission of the States (1997, 8) has noted, "The dominant education governance structure in this country is hierarchical and bureaucratic, designed to resist change and promote stability . . . [which] may be its undoing." The bureaucratic, hierarchical structure of today's educational system was established between 1890 and 1920 to create a centralized decision-making power—school boards and superintendents—designed to produce an efficient, ordered society. This model limited public involvement to the election of school board members and insulated policy makers from the demands of daily operations (Snauwaert 1993). Though this centralized model generally served the needs of the 20th-century educational system, current trends suggest the need for a shift toward decentralization. Figure 1.2 on page 8 outlines examples of proposed reform movements during the past two decades and their relationship to decentralization.

A shift toward decentralization innately implies a shift toward a more participatory style of governance. Though there may be other approaches to decentralization or centralization of school structuring, we will examine three areas currently receiving widespread attention: (1) privatization through charter schools, vouchers, and home schooling; (2) governance and management through school-based councils; and (3) the impact of technology.

The present mixture of support and dissatisfaction with public schools has serious implications for the future. A 1997 telephone survey of 900 college professors of education reported 95 percent agreement that public education is our nation's most critical democratic institution and should be protected at all costs (Farkas, Johnson, and Duffett 1997). In contrast, more than half of voters participating in a 1996 poll felt that the current public education system needed a complete overhaul and that U.S. citizens should look outside the public system to improve the quality of education. Of those polled, 27 percent felt that home schooling and vouchers for private and parochial schools should be given an opportunity to succeed as alternatives to public education (Education Commission of the States 1997). The difference between these two perspectives may be evidence of the "cartel syndrome," wherein those involved in operating the system are having trouble going beyond the authoritative model of the past, while the general populace understands that the parameters of the system may need to be altered.

Charter schools. Based on state legislation requirements, charter schools offer additional options for families by permitting local communities to receive public funds to operate independent schools. A sponsor—usually a local school district,

Figure 1.2

Movement	Catalyst for Change	Result of Movement	Centralized or Decentralized Responses
Report: *A Nation at Risk* (NCEE 1983)	Risk of U.S. losing place in global, political, and economic order due to eroded educational foundation	Increased emphasis on: accountability of student achievement; teacher certification standards; higher graduation standards; and proposals for merit pay and salary increases for teachers	Centralized response emphasizing bureaucratic control
School-Choice Movement	A feeling that hierarchical, bureaucratic school governance undermines autonomy and the professional nature of teachers	A laissez-faire choice system based on free-market competition	Decentralized
School-Based Management	A belief that decision making should be shifted from the school board and central office to teachers, parents, principals, community members, and students at individual schools	School-level autonomy and participatory decision	Decentralized

state-level authority, or public university—has the role of public overseer. The focus of charter schools is diverse: some emphasize the basics; others focus on small, nurturing environments with close student-teacher contact; and still others use technology to permit students to study off-site (Williams 1994).

Minnesota was the first state to pass charter-school legislation in 1991. By 1998, a full 30 states had passed charter legislation, funding 750 operational charter schools serving more than 150,000 students (Nathan 1996; U.S. Department of Education 1997). This growing public interest in charter schools prompted the U.S. Congress to authorize funds to study their impact, amending in 1994 the Elementary and Secondary Education Act. The first-year report of this study, sponsored by the U.S. Department of Education (1997), revealed some interesting findings:

• Charter schools are small compared to typical public schools. About 60 percent of the 225 charter schools participating in the study enrolled fewer than 200 students, compared with 16 percent of other public schools.

• Most charter schools are newly created. More than 56 percent of the charter schools were created as a result of charter legislation. The remaining ones were conversions of preexisting public schools (32.5 percent) or preexisting private schools (11.1 percent).

• Charter schools serve, on average, a slightly lower proportion of students with disabilities in the majority of states.

• Charter schools have, on average, a racial composition roughly similar to state-wide averages or a higher proportion of students of color in some states.

• Charter schools serve, on average, a lower proportion of limited-English-proficient students in the majority of states.

• Charter schools enroll approximately the same proportion of low-income students that public schools do.

Vouchers. School vouchers involve the payment of state or federal money to parents of children in private schools, including religion-affiliated schools, to offset educational expenses. Proponents of school-voucher programs choose vouchers over public schools for three reasons: (1) public schools have a set enrollment based on geographic areas, so they have no incentive to improve the quality of education; (2) if a family with a modest to low income is dissatisfied with public schools, parents have no options for opting out of the system and, therefore, there is little incentive to improve the quality of education; and (3) maximum freedom of choice can be offered through vouchers, which will improve the quality of education. Detractors, of course, object to any plan for public funding of church-based education as a violation of the separation of church and state.

Home schooling. From 1850 to 1970, most children were not educated at home by their parents. However, in the late 1960s and early 1970s, home schooling began to emerge as a viable option for families concerned with values, safety, and the quality of education. In 1986, an estimated 120,000 to 260,000 children were being educated at home. In many ways, home schooling supports tenets considered "best practices" by many educators. For example, home schooling is usually learner-centered, respectful of personal values and histories, and supportive of experimental and natural curiosity toward learning. The main disadvantage is cited as a lack of opportunities to socialize with other children, which parents must actively compensate through other group activities in the community (Williams 1998).

Governance and Management

Changes in management are an integral part of decentralization. Many scholars are emphasizing the need for participatory leadership at all levels, including with students, teachers, district administrators, and parents. In an information-based society, schools must be managed from a visionary perspective with purpose and values that support the ever-changing needs of all participants. This approach to management implies a system in which teachers and parents assume leadership roles, students and their needs remain central to the purpose of the school program, and administrators see themselves as leaders among leaders who rely on mutually respectful governance (Schlechty 1990; Snauwaert 1993).

Recent reform efforts include aspects of restructuring that reflect a mixture of traditional approaches (for example, programs that reinforce the Industrial Age hierarchical pyramid of management) and innovative changes (an emphasis on joint school decision-making councils). Attempts of governance decentralization are especially evident at state and local levels where joint decision making by local school district administrators, principals, teachers, and parents is being encouraged. How can governance changes be promoted most effectively? What are the benefits of participatory governance?

Contrast the following two approaches to governance-management changes. In 1990, the Kentucky Education Reform Act was enacted, mandating the development of school-based decision-making councils. This requirement had a tenuous beginning, perhaps due to the fact that state law dictated a change in governance, coupled with lack of training and inexperience on the behalf of staff members and parents (Kannapel, Moore, Coe, and Aagaard 1992). Studies indicate that, when a state law dictates system-wide changes, a sense of powerlessness filters through the system, causing resistance and confusion (Aagaard, Coe, Moore, and Kannapel 1994; Smith, Rhodes, and Jensen 1994). For example, one five-year longitudinal study in four rural-Kentucky school districts examined the extent of shared decision making during the process of establishing school-based decision-making (SBDM) councils. Of the four districts studied, only one school voted to begin SBDM during the first year. The other three districts imposed a forced decision on schools as required by the state law. Two years later, resistance to change persisted, and only 10 of the 20 schools in all four districts had begun SBDM councils.

By comparison, a five-year case study (Wertheimer and Zinga 1997) investigated a district-wide school-reform effort in Pittsburgh, Pennsylvania, in which there was no legislative mandate or top-down decision. Schools were encouraged but not mandated to participate in this system-wide technology project funded by the National Science Foundation. The ideological basis of the project implementation was constructivist, encouraging: mutual participation at all levels; ideas to be implemented by the people who created them; open access to resources; and empowerment and creativity at all levels of the organizational system. By the project's fifth year, the response was overwhelming, as evidenced by 41 of the 69 eligible schools applying for funding. School-district staff members reported a sense of joint empowerment as district administrators, school principals, and individual teachers chose to participate in this project.

Demands for changes in the form of legislative mandates and voluntary initiatives will continue in the future. The question is how to respond responsibly to these experiences. Changes in governance may require educators to reach beyond traditional, control-centered models toward greater decentralization through participatory decision making.

Some school districts addressing the needs of inner-city schools have begun to implement initiatives that include decentralizing governance systems. In Wisconsin, Ohio, and Puerto Rico, for example, private-school voucher programs are being used. In Maryland, Connecticut, and Wisconsin, district operations have been privatized. In other areas of the country, urban districts are exploring options to break large districts into smaller units (Education Commission of the States 1997). These school districts may provide guidance for decentralization by sharing the experiences they encounter when incorporating initiatives into the factory model and adjusting them through the constructivist cycle until a viable new approach is developed.

The Role of Change Agents

Each person interacting with the educational system is a change agent. Students, parents, administrators, policy makers, community members, and teachers all have a critical role in the success or failure of our educational system. Banathy (1991) described value systems as the means by which society shapes ethical norms and creates new images of sociocultural characteristics. Thus, belief and value systems of individual change agents become the contextual environment for change. Research has shown that oppressive, forced changes basically stifle creativity and disempower change agents (Clune 1993). The goal of education then becomes a "filling of the vessel" with product-oriented expectations that frequently omit recognition of diversity of family and cultural heritages as well as differences in learning styles, personal interests, and aspirations. Fullan (1993) suggested that the only effective method of enacting changes in education is to create a context that enables and stimulates people to consider personal and shared visions while developing skills through practice over time. Therefore, implementation of changes in U.S. education during the next millennium will require a shift in emphasis from an authoritative-leadership model to a participatory decision-making model. Change agents will need to feel encouraged to think and behave differently from the status quo of the past.

Change agents often have multiple and sometimes conflicting roles in the change process. For example, teachers may be interested in the idea of portfolio assessment but cling to traditional assessment methods as the final word. Parents are sometimes the leaders of innovative change and other times fully withdrawn from the change process (Aagaard et al. 1994; Kannapel et al. 1994). The multiplicity of roles for individuals or groups of individuals in the change process is consistent with postmodernism and complex systems theory, which recognizes uncertainty and multiplicity as natural (Burbules 1996; Kauffman 1995; Prigogine and Stengers 1984; Stone 1992). Therefore, a mixture of traditional and nontraditional approaches by the same agents or groups of agents should be expected.

How can the potential of change agents be enhanced during the new millennium? Further investigation of individual creativity in organizational systems may provide strategies to help answer this question. Researchers have found that individual creativity and innovation in organizational systems are inherently connected (Amabile 1988; Schoenfeldt and Jansen 1997; Slabbert 1994; Tesluk, Farr, and Klein 1997). Furthermore, creativity in organizations is a function of individual creative behavior as well as group and organizational culture characteristics (Schoenfeldt and Jansen 1997). Individual qualities such as self-motivation, persistence, curiosity, and an affinity for problem solving promote the overall success of organizational systems. In contrast, qualities such as inflexibility, pessimistic attitudes, external motivations such as money, and lack of training contribute to serious problems in organization (Amabile 1988; Ebert 1994; Tesluk et al. 1997).

Proposed changes undergo many alterations before moving on to the next stage of integration into the open, complex system (Kauffman 1995). Creativity is essential to this part of the change process, because the more options a system can generate, the more likely the change will occur (Amabile 1988; Capra 1996; Schoenfeldt and Jansen 1997; Woodman, Sawyer, and Griffin 1993). Qualities in organizational climates that support creativity include: freedom of choice; a sense of control over one's work and ideas; sufficient resources and time; an atmosphere that supports experimentation; recognition of success; a sense of challenge; and an urgency about work-related tasks (Amabile 1988; Schoenfeldt and Jansen 1997; Tesluk et al. 1997; Woodman et al. 1993). Conversely, inappropriate reward systems, little regard for innovation, constraints about work scopes, poor management, and an overemphasis on status quo are reported as inhibitors of creative environments (Amabile 1988). As we move into the next century, educators must foster more creativity to meet future generations' changing needs.

The Impact of Technology

Technology will continue to be a dramatic catalyst for change (Burbules and Callister 1996; Oliver 1999). In the past two decades alone, computer usage has increased at a staggering pace, changing numerous aspects of life, including methods for information dissemination, communication systems, and even the way we conduct banking and shopping. Libraries, textbooks, maps, reference materials, and college coursework can already be accessed with a few clicks of the computer mouse. As we look toward the new millennium, an increasing number of families, businesses, and educational entities will become even more dependent on computers.

Though many people are skeptical of technology and globalization, it is important to note that these changes are not designed to create moral dilemmas or to undermine past traditions. Technology simply exists, and, through its presence, instant, global understandings are born that profoundly affect our lives. How will these changes affect the structure and implementation of education in the 21st century? Will technological advances make time and place irrelevant? Will it even be necessary to have teachers in classrooms? If there are no classrooms, how will children learn the social skills necessary to live in a community of peers? How will children learn and practice the basic premises of democracy if they are not participating in a regular group activity during their development (Education Commission of the States 1997)? To incorporate technology in our educational system successfully during the next millennium, we must examine the potential changes in the current system's structure, classroom interactions, and parent and community involvement.

Structural changes. The influx of technology will present a mixture of benefits and challenges concerning the provision of educational services (Scully 1995). Changes in how classes are offered have already expanded to include computer courses in higher education and even some charter schools for high school students. College and university students can be anywhere in the world and log on to the Internet any time, day or night, to complete assignments or converse with experts via the World Wide Web. Whereas high school classes via computer are not prevalent, it may be only a short time before high school courses can be offered through computer technology. This change raises questions about the role of local schools in relation to individual students, enforcement of state standards, and issues concerning state and even national boundaries for tuition and accreditation purposes, grading systems, enrollment processes, and transfer procedures. However, existing structures do provide insight in accommodating this systems change. For example, many states have combined independent colleges and universities into one large system. Considerations for grading systems and tuition have already been addressed and policies developed. As course offerings through computer links and distance learning become more prevalent, existing statewide systems can provide models for addressing issues that traverse state and national boundaries. However, it will require a willingness to revise traditional educational-system processes. Public education may need to let go of old "turfdoms" as the focus shifts to course offerings rather than schools.

Classroom interactions. One advantage of courses taken by computer may be increased individualization according to the student's unique abilities (Reigeluth and Garfinkle 1994). For example, one third-grade student might be working on addition computation, another on multiplication tables, and another on problem-solving activities during the same block of time for math lessons. Students could work at their own pace until they achieve mastery of the subject matter rather than be forced to adhere to the learning pace of other students. Students could use software programs or access information via the Web, according to their learning-style preferences and interests.

Computer usage could enable students to be better equipped to create independent solutions. Burbules and Callister (1996) provided some interesting insights regarding the potential impact of computers on the learning process. They suggest a careful examination of methods for using hypertext to promote a dialogic atmosphere in which the learner is actively engaged in constructing knowledge. The influence of hypertext on how information is organized may require changes in conceptualizing educational activities. In traditional methods, the information-gathering process is fairly linear and sequential. For example, a person reads a unit of text before going to another; in hypertext, links to new information may "hopscotch" from one topic to another according to a word or phase. A student looking for information on the U.S. Civil War may start with Abraham Lincoln, then move to Kentucky history, then to Jefferson Davis, and then to Robert E. Lee—all in a matter of minutes. This process is nonlinear in nature and may require assignments to be broader in focus. In addition, students may need longer periods of time to weed out pertinent information. Furthermore, the instantaneous nature of hypertext links can offer students opportunities for greater depth when learning about a particular topic. The seamless shifting from topic to topic can broaden the playing field for information. However, a caution is given: teachers may want to place parameters on Web searches, so that students avoid becoming fragmented in their efforts and lost in the vastness of cyberspace hyperlinks.

It is very likely that students of the 21st century will have individual notebook computers similar to the widespread use of calculators in today's society (Collins, Morrison, and Newman 1994). These individual computers could enhance the connections between school and home while promoting interaction among different cultures. For instance, a student could easily continue working on a project at home either individually or with peers. Because computer technology transcends geographic and political borders, projects between global communities of unprecedented scope could become a regular occurrence. In an ideal world, one could speculate that more frequent communication among different cultures could lead to greater acceptance of differences.

As classrooms become more inundated with computer technology, the role of teachers will change. Teachers could have more time to coach and facilitate learning individually or with small groups instead of leading large-group lessons that may not be appropriate for all students in the classroom. Teachers may be challenged by students to acquire new knowledge in response to the larger and more diverse amounts of information students will access via the Web. Teachers also may find themselves spending more time communicating with various groups of people affiliated with school activities, such as parents and community organizations.

Parental and community involvement. The vital role of parent-school partnerships in education has long been recognized (Day 1995). Computer technology may enhance parental and community involvement in education by providing unlimited communication between home, school, and community environments (Collins et al. 1994). Direct links into the school network could provide access to school announcements, homework assignments, and communications from teachers while fostering better parental participation in school decisions. Parents could also use electronic communication to ask questions or share their perspectives with individual teachers or the entire school. Community organizations could participate in school activities along similar lines. In addition, community organizations could provide information on topics of study or communicate opportunities for students in community activities that relate to their schoolwork.

Curriculum and the Role of Assessment

Central to the shift in education from a factory model to an information-based system is the curriculum (Reigeluth and Garfinkle 1994; Schlechty 1990). Rather than presenting a predetermined, set curriculum for students to learn through drill and rote memorization, the curriculum of the future should focus on learning processes with students as co-constructors of knowledge. This approach incorporates individual differences such as variations in interests, cultural heritage, and skill development (Day 1995). As Schlechty (1990, 42) noted, "In the knowledge-work school, the curriculum becomes a body of material to be worked on by students, processed by students, molded and formed by students." In this approach, teachers also become innovators, creating a rich and diverse curriculum that offers a multitude of opportunities for students to learn and invent new knowledge. Teachers should encourage students to use their unique abilities to experiment, to create new ways to use resources, and to process knowledge embedded in the curriculum according to their unique characteristics. Practices such as ability grouping, multiage grouping, nongraded programs, and the use of technology in the classroom must be reexamined to create a dynamic approach to education in the 21st century (Day 1998).

In reflecting on best practices in the 21st century, we must focus on methods of assessment that will be a meaningful component of the learning process.

This approach, unfortunately, contrasts sharply with some of the current trends in school reform. State standards, accountability programs, and an emphasis on "the basics" have become prominent features of reform efforts since the release of *A Nation at Risk* (National Commission on Excellence in Education 1983). This perspective assumes that, if student test scores show gains throughout the grade levels and high school graduates reflect a predetermined level of knowledge according to standardized measures, then students have received a quality education that will make them acceptable, meaningful citizens (Clune 1993; Ryan 1996; O'Day and Smith 1993). These policies are built upon the factory model of the Industrial Age that emphasizes the product—in this case, the students.

Leaders of statewide accountability programs report improvements in curriculum and instructional methods as their primary reason to assess child progress (Bond and Braskamp 1996). In reality, though, assessment surfaced as the primary focus of these efforts to measure test-score achievement against local, state, national, and international norms, and, in some states, to judge teacher effectiveness (Abelmann and Kenyon 1996; Bond 1995; Clune 1993; Haladyna, Nolen, and Haas 1991; Jones and Whitford 1997). Bond and Braskamp (1996) cited three reasons for the prominent role of assessment in school reform: (1) the shift from federal control to control by states and, ultimately, to local school districts; (2) the use of assessment as a focal point that motivates students, teachers, parents, and others to help children learn an identified set of skills; and (3) the convenience of assessment as a tool to measure the progress of successful schooling. By the academic year 1994–95, 45 states were conducting some type of statewide accountability assessment in their public schools; of the five remaining states, three were in the process of reformulating statewide assessment programs (Bond and Braskamp 1996).

Given the enormous amount of time, money, and effort now invested in these statewide reform programs, it is unlikely that they will dissipate in the near future. Therefore, in reflecting on best practices in the 21st century, we must focus on methods of assessment that will be a meaningful component of the learning process. To date, a variety of methods to measure student progress have been used in U.S. education, including multiple-choice questions, essays, assigned papers, reports, projects, and laboratory experiments (Kane, Khattri, Reeve, and Adamson 1997). However, standardized testing composed of multiple-choice questions has dominated other methods of assessment. For instance, though many states incorporate some type of performance-based assessment in their statewide accountability programs, the majority of states use multiple-choice testing in combination with authentic-assessment methods (Bond and Braskamp 1996). Even in states such as Kentucky, California, and Arizona, where portfolio assessment was included in reform legislation, the struggle for consistent scoring techniques and clear accountability reporting has caused a return to multiple-choice testing components (Bond and Braskamp 1996; Jones and Whitford 1997).

In the information-based society of the new millennium, however, an emphasis on authentic testing practices will provide more in-depth assessments of student knowledge, especially in the areas of the students' abilities to use problem-solving strategies and other critical-thinking skills. Authentic assessment includes three distinctions from multiple-choice testing (Kane et al. 1997): First, authentic assessment requires students be engaged actively in constructing, demonstrating, or performing a solution or product according to specified requirements. Second, this method supports knowledge acquisition through tasks that have a "real world" connection. Third, authentic assessment is viewed as a method that requires thoughtful, reflective responses of the person being tested.

Arts Education

Arts education offers tremendous possibilities for teaching and learning in the new millennium. It offers a means to achieve many educational goals.

First, exposure to the arts enhances students' appreciation of cultural difference and the ability to understand other ways of viewing the world. Globalization has brought the farthest corners of Earth into our living rooms and schools. Students must be equipped to function in the global community: In the offices of tomorrow, they will be working with people from all over the world. Thus, arts literacy can help them gain the symbolic comprehension skills and creativity necessary to function in a multicultural environment. Moreover, artistic expression highlights universal aspects of humanity and can serve as a powerful unifying force.

Second, public education is the only entrée to arts literacy for the vast majority of students. As Elliot Eisner (1985) has noted, "The arts represent man's best work.

Our children ought to have access to the intellectual and artistic capital of our culture." Without a foundation in art appreciation during their early years, students may not be able to enjoy art in the future. Furthermore, students bereft of art opportunities will not develop the higher-order, holistic-thinking skills that artistic endeavors foster.

Technological advances have also touched the arts. Today, to record professional-quality music one needs only a computer, the right software, and a musical instrument. Children have a strong interest in music, whether it is pop, rock, jazz, classical, hip-hop, rap, country, blues, opera, or otherwise—and music education gives students a foundation for contextualizing and pursuing their own musical interests. With adequate access to technology and education in music and the arts, students can simultaneously express themselves artistically and learn valuable computer skills applicable in the professional world. As educators, we must stay abreast of these technological advances to guide students' interests and their innate curiosity about the world.

Higher Education

As U.S. society prepares to alter its public education system during the next century, the role of higher education will become even more critical to the successful implementation of systemic changes. Two issues concerning the relationship of higher education to changes in public schooling are particularly vital: teacher preparation and future research endeavors.

Teacher preparation. Since the mid-1980s, several national reports have called for systemic changes in teacher education to meet the changing needs of our public education system and to improve the professional image of teaching. A number of these reports—such as *A Nation Prepared: Teachers for the 21st Century* (Carnegie Task Force on Teaching as a Profession 1986) and *A Call for Change in Teacher Education* (National Commission on Excellence in Teacher Education 1985)—urged more rigorous academic standards for teachers (Lucas 1997), including the development of an expanded graduate curriculum in schools of education. *Tomorrow's Schools of Education* (Holmes Group 1995) made five recommendations for restructuring teacher education: (1) to make teacher-preparation programs more intellectually challenging; (2) to accommodate more fully differences in the skills, knowledge, and career commitments of teachers; (3) to create entry-level standards for teachers; (4) to create better linkages between schools and institutions of higher education; and (5) to make schools more appealing to teachers as places to work and learn. All of these reports urged policy makers to upgrade teacher training by requiring graduate degrees for teachers. The development of a career-advancement system, graduated salary increases, and national certification programs were also recommended in these reports.

Ironically, in contrast to these recommendations, there has been a national shift toward professional-development schools and partnerships between local school districts and universities that allow teachers to be trained within the community. Lucas (1997) reported that, by the 1990–91 school year, between 34 and 48 states had developed more than 40 alternative-certification programs administered by combinations of state agencies, institutions of higher education, private organizations, and school districts. The Teach for America (TFA) program developed by Kopp (1994) provides an example of a successful enterprise funded by corporations, foundations, and private donors. TFA recruits graduating seniors from colleges and universities who are not education majors. After a six-week preservice institute and a two-week supervised practicum at a selected school, graduates are placed in teaching positions as regular teachers with a minimum of a two-year employment agreement.

Given recent federal support for reduction of class sizes, these types of certification programs will probably become even more prevalent to meet teacher shortages. Such alternative programs raise many questions about the quality of teachers and the credibility of the teaching profession. As we move into the next millennium, teacher-training programs must carefully examine the benefits of institutions of higher education versus the need for more teachers. Some of the questions that will need consideration include:

• What is the impact of placing inexperienced teachers with little or no training in classrooms?

• Can institutions of higher education and other certification programs pool resources to create a viable solution to the increased demand for teachers?

• Could pedagogical centers be created in communities as part of public education to prepare teachers?

• Would it be more effective to spread teacher preparation across academic departments in universities rather than having separate schools of education?

• Should additional federal and state funding be allocated to institutions of higher education to create more comprehensive teacher-training programs, such as five- or six-year degrees?

• How can teacher-preparation programs integrate courses devoted to societal needs, such as culturally relevant teaching practices, heightened ecological awareness, knowledge about interpersonal-skill development to combat violence and prejudice, and globalism?

Research. Though the U.S. Department of Education began investing in research as early as the 1860s, less than 10 percent of postsecondary education is funded by the federal government (Gladieux and King 1995). For example, approximately $15 billion was allocated for university-based research and development in 1993. As we look to the future of research in higher education, potential funding sources will continue to be more competitive. Yet the role of research will become even more vital to meet the changing needs of our society. In essence, we have a choice of diluting education through inadequate funding for teacher training and research or making powerful changes that will increase the quality of education.

CALLS FOR ACTION

From the family dinner table to the halls of the U.S. Congress, a call for action is reverberating throughout the country: "How can our educational system be improved to ensure an appropriate education for every child in the next century?" This call is being driven by the belief that public education is a cornerstone of our democratic society. As we have discussed, some alarming facts indicate the troubled state of our current educational system and the need for improvements. However, despite the problems and inefficiencies of our educational system, there is hope for the future. This hope is built upon the even larger number of success stories for education during the 20th century. Change is a natural occurrence in complex systems like our educational system. Its effect on active participation in U.S. education has sometimes been small and nearly undetectable, evolving over a long period of time, and other times has been dramatic—such as the recent implementation of statewide accountability programs across the nation. The question to ask is not how we can maintain the status quo of the past; rather, how can we meld the accumulated knowledge from the successes of the past century with current and future resources to build a more effective educational system? In this discussion, we have offered some answers through the lens of systems thinking to help educators, parents, and policy makers prepare future generations.

References

Aagaard, L., P. Coe, B. D. Moore, and P. J. Kannapel. 1994. A qualitative look at Kentucky's primary program: Interim findings from a five-year study. Paper presented at the Annual Meeting of the American Educational Research Association, New Orleans, 4–8 April. ERIC ED 371 013.

Abelmann, C. H., and S. B. Kenyon. 1996. Distractions from teaching and learning: Lessons from Kentucky's use of rewards. Paper presented at the Annual Meeting of the American Educational Research Association, New York, 4–12 April. ERIC ED 396 454.

Amabile, T. M. 1988. A model of creativity and innovation in organizations. *Research in Organizational Behavior* 10: 123–67.

Banathy, B. H. 1991. New horizons through systems design. *Educational Horizons* 69(2): 83–89.

Banathy, B. H. 1994. The three imperatives of the design of educational systems: Transcend-envision-transform. *Educational Horizons* 72(4): 186–95.

Bell, D., and S. R. Graubard, eds. 1997. *Toward the year 2000: Work in progress*. Cambridge: MIT Press.

Bond, L. A. 1995. *Challenges in the development of state assessment programs that support educational reform*. Oak Brook, Ill.: North Central Regional Educational Laboratory.

Bond, L. A., and D. Braskamp. 1996. *The status report of the assessment programs in the United States: State student assessment programs database school year 1994–1995*. Washington, D.C.: Council of Chief State School Officers.

Burbules, N. C. 1996. Postmodern doubt and philosophy of education. In *Philosophy of education 1995*, ed. A. Neiman, 39–48. New York: Philosophy of Education Society.

Burbules, N. C., and T. A. Calister Jr. 1996. Knowledge at the crossroads: Some alternative futures of hypertext learning environments. *Educational Theory* 46(1): 33–50.

Capra, F. 1996. *The web of life*. New York: Anchor Books.

Carlson, J. B. 1995. Launching leadership. In *Education for the 21st century: Key issues, leadership, literacy, legislation, learning*, ed. B. D. Day, 13–40. Dubuque, Iowa: Kendall/Hunt.

Carnegie Task Force on Teaching as a Profession. 1986. *A nation prepared: Teachers for the 21st century*. New York: Carnegie Corporation of New York. ERIC ED 268 120.

Clune, W. H. 1993. The best path to systemic educational policy: Standard/centralized or differentiated/decentralized? *Educational Evaluation and Policy Analysis* 15(3): 233–54.

Collins, A., D. Morrison, and D. Newman. 1994. Putting technology to work for school reform. In *Systemic change in education*, ed. C. M. Reigeluth and R. J. Garfinkle, 71–82. Englewood Cliffs, N.J.: Educational Technology Publications.

Day, B. D., ed. 1995. *Education for the 21st century: Key issues, leadership, literacy, legislation, learning*. Dubuque, Iowa: Kendall/Hunt.

Day, B. D. 1998. Revisiting the multi-age classroom: An old concept for the new millennium. *Delta Kappa Gamma Bulletin* 64(4): 37–41.

Ebert, E. S. 1994. The cognitive spiral: Creative thinking and cognitive processing. *Journal of Creative Behavior*

28(4): 275–90.

Education Commission of the States. 1997. *Transforming the education system: The 1997 education agenda*. Denver: ECS.

Eisner, E. W. 1985. Why art in education and why art education. *Beyond creating: The place for art in America's schools*. Los Angeles: Arts Ed Net, J. Paul Getty Trust. Available at: *http://www.artsednet.getty.edu/ArtsEdNet/Read/Beyond/whyart.html*.

Farkas, S., J. Johnson, and A. Duffett. 1997. *Different drummers: How teachers of teachers view public education*. New York: Public Agenda.

Fleener, M. J., and R. G. Pourdavood. 1997. Autopoiesis and change: Ontological considerations and implications of school reform. Paper presented at the Annual Meeting of the American Educational Research Association, Chicago, 24–28 March.

Fry, P. G., and M. J. Fleener. 1997. An analysis of pre-service teacher-class interaction metaphors. *Journal of Classroom Interaction* 32(1): 23–28.

Fullan, M. 1993. *Change forces: Probing the depth of educational reform*. Bristol, Pa.: Falmer Press.

Gladieux, L. E., and J. E. King. 1995. Challenge and change in the federal role. *New Directions for Institutional Research* 85(Spring): 21–31.

Gleick, J. 1987. *Chaos: Making a new science*. New York: Penguin Books.

Haladyna, T. M., S. B. Nolen, and N. S. Haas. 1991. Raising standardized achievement test scores and the origins of test score pollution. *Educational Researcher* 20(5): 2–7.

Holmes Group. 1995. *Tomorrow's schools of education: Principles for the design for professional development schools*. East Lansing, Mich.: HG.

Hopkins, B. J., and F. C. Wendel. 1997. *Creating school-community-business partnerships*. Bloomington, Ind.: Phi Delta Kappa Educational Foundation.

Jones, K., and B. L. Whitford. 1997. Kentucky's conflicting reform principles: High-stakes school accountability and student performance assessment. *Phi Delta Kappan* 79(4): 276–81.

Kane, M. B., N. Khattri, A. L. Reeve, and R. J. Adamson. 1997. *Assessment of student performance: Studies of education reform*, vol. 1. Washington, D.C.: U.S. Department of Education.

Kannapel, P. J., B. D. Moore, P. Coe, and L. Aagaard. 1994. School-based decision making in rural Kentucky schools: Interim findings of a five-year longitudinal study. Paper presented at the Annual Meeting of the American Educational Research Association, New Orleans, 4–8 April. ERIC ED 371 932.

Kauffman, S. 1995. *At home in the universe: The search for laws of self-organization and complexity*. New York: Oxford University Press.

Kopp, W. 1994. Teach for America: Moving beyond the debate. *The Educational Forum* 58(2): 187–92.

Lucas, C. J. 1997. *Teacher education in America*. New York: St. Martin's Press.

Mann, D. 1984. It's up to you to steer those school/business partnerships. *American School Board Journal* 171(10): 20–24.

Mann, D. 1987. Business involvement and public school improvement, part I. *Phi Delta Kappan* 69(2): 123–28.

Nathan, J. 1996. Possibilities, problems, and progress: Early lessons from the charter movement. *Phi Delta Kappan* 78(1): 18–23.

National Commission on Excellence in Education. 1983. *A nation at risk: The imperative for educational reform*. Washingon, D.C.: U.S. Department of Education. ERIC ED 226 006.

National Commission on Excellence in Teacher Education. 1985. *A call for change in teacher education*. Washington, D.C.: U.S. Department of Education. ERIC ED 252 525.

O'Day, J., and M. S. Smith. 1993. Systemic reform and educational opportunity. In *Designing coherent education policy*, ed. S. H. Fuhrman, 250–312. San Francisco: Jossey-Bass.

Oliver, R. W. 1999. *The shape of things to come: Seven imperatives for winning in the new world of business*. New York: Business Week Books.

Prigogine, I., and I. Stengers. 1984. *Order out of chaos*. New York: Bantam Books.

Reigeluth, C. M., and R. J. Garfinkle, eds. 1994. *Systemic change in education*. Englewood Cliffs, N.J.: Educational Technology Publications.

Ryan, J. 1996. Putting Humpty Dumpty together again: Order, anxiety, and systemic reform. *International Journal of Educational Reform* 5(4): 453–62.

Schlechty, P. C. 1990. *Schools for the twenty-first century: Leadership imperatives for educational reform*. San Francisco: Jossey-Bass.

Schlechty, P. C., and B. Cole. 1991. Creating a system that supports change. *Educational Horizons* 69(2): 78–82.

Schoenfeldt, L. F., and J. K. Jansen. 1997. Methodological requirements for studying creativity in organizations. *Journal of Creative Behavior* 31(1): 73–90.

Scully, M. G. 1995. Postsecondary education and society: The broader context. *New Directions for Institutional Research* 85(Spring): 75–84.

Sipple, J. W., C. G. Miskel, T. M. Matheney, and P. C. Kearney. 1997. The creation and development of an interest group: Life at the intersection of big business and education reform. *Educational Administration Quarterly* 33(4): 440–73.

Slabbert, J. A. 1994. Creativity in education revisited: Reflection in aid of progression. *Journal of Creative Behavior* 28(1): 60–69.

Smith, J. L., J. W. Rhodes, and T. Jensen. 1992. Restructuring the urban primary school: A collaborative approach to developing a nongraded curriculum. Paper presented at the Annual Meeting of the American Educational Research Association, San Francisco, 20–24 April. ERIC ED 347 231.

Snauwaert, D. T. 1993. *Democracy, education, and governance: A developmental conception.* Albany: State University of New York Press.

Stone, L. 1992. The essentialist tension in reflective teacher education. In *Reflective teacher education*, ed. L. Valli, 198–261. Albany: State University of New York Press.

Tesluk, P. E., J. L. Farr, and S. A. Klein. 1997. Influences of organizational culture and climate on individual creativity. *Journal of Creative Behavior* 31(1): 27–41.

U.S. Department of Education. 1997. *A study of charter schools: First year report—May 1997.* Washington, D.C.: USDE.

Wertheimer, R., and M. Zinga. 1997. Attending to the noise: Applying chaos theory to school reform. Paper presented at the Annual Meeting of the American Educational Research Association, Chicago, 24–28 March. ERIC ED 408 707.

Williams, S. 1994. Do charter schools offer real promise or false hope? In *Systemic change in education*, ed. C. M. Reigeluth and R. J. Garfinkle, 83–94. Englewood Cliffs, N.J.: Educational Technology Publications.

Williams, T. 1998. Home schooling: An overview. Available at: *http://www.ohioline.ag.ohio-state.edu.*

Woodman, R. W., J. E. Sawyer, and R. W. Griffin. 1993. Toward a theory of organizational creativity. *Academy of Management Review* 18(2): 293–321.

2

Education Reform on the Move

By *Michael Fullan*

The broad history of educational reform over the last third of this century is instructive. Periods of school reform in North America can be divided into four approximate phases: (1) large-scale adoption, (2) small-scale change, (3) narrow assessment, and (4) large-scale reform.

The first phase of reform, which covers much of the 1960s, is called "large-scale adoption" because there were many aspirations for large-scale improvement of education. Only rarely, however, did reform move beyond the stages of "adoption" or being "on the books." Into the limelight came new math, new biology, and new chemistry curricula, along with open-plan schools, team teaching, and similar concepts. Seldom, though, did these educational initiatives result in changes in the classroom (Fullan and Stiegelbauer 1991).

Around 1970, the second phase of modern education reform emerged. Movement toward small-scale change reflected a recession—economically, intellectually, and certainly in terms of aspirations. It was a period of recognizing failures in implementation strategies, along with the odd individual school success. Indeed, some schools—scattered and unconnected—*were* able to improve. Yet there was no statistical evidence to back up these improvements, nor any attempt to try them on a larger scale. Moreover, there was no reason to believe that successful schools could sustain their efforts.

The third phase, narrow assessment, can be marked around 1983 with the publication in the United States of *A Nation at Risk* (National Commission on Excellence in Education 1983). This publication signaled a growing dissatisfaction on the part of the public—and, thus, policy makers—regarding education. In other words, schools needed serious improvement. As society became more complex and chaotic, the education system was seen as lagging behind. There was a growing sense of urgency that something needed to be done.

The decade of 1983–93 was essentially a series of missteps. U.S. and Canadian governments tried to fix problems by increasing standards, establishing assessment and accountability procedures, and generally putting pressure on educators and schools to perform better. Micklethwait and Wooldridge (1996, 294) commented on the propensity of governments to favor quick and dramatic solutions—which are bound to fail—and the two problems plaguing policy making: "The first is that the state is an incredibly blunt instrument; it gets hold of an overarching idea and imposes it without any sensitivity to the local context. The second is the desperate craving of politicians for a magical solution."

The fourth phase—the current one—is large-scale education reform. Though still in the early stages, this phase of modern-era reform has become increasingly evident in several countries, states, and provinces during the past five years. It is a return to striving for large-scale reform, but tempered with some of the knowledge and lessons from the previous three phases. Phase four draws on the ambitious aspirations of the first phase: it acknowledges the importance of school-by-school or local implementation; it builds in accountability, acknowledging the urgency of the situation, but realizes that accountability by itself will not work. There are still many misfired policy attempts that focus largely on structure, governance, finance, and other formal elements of the system without having a corresponding set of strategies to address local capacity-building. Yet there exists a growing realization that large-scale reform will require both central policy and local development.

The next five years represent a new defining period for the field of education, presenting a quantitatively new opportunity to bring about large-scale fundamental change. On the discouraging side of the ledger are:

(1) a history of failed reform;

(2) demoralization of teachers as a result of the narrow assessment phase; and

(3) the incredible complexity of transforming education in today's chaotic conditions.

On the positive side are:

(1) a greater accumulation and appreciation of the knowledge base needed to develop strategies for reform;

(2) changing demographics around the educational ranks that open the doors for scores of new teachers, administrators, and professors of education (Admittedly, this shift also represents a large challenge to attract, prepare, and support the development of thousands of new educators.); and

(3) a growing sense of urgency and purpose on the part of many leaders and constituencies that now is the time to tackle these problems on a large scale.

In short, there are indications that both the skill and the will may be present in enough quantities that something substantial could be attempted and sustained over the next decade.

EDUCATION REFORM AT THE POLICY LEVEL

Four main policy areas are essential for education improvement: curriculum and instruction, assessment, teacher education, and community development, including early childhood education (Fullan 1998). Each domain has its own movement.

Curriculum and instruction, particularly at the elementary level, is moving toward the right track. For example, curriculum documents have become clearer, reflect best ideas in the different areas of learning, link goals and outcomes better, refer to key instructional methods, and provide sufficient flexibility for teachers, schools, and districts to adapt or to develop local versions. Secondary school curriculum reform lags behind in development in many jurisdictions, but it too has been receiving stronger attention. In brief, curriculum is becoming stronger and better, at least at the policy-development level.

Similarly, assessment policies are robust. One advantage Canada has in this area, compared to the United States, is a later development of assessment practices, which helped the country avoid or minimize many of the pitfalls of high-stakes testing. The technology of assessment is growing in sophistication, and a much better fit has been made between the curricula and the assessments. This trend does not yet reflect implementation, but the potential for doing good is there. Currently, the same cannot be said about the remaining two areas of policy.

Teacher education—from pre-service to continuing education—sometimes can seem the worst problem and the best solution. From a policy point of view, it remains politically unattractive. In states and provinces, the barest of structural requirements are addressed in policy. These requirements of specific courses and quality certification are necessary. Indeed, they must be strengthened and are at the lower end of what will be required for teacher renewal in the next millennium.

The Rise and Stall of Teacher Education Reform (Fullan, Galluzzo, Morris, and Watson 1998), a recent report for the Ford Foundation, examined teacher education in the United States. Two conclusions were reached. First, the main components of reform should entail:

• developing a stronger knowledge base for teaching and teacher education;

• attracting able, diverse, and committed students to the career of teaching;

• redesigning teacher-preparation programs so that the linkages to arts and sciences, and to the field of practice, are both strengthened;

• reforming the working conditions of schools;

• developing and monitoring external standards for programs as well as for teacher candidates and teachers on the job; and

• focusing rigorous and dynamic research on teaching, teacher education, and assessment and monitoring of strategies.

Second, there is significant policy action under way, especially in relation to the follow-through in the United States of the National Commission on Teaching and America's Future. In Canada, similar actions have been outlined in *The Rise and Stall of Teacher Education Reform*. Without significant new policy development, however, both nations will squander the tremendous demographic opportunities for reshaping the teaching force during the next few years.

Finally, community development is far behind the times. School councils certainly can be useful, but they remain, perhaps, superficial manifestations of what will be needed to direct policy toward community mobilization. Early childhood policy, as part of this community-development sphere, is similarly underdeveloped, though it has been receiving more attention recently. Unlike teacher education, early childhood initiatives should be more politically attractive. Many European countries have recognized the critical importance of investing in crucial early childhood policy expectations and incentives. Still, Canada and the United States lag behind.

EDUCATION REFORM AT THE LOCAL LEVEL

Policy initiatives and local school operations occupy divergent worlds. Local implementation of education reform depends upon the development of learning communities and collaborative cultures at the school, community, and district levels. When learning communities do develop, they make a powerful difference. They mean teachers working in concert to examine student work and achievement, and, in turn, making corresponding changes in their teaching methods and in other aspects of the school. Moreover, research literature is conclusive in finding that teachers, principals, parents, and others can make a significant difference in student learning when they: (1) work together, (2) focus on the best pedagogy, and (3) take a close look at what students are learning and are motivated to learn.

The Manitoba School Improvement Program (MSIP) is a good case in point. Under conditions of local external pressure and support, teachers in several MSIP secondary schools became energized to focus on student learning and engagement to make changes and get results (Zimmerman and Lee 1998). Another example is the work of Newmann and Wehlage (1995) and their colleagues Louis and Kruse (1995), who similarly found that schools in which "professional learning communities" developed achieved greater success with students in science, mathematics, and social studies. Indeed, it is crucial that we work on "reculturing"—developing learning communities—rather than stopping at "restructuring"—changing formal structures (Fullan and Hargreaves 1992).

Previous outside forces are now in teachers' faces every day. This new environment is complex, turbulent, and unpredictable, yet increases the demands for better performance and accountability.

In addition to inside-the-school development, schools must "go wider" or cultivate what might be termed "the inside-out relationship" (Hargreaves and Fullan 1998). While the first conclusion is that schools would be well advised to turn their focus on reculturing, a related conclusion is that they cannot do it alone.

The external-to-the-school context has changed dramatically over the past five years. The walls of the school have become more permeable and more transparent. Teachers and principals now operate under a microscope in a way previously unknown. In other words, the "out there" is now "in here." Previous outside forces are now in teachers' faces every day. This new environment is complex, turbulent, contradictory, relentless, uncertain, and unpredictable, yet it increases the demands for better performance and accountability of its schools. In light of this new reality, teachers and principals must reframe their roles and orientations to the outside (Hargreaves and Fullan 1998).

The first lesson of the inside-out story is counterintuitive. Most outside forces threaten schools, but they are also necessary for success. To turn disturbing forces to one's advantage, it is necessary to develop the counterintuitive mind-set of "moving toward the danger" (Hargreaves and Fullan 1998). Schools must link to at least the following five powerful external forces:

- parents and community;
- technology;
- corporate connections;
- government policy; and
- the wider teaching profession.

When rapport manifests among parents, community, teachers, schools, and the student, learning occurs. The problem is what to do when such rapport does not exist. As Dolan (1994, 60) remarked, educators have to involve parents in as many activities as possible and "work through the discomfort of each other's presence." Effective schools use their internal collaborative strength to seek out relationships with the community. They see parents as part of the solution more than part of the problem. They pursue programs and activities based on two-way capacity building to mobilize the resources of both community and the school in the service of learning (Epstein 1995).

The establishment of school councils is a good example of restructuring rather than reculturing. School councils by themselves are not sufficient. Having a few representatives in advisory or decision-making roles will not impact student learning. It is only when the majority of teachers and the majority of parents begin linking to one another, as Epstein (1995) stated, that students will experience any substantial improvement in learning.

The second external factor is technology. It is, of course, ubiquitous. The main issue, though, is how to contend with it. In the book *What's Worth Fighting for Out There*, the conclusion is that the more powerful technology becomes, the more indispensable good teachers become (Hargreaves and Fullan 1998). Technology generates a glut of information, but is not particularly pedagogically wise. This context is especially true of new breakthroughs in cognitive science about how learners must construct their own meaning for deep understanding to occur. Teachers, therefore, must become the pedagogical design experts, using the power of technology—something they are not yet prepared to do. However, it is part of the "getting out there" story.

Third, corporate partnerships continue to increase, and if schools are to hold their own in this new arena, they must *know* what they are doing. Getting out there means developing the criteria and confidence to form productive alliances. Collaborative schools are less vulnerable, more confident, and more open to outside relationships.

Fourth, government policy has also become increasingly demanding. Accountability and assessment policy is a good example. Assessment literacy, as mentioned earlier, has an inside-out dimension. To put it directly, teachers must become experts about external standards. On the political side, they must move toward the danger by entering the fray and by participating in the debate about the uses and misuses of achievement results. They must also take advantage of external standards to help inform what they are doing.

Collaborative schools are active and critical consumers of external standards. They use standards to clarify, integrate, and raise their expectations. They want to know how well they are doing so they can celebrate and/or work at getting better. Newmann and Wehlage (1995) also argued that external standard-setting by professional organizations and states (and provinces) is an essential component of reform. From the inside-out perspective, schools that do well seek and make use of standards as part and parcel of their school improvement plans. They become assessment literate as they relate their performance to external standards. As Newmann and Wehlage (1995, 41) put it, "Without clear, high standards for learning, school restructuring is like a rudderless ship."

The final set of key external forces concerns the current preoccupation with developing the teaching force. School improvement will never occur on a wide scale until the majority of teachers become contributors to and beneficiaries of the professional learning community. Again, effective schools see themselves as part and parcel of this wider movement. They, of course, create conditions for continuous learning for their own members—but they do more than that. They engage in partnerships with local universities and/or become members of other reform networks. They see themselves as much in the business of teacher education as in the business of school improvement. Effective schools have explicit criteria for hiring, pay attention to induction, support learning opportunities for their members, look for reform-oriented union leadership, provide a laboratory for student teachers, and so on. In short, they take advantage of new developments in the teaching profession, but they also give as much as they get through active participation in helping to reshape the profession as a whole.

INCREASING THE RAPPORT BETWEEN POLICY AND LOCAL DEVELOPMENT

Finally, educators must consider how large-scale reform can be pursued to embrace the likelihood that there will be some degree of linkage between policy and implementation. Bryk, Sebring, Kerbow, Rollow, and Easton (1998) have developed the best formulation of this direction. They identify four main elements of the external structure that can be extrapolated for the whole system: (1) policies focusing on decentralization, (2) local capacity building, (3) rigorous external accountability, and (4) stimulation of innovation.

The first step is to realize that the goal must be to help schools to develop collaborative cultures within the school and partnerships external to the school. Clearly, schools cannot be *made* to operate in this manner; but there is no chance whatsoever of large-scale reform without movement in these directions. Thus, the first element is to maintain and develop *decentralization policies*. This step would involve retaining or strengthening site-based emphasis and local district responsibilities (but remember reculturing).

Whereas the first element says to trust decentralization, the other three, in effect, say "but not completely." Educators have known for some time that decentralization per se does not produce large-scale change—or much small change, for that matter. The trick is not to abandon it but to strengthen it. The second aspect, *local capacity building*, does just that. Here, the investment is in policies, training, professional development, ongoing support, and other related areas to develop the capacity of schools, communities, and districts to operate. These activities range from school-team training, local school councils, redesign of initial teacher education, and the panoply of new activities that will be needed to prepare teachers, principals, parents, and others to function as professional learning communities inside and outside the school.

Third, a *rigorous external accountability system* must be built into the infrastructure. Schools do best when they pay close attention to standards and performance. The external accountability system generates data and procedures that make this practice more likely and more thorough. However, such a system must be primarily—though not exclusively—based on a philosophy of capacity building, of using "assessment for learning" and otherwise enabling educators to become more assessment literate. No external, formal accountability system can have an impact in the long run unless it has a capacity-building philosophy. Though this is the foremost primary goal, the external accountability system must also have the responsibility to intervene in persistently failing situations. Balancing accountability support and accountability intervention is obviously a tough call, but this is precisely how sophisticated the external infrastructure must become.

Fourth, ideas remain important; scientific breakthroughs about learning continue to rise, and innovations are being attempted around the world. Therefore, the *stimulation of innovation* must be a strong feature of the infrastructure. Investments must be made in research, development, innovative networks, and other areas so that the marketplace of educational ideas is constantly being stimulated. The external system must help schools and school districts access ideas and, through capacity building, support the development of accountable professional communities.

REFORM MOVEMENT

It would be premature to conclude that large-scale educational reform is substantially "on the move." There is enough promise, however, to conclude that the conditions are more favorable, albeit complex and fragile, than ever imagined. Some of the key policies are being put in place. Much is known about the kinds of local action needed, and there is an appreciation of the need to connect the two worlds of policy and implementation.

Unfortunately, for reform to be successful, educators will need to coordinate and otherwise establish rapport between simultaneous top-down/bottom-up strategies. This action must occur at the local level between districts and their schools as well as at the provincial/state level between governments and local jurisdictions. It will be difficult, because the forces of change are complex and the strategies needed must constantly engage in a balancing act between too much and too little structure, between top-down desires and bottom-up inclinations.

The next several years represent an ideal time to develop new and more powerful strategies. Both the will—the sense of urgency and purpose—and the skill—the knowledge base and competencies to act—can be mobilized for improvement. The movement is by no means automatic, but for the first time in almost half a century there is a real opportunity to engage in large-scale reform.

REFERENCES

Bryk, A. S., P. Sebring, D. Kerbow, S. Rollow, and J. Easton. 1998. *Charting Chicago school reform*. Boulder, Colo.: Westview Press.

Dolan, W. P. 1994. *Restructuring our schools: A primer on systemic change*. Kansas City, Mo.: Systems & Organizations.

Epstein, J. 1995. School/family/community partnerships. *Phi Delta Kappan* 76(9): 701–12.

Fullan, M. 1998. Education reform: Are we on the right track? *Education Canada* 38(3): 4–7.

Fullan, M., and A. Hargreaves. 1992. *What's worth fighting for in your school*. New York: Teachers College Press.

Fullan, M., and S. Stiegelbauer. 1991. *The new meaning of educational change*. New York: Teachers College Press.

Fullan, M., G. Galluzzo, P. Morris, and N. Watson. 1998. *The rise & stall of teacher education reform*. Washington, D.C.: American Association of Colleges for Teacher Education.

Hargreaves, A., and M. Fullan. 1998. *What's worth fighting for out there*. New York: Teachers College Press.

Louis, K. S., and S. D. Kruse, eds. 1995. *Professionalism and community: Perspectives on reforming urban schools*. Thousand Oaks, Calif.: Corwin.

Micklethwait, J., and A. Wooldridge. 1996. *The witch doctors: Making sense of management gurus*. New York: Times Books.

National Commission on Excellence in Education. 1983. *A nation at risk: The imperative for educational reform*. Washington, D.C.: NCEE.

Newmann, F. M., and G. Wehlage. 1995. *Successful school restructuring*. Madison, Wisc.: Center on Organization and Restructuring of Schools.

Zimmerman, M., and L. Lee. 1998. Making a difference. *Education Canada* 38(3): 26–27.

3

Early Experience and Brain Development

By *Bettye Caldwell**

Current professional and lay excitement about the role of early experience in brain development may be the best thing that has happened to the field of early education in a long time. New research methods and findings are providing a level of validity to the field that might never have occurred otherwise. Anyone who works with young children does so out of the conviction that experiences of this period exert a lasting and pervasive influence on development, even though memory for specific events may be lost with time. It is gratifying to have sophisticated scientists use new methods to look at what is going on inside the brain and relate these internal events to the behavioral changes we can observe.

A statement often heard these days is that the "brain is not hard-wired at birth." One problem with this metaphor is the opinion that often follows it, which claims that, until recently, everyone thought the wiring was complete at birth. It is difficult to believe that anyone ever really thought this way, as we have known for a long time that a baby's brain wiring is not unlike a new computer, which cannot do very much until loaded with software—that is, experience. Undoubtedly, Mozart came hard-wired to be a musical genius, but if he had grown up in an environment devoid of pianofortes, violins, and a father who could introduce him to musical notation, we probably would not have been blessed with 50 symphonies, countless concerti, and other works.

THE LONG MARCH TO BRAIN PRIMACY

We have come a long way in our awareness of the brain's importance and our knowledge of how it functions. When the Egyptians developed their incredible system of mummification 5,000 years ago, they put the organs they considered impor-

---

* The author wishes to express her appreciation to Ms. Marian Keeton, for her valuable help in tracking references, and Dr. Frank Scalzo, for ensuring the accuracy of her interpretations of contemporary neuroscientific concepts and findings.

tant into four canopic jars—heart, intestines, liver, and lungs. They threw the brain away, because they considered it not very important!

One of the first papyrus scrolls ever deciphered, written around 3000 B.C.E., reported the findings of 48 head and neck injury cases (Changeux 1997). The surgeon commented that, if the skull was smashed in the temple, the patient could not speak. He also described the cerebral fissures and convolutions and reported the seemingly contradictory finding that an injury to the top of the skull was associated with dysfunction in the lower limbs. Changeux (1997) noted that the scribe mentioned this inversion four times, as though anticipating disbelief that the symptom would occur so far from the lesion. Still, the observer believed his data and commented that, if others would observe similar injuries, they would find similar symptoms.

These early empirical findings either did not reach many people or offer much credibility circa 8th century to 4th century B.C.E. Most of the powerful Greek philosophers, along with Mesopotamian and Hebrew thinkers, espoused Homer's position that the heart was the source of thought and feeling. Both Democritus (who gave us the term "atom") and Hippocrates (generally called the father of modern medicine) spoke in favor of the brain. Their ideas, however, were essentially powerless against those of the great Aristotle, whose thinking governed the intellectual world for 2,000 years. Though Aristotle is reported never to have seen or dissected a human brain, as Hippocrates had, he revived and strengthened the cardiocentric view of humanity. His position held sway for nearly two millennia, despite the fact that just 200 years later scientists found the brain's ventricles, cerebellum, and cortex convolutions, and noted that nerves were different from blood vessels. Changeux (1997, 7) reported that, "It was not until the 17th century that this level of anatomical knowledge of the human brain was surpassed." Of course, anatomical dissection alone cannot point up patterns of association between structure and function. Without this knowledge, debates about whether the brain or the heart is the primary organ are merely rhetorical. The power of the Aristotelian position to override the evidence of the early anatomists may be the first recorded example of politically correct science. After all, Aristotle was, among other things, Alexander the Great's tutor. It takes a lot of evidence to overcome the opinions of the powerful.

New knowledge almost always involves a fight to gain acceptance as scientific truth. Perhaps it is fitting to conclude this historical section with a more recent quote from Jean Baptiste de Lamarck, another scientist whose ideas were discredited for more than a century but have become compatible with the new wave of brain research. In 1809, Lamarck summarized, "One can doubtless possess at birth a particular disposition for features that one's parents transmit by their organization, but it is certain that, if one does not exercise strongly and habitually the faculties that such a disposition favors, the particular organ that executes the acts would not develop" (Changeux 1997, 205). Most of us were taught as students to discredit Lamarck's point of view, generally referred to as the inheritance of acquired characteristics. Yet his assertion that exercise of the faculties strengthens the anatomical basis for the faculty is very much in line with the exciting contemporary attention to the role of experience in brain development.

This introduction is but a sketchy and admittedly selective history of the remarkable advance of brain research over the centuries, omitting many important names of individuals whose contributions have been monumental. However, it provides a template for understanding the point on a moving trajectory that we have reached today. It illustrates the continuing battle fought between ideas and evidence and the dependency of true advance on methodological progress. Undoubtedly, we have learned more in the past 50 years than in all the years of recorded history leading to that interval. Yet no more than Hippocrates or Lamarck have we reached the final destination of neuroscientific research. Considering the history of brain research, with its detours and cul-de-sacs along with its advances, we can put progress into perspective and realize that what exists immediately ahead is all we can see, but it is not the end.

Old Ideas, New Methods

Science advances in alternating cycles of method development and the application of these methods to the derivation of newer and better concepts. Today's high-tech world offers the opportunity for a quantum leap forward in the development of new and better methods for the study of the brain. The result inevitably will be refinement of concepts and strengthening of the knowledge base in early childhood.

A method that has been around for a long time, but which has recently seen improvements that make it more suitable for use with infants and young children, is the electroencephalogram (EEG), which records electrical waves in different parts of the brain. Researchers have modified traditional procedures—attaching electrodes to the scalp with sponges held in place by little caps, causing minimal discomfort in the subjects—and made this way of looking at brain function appropriate for use with even very young infants (Dawson, Hessl, and Frey 1994). Illustrating the kind of information that can be extracted via this procedure is the discovery that children of depressed mothers show decreased cortical activity, which essentially parallels their mothers' (Dawson et al. 1994). An adaptation of the standard EEG procedure is the high-density event-related potential, which differs from standard EEGs in that it records brain waves in response to a specific stimulus—that is, it is evoked by certain stimulus events.

Techniques involving magnetic resonance imaging (MRI) are playing an important role in new brain research. MRIs have been used to study brain structure, and functional MRIs permit the measurement of cerebral blood flow as an indication of neural activity. A related method offering a great deal of promise is Positron Emission Tomography (PET), as used by Chugani (1994) and his colleagues. This somewhat invasive method requires the injection of radioactive isotopes and, thus, is not widely used with children unless they have some kind of clinical condition needing remediation. In addition, PET must be used with children who are awake and who can remain still for considerable time, thus ruling out young infants. The brain responds to the positrons produced by the injected isotopes in essentially the same way it responds to glucose, the brain's chief fuel. The resulting computerized image permits both brain structure and the metabolic activity of different brain parts to be visualized. Even though ethical considerations have limited use of this method, enough studies have been made of infants and children already receiving radiation (tumor treatment, for example) to show rapid growth in glucose metabolism during the first two to three years of life. These levels remain high until 8–10 years of age and then gradually decline to adult levels by ages 16–18. This early excess over adult values is seen as one provision for the extra cerebral energy required during periods of rapid growth (Chugani 1994).

Neuroscientists have also conducted painstaking research involving actual counting of synapses—connections between nerve fibers, of which we eventually have trillions—charting changes in the numbers found at different ages (Huttenlocher 1984; Goldman-Rakic 1987). Research using this model has shown developmental changes that roughly parallel those noted when PET is used—that is, a dramatic increase in synapses during the early months and years of life, a peak around ages six to eight years, followed by a decline to adult levels. There is currently a great deal of interest not only in synaptic connection increase occurring during the early years—essential for cross-sensory associations and complex ideation—but also in the decline or "pruning" that occurs in middle childhood. Does this decrease represent consolidation and greater efficiency of function, or failure to provide experiences that maximize cortical opportunity? Data produced from studies using these newer methods consistently support the proposition that experience plays a crucial role in shaping brain development (Johnson 1997).

Conducting such research with representative samples of normal and healthy children is not easy and, as a consequence, can only provide inferential information about vibrant children in our early childhood programs. PET studies of young children have been conducted primarily with children having some known neurological complication; synapse counts can be done only with nonliving organisms. However, knowledge gained via these and other methods for studying brain development yields hypotheses that can then be tested in other naturalistic and experimental settings involving children and adults. From such observations come reality checks that further guide neuroscience. As previously stated, knowledge advances through the alternating process of finding new and better study methods in a given field and applying these methods to seek more precise facts. If the methods are poor, the "facts" derived from them will be short-lived. We can hope that new methods now being used will produce facts that can stand the test of time.

THE HIERARCHY OF BRAIN STRUCTURES

Though the brain is a bodily structure, its development is a process—a process that continues from conception to death. It first makes its appearance when the embryo is a few weeks old as a clumping together of cells at the top of a tube—the spinal cord—that eventually will become its major highway, connecting it with the remainder of the body. The brain, and other anatomical structures that surround it, lead the embryonic parade, with the brain acting as Mission Control. The brain seems to have a way of being first in line to get its share of what the new organism gets from the mother. This primacy of the head region has led to the designation of embryonic development as being *cephalo-caudal*, literally "head to tail." The spinal cord, which runs down the trunk from the lower part of the brain relaying commands to muscles and information back to the control center, is similarly favored. The preferential growth it manifests is referred to as the *proximo-distal*, or central to periphery, law of development.

The clump of cells that will develop into the brain divides repeatedly during early prenatal development. With each division, a certain amount of flexibility is lost and the eventual fate of the various cells, more limited. Experiments conducted years ago (Hamburger 1963) with various nonhuman species showed that, very early in embryonic development, cells in the region programmed to form an eye, for example, could be transplanted to the area expected to produce lower limbs and those transplanted cells would develop into a limb. The same transplantation done at a later stage would result in the development of a fragmented eye where the lower limbs should be.

By the time of birth, the human brain is the heaviest nonskeletal part of the body. In the birth process, it is protected from injury during descent through the birth canal by the bony skull. The length of the skull is about one-third the length of the infant, though during adulthood it will be only about one-tenth of a person's height. The brain possesses at birth all the neurons, or nerve cells, it will have in life—an estimated 100 billion to 1 trillion (give or take a few million).

The name of the brain game is to get all those neurons interconnected, or at least a goodly portion of them. To accomplish that feat, each neuron sends out shoots of various lengths, called nerve fibers. On both ends of the fiber, fuzzy branches develop, called axons at one end and dendrites at the other. Axons and dendrites do not actually hold onto one another; between them lies an infinitesimally small space, across which a chemical reaction is conducted that transmits the impulse from the nerve fiber. This interchange area where axons and dendrites interact is called a synapse, and the increase in complexity in the brain consists largely of an increase in its number of synapses. Through this process, all parts of the brain eventually develop the possibility of being connected with all other parts.

This increase is most dramatic during the first four years or so of life. At the end of the early childhood period, a child's brain has many more synapses than it had at birth and a richer network than it will have when physiological maturity is achieved. This reduction in the number of synapses after the early childhood years is not completely understood. Devotees of early childhood research have speculated the pruning could indicate that experience—that is, the learning environment—was no longer optimally supporting the developing brain. Most neuroscientists, however, interpret this reduction as an indication of greater neural efficiency and a removal of some of the redundancy often present in early physiological development. Goldman-Rakic (1987), for example, cited the finding that individuals with severe mental impairment have sometimes been found to have either unusually high or low synaptic density as evidence for the hypothesis that more is not necessarily better. The exact meaning of this pruning process awaits further work in the next decade.

Structurally, the brain is built up in layers or tiers from, more or less, the bottom to the top and from the inside to the periphery. Complexity increases moving from the central core to the outer layer, the cerebral cortex. The regions in the interior—spinal cord, brainstem, cerebellum, midbrain, hypothalamus, and thalamus—are all older, evolutionarily speaking. They are, for the most part, unitary, whereas the more recent structures are neatly divided into two hemispheres. Situated between these older structures and the cortex are a number of small nuclei known collectively as the limbic system. The word "limbus" means border or edge, and the cells comprising this system appear to have some characteristics of the brainstem and midbrain and some of the cortex.

The cortex is sometimes referred to as the "new brain." Certainly, it is new in the sense that it constantly reconstitutes as synapses form or are forfeited, as use patterns increase, and as new stimuli force reorganization of existing connections. Much, but not all, of the work in education consists of building up and strengthening cortical connections. Indeed, it is in the cortex that the acquisition and storage of information, problem solving, and reasoning occur. These cognitive processes contribute to the structure of the cortex, just as the cortex influences an individual's ability to carry out the processes. The precise coordination of all the genetic and experiential factors that result in a well-functioning brain and nervous system represents the miracle of life in all of its splendor.

IMPLICATIONS FOR EDUCATION

There are several implications in early childhood education practices concerning the new wave of research in the brain/experience arena:

Anyone who cares for and works with young children is, in the truest sense of the term, a brain researcher.

1. **A child's behavior provides the cleanest window into the brain.** By comparison, most other techniques are like looking through isinglass. Although new high-tech research methods provide exciting information about activity in the brains of children (and adults), even the most sophisticated method would be of limited value without behavioral confirmation of *what* is happening. That is, observable behavior provides a window to activity inside the brain. This means that anyone who cares for and works with young children is, in the truest sense of the term, a brain researcher. Every parent, every teacher, every caregiver in a high-quality early childhood program is conducting naturalistic research on the effects of early experience on brain development. Furthermore, they are doing this without the injection of radioactive isotopes, without connecting wires, and without dissecting nonliving brains.

A synapse is rather like a purple cow—most of us have never seen one. But we have seen smiles, signs of recognition, increased eye-hand coordination, evidence of object permanence, and many other indications that something good is happening inside the brain. The kinds of behavior we observe will more reliably report what occurs inside the brain than glucose metabolism changes will indicate what occurs behaviorally.

Behavior not only indicates that something has happened inside the brain, but paints a picture of *what* has happened. For example, take a simple item that appears on a number of infant-development scales: "Child turns head and leans over to look for a fallen spoon." Success on that item requires impressive brain organization and control. To perform these tasks, the baby must be able to form some kind of mental image of a spoon that remains when the spoon is not present (object permanence) and turn its head on command, stimulated either by an idea ("The spoon is not visible but still exists somewhere") or a stimulus (the sound of the spoon hitting the floor). Unless these reactions occur inside the brain, the baby will not turn his or her head to peer over the side of the chair. This behavior signifies advances in neural circuitry. Teachers and parents, however, usually just notice the behavior without reflecting on its significance to brain development.

2. Educators must learn more, and new personnel must be educated better, about brain development. A corollary of the first point is that, as teachers, we must learn more about brain development and its manifestations in behavior. Not very many of us, in achieving whatever credentials we possess, were required to learn much about the brain. Moreover, most of us who provide training to people entering the field search frantically for a consultant when units on the brain receive even a smattering of lip service. We must do better. Understanding the underlying neural circuitry for developmental advance should not be any more difficult than understanding what Piaget meant by a "secondary or tertiary circular reaction." A solid grounding in physiology used to be a requirement for a doctorate in psychology. After decades of brainwashing (pun intended) about the necessity of attending only to manifest behavior, such grounding no longer is the case. In education courses, an interest in the mechanisms underlying learning has been virtually nonexistent since the early years of the 20th century.

The new wave of interest in the brain is proof that the time has come to change that. When newspaper and magazine reporters know more about brain development than the people who help arrange children's experiences, something is wrong and must be changed. It is time we seek out excellent sources available, including: *Baby Signs* (Acredolo and Goodwyn 1996), *Magic Trees of the Mind* (Diamond and Hopson 1998), *The Psychology of Behavioral Development* (Gandelman 1992), and *Developmental Psychobiology* (Michel and Moore 1995).

3. Educators need to keep—and strengthen—the focus on the inter-connectedness of development. As already indicated, brain development is all about forming connections—between different sensory modalities, between receptors and muscles, between internal and external events. In their daily teaching activities, teachers should always try to help children see how information or skills they are using relate to one another and to other aspects of their lives. Have you ever wondered why it became so important to know that the square of the hypotenuse is equal to the sum of the square of the other two sides of a right angle triangle, except to pass a mathematics test? Your answer is probably "yes," and chances are that nobody bothered to help you see how that "fact" connected with others.

One of the cardinal concepts of the Developmentally Appropriate Practices distributed by the National Association for the Education of Young Children is that children must be dealt with holistically. The following (Bredekamp and Copple 1997, 10) is listed as the first principle of child development that should guide practice: "Domains of children's development—physical, social, emotional, and cognitive—are closely related. Development in one domain influences and is influenced by development in other domains." That principle parallels nicely with brain functioning during infancy and early childhood. A visual stimulus impinges on the occipital region, but if any sort of decision is needed ("Do I want the red or the blue?") the frontal region is involved. In other words, everything is connected.

This connection can be seen clearly in data considering the influence of such factors as poverty (with its associated package of developmental inhibitors) on various forms of social behavior. In their long-term follow-up of children who grew up in poverty, Sroufe and Egeland (1991) found that fewer children of poverty established secure attachments to their mothers and that more of them had either academic or social problems in school (the relatedness of cognitive and emotional factors). One characteristic of resilience, when found, was a strong and secure attachment to a primary caregiver. Gunnar (1996) has shown that stressful experiences in childhood are associated with high levels of cortisol (measured by taking saliva samples). In turn, high cortisol levels are associated with a reduction in the number of available synapses in parts of the brain and, hence, with both cognitive and social developmental problems. Thus, whatever happens, the child acts as a total organism.

In early childhood programs, we may think we are working only with and for the cortex, but, unfortunately (or fortunately), that is not the case. The old brain, with its ability to facilitate or interfere, is always there, remaining a major player in the drama. Perry (1997, 129) has argued persuasively that an imbalance in favor of the lower brain structures tends to occur when infants and young children have been emotionally neglected or victims or witnesses of violence. In such instances, the "cortically mediated, inhibitory capabilities that modulate the more primitive, less mature, reactive impulses of the human brain" are not powerful enough to subdue immature and violent behavior.

It would be extremely helpful for teachers to know whether children in their classrooms were securely attached to their parents or had been either victims or witnesses of violence prior to enrollment; unfortunately, it is all too easy to discover whether they have been inadequately stimulated. Oftentimes, such information is kept from teachers on the grounds that parental rights would be violated if shared. However, teachers need to be alert whenever they have an inattentive child or one who lacks poor impulse control. Such a child may be suffering from the imbalance described by Perry and merely maintaining high vigilance in anticipation of being hurt or injured. Again, behavior gives signals as to what is happening in the brain. Fostering better impulse control via the higher brain centers without dealing somehow with demands of the more primitive parts will result only in frustration for the educator.

4. Educators must give more creative thought to programming during the first three years of life. Completion of the brain's "hard-wiring" probably begins prenatally, but the rate increases exponentially at birth. The need for an interpersonal and physical environment attuned to the brain's demands for experiences of certain types and intensities is critical. Most parents realize this, either through intuition or instruction, and most are exquisitely sensitive to their infant's developmental cues. Some parents, unfortunately, are not, believing infants only eat and sleep and that, as adults, they need to keep quiet around the child. In many of these instances, the infants are not held, cuddled, talked to, sung to, rocked, or even played with regularly. Sometimes, parents have so many responsibilities with other children or jobs or have so many emotional problems of their own that they cannot respond to their infants appropriately. Furthermore, as is well known, when parental problems are really acute and the infant's behavior does not respond to their expectations (the child will not stop crying or respond to the command of "no"), abuse may occur.

Certain behaviors play havoc with the developing brain. Fortunately, infants' brains are, to some extent, forgiving. If they get the proper experiences and can form satisfying relationships with people other than their parents, some of the possibly detrimental effects can be attenuated, if not avoided altogether. This reality mandates the availability of supplementary-care services attuned to providing experiences that can nourish the developing brain. Not just any kind of care will suffice. Only if caregivers providing these services sufficiently appreciate the importance of their work and learn as much as possible about the kinds and the extent of experiences children need will they be able to help redirect brain development toward good thinking, good judgment, and adequate control of antisocial impulses.

5. Brain-experience relations should increase our recognition of, and respect for, individual differences. Respect for individual differences is one of the shibboleths of the education profession. However, it is violated daily to the detriment of children. "Group think" prevails in most classrooms, as do group assignments, group grading, and group evaluations. Dolly, the famously cloned sheep, notwithstanding, humans are not clones of one another; even identical twins have differences in brain structure and functioning. Using MRI scans, Tramo, Loftus, Thomas, Green, Motrt, and Gazzaniga (1994) found considerable variation in cortical areas in identical twins. In one twin, the occipital lobe occupied about 20 percent of the cortex; in the other, it occupied only 13 to 17 percent. Certainly no two individuals, twins or otherwise, have exact experiential histories. Although chronological age is generally used as the admission key to various educational programs, the integration of brain development and experience, once it can be accurately assessed, should provide a far more useful criterion of "readiness" for any particular type of proffered education.

Recognition of this reality presents a major challenge for educators to adapt their teaching, at any grade level, to a wide range of learning participants. Some of their children may have happy and satisfied lower brains yet have cortexes begging for new connections. Others will still be struggling to develop enough self-regulation to free cortical centers for attention and new learning. Again, the behavior of the children will provide the initial clue. Within the new paradigm, however, behavior clues will need to be coupled with relevant experiential history to help devise educational remediation for observed problem behavior.

Caveat Emptor

Has the excitement and the attention of new research made us go overboard in our zeal to build educational programs on a foundation of brain development? Are these educational implications derived from a secure knowledge base, or are they merely wishful thinking? Without question, they are far from the latter. Trying to create effective pedagogy that ignores the neurological foundations of learning is an experience in futility. Equally foolish is to emphasize the importance of brain development without acknowledging the role of experience in shaping that development.

Still, we are far from having a template based on neuroscience that mandates a precise sequence of activities to follow for children to develop optimally. This point has been expressed by many educators (Caine and Caine 1994; Bruer 1997) as a precaution against the wholesale discarding of several generations of research on how children learn just to jump on the brain bandwagon. Bruer (1997, 4, 15) has been especially eloquent in suggesting that any attempt to base educational practices on brain science is

> *trying to build a bridge too far. Educational applications of brain science may come eventually, but as of now neuroscience has little to offer teachers in terms of informing classroom practice. . . . Neuroscience has discovered a great deal about neurons and synapses, but not nearly enough to guide educational practice. Currently, the span between brain and learning cannot support much of a load. Too many people marching in step across it could be dangerous.*

This bit of circumspection is offered as a caveat against an emotionally charged endorsement of contemporary neuroscience to become *the* basis for educational practices. However, it in no way minimizes the importance of experience during the early years for the development of the whole child and for the whole child's brain. If we walk on the bridge cautiously, avoiding the potholes that represent insufficient evidence, we ought to be able to keep the two domains in contact with one another in a symbiotic pattern of mutual support.

FUTURE IMPLICATIONS

In Moliere's *The Bourgeois Gentleman* (1999), there is a character who wanted desperately to speak prose, only to learn eventually that he had been speaking prose all his life. This metaphor is apt for early childhood educators. Because neuroscience is so neglected in their training, they do not appreciate or take credit for the fact that they always knew the brain was not hard-wired at birth and that they, along with the parents, help provide the "software" necessary for optimal functioning of the system. Early childhood educators have been speaking eloquent brain prose for a long time—that is, doing everything they know to nourish brain development by providing needed early experiences. These educators stand close by the window-to-the-brain—behavior—and that can never be ignored by even the most advanced research methods. So, whether they want to be classified as such, early childhood teachers operate in roles akin to those of naturalistic brain researchers.

Just as observed behavior has helped clarify roles played by different parts of the brain over the centuries, new methods spawned by technological advances allow us to know what is happening in the brain when certain behaviors are observed. An alliance of neuroscientists and early childhood personnel will lead to more reliable knowledge than either group can achieve alone. This alliance can result in the avoidance of irrational and competitive "either/or" positions, neither adequate without the other. The implications of this alliance are clear:

• Educators need to know more about nervous-system development.

• They need to continue to stress holistic learning and connectedness among seemingly disparate areas of skills and knowledge.

• They need to give more creative attention to learning experiences during the first three to four years of life—the period of the most rapid synaptic development.

• They need to gear educational offerings to the wide range of brain-experience consolidation likely to exist in classrooms.

Using new brain research as a guide, along with decades of research and experience dedicated to clarifying how children learn, we can develop an early childhood pedagogy that respects these needs. The results are exciting to contemplate.

REFERENCES

Acredolo, L., and S. Goodwyn. 1996. *Baby signs: How to talk with your baby before your baby can talk*. Chicago: Contemporary Publishing.

Bredekamp, S., and C. Copple. 1997. *Developmentally appropriate practice in early childhood programs*, rev. ed. Washington, D.C.: National Association for the Education of Young Children.

Bruer, J. T. 1997. Education and the brain: A bridge too far. *Educational Researcher* 26(8): 4–16.

Caine, R., and G. Caine. 1994. *Making connections: Teaching and the human brain*. Menlo Park, Calif.: Addison Wesley Longman.

Changeux, J.-P. (trans. L. Garey) 1997. *Neuronal man: The biology of mind*. Princeton, N.J.: Princeton University Press.

Chugani, H. T. 1994. Development of regional brain glucose metabolism in relation to behavior and plasticity. In *Human behavior and the developing brain*, ed. G. Dawson and K. W. Fischer, 153–75. New York: Guilford Press.

Dawson, G., D. Hessl, and K. Frey. 1994. Social influences on early developing biological and behavioral systems related to risk for affective disorder. *Development and Psychopathology* 6(4): 759–79.

Diamond, M., and J. L. Hopson. 1998. *Magic trees of the mind: How to nurture your child's intelligence, creativity, and healthy emotions from birth through adolescence*. New York: Dutton.

Gandelman, R. 1992. *The psychobiology of behavioral development*. New York: Oxford University Press.

Goldman-Rakic, P. S. 1987. Development of cortical circuitry and cognitive function. *Child Development* 58(3): 601–22.

Gunnar, M. R. 1996. Quality of care and the buffering of stress physiology: Its potential in protecting the developing human brain. Minneapolis: University of Minnesota Institute of Child Development.

Hamburger, V. 1963. Some aspects of the embryology of behavior. *Quarterly Review of Biology* 38(4): 342–65.

Huttenlocher, P. R. 1984. Synapse elimination and plasticity in developing human cerebral cortex. *American Journal of Mental Deficiency* 88(5): 488–96.

Johnson, M. H. 1997. *Developmental cognitive neuroscience: An introduction*. Cambridge, Mass.: Blackwell Publishers.

Michel, G. F., and C. L. Moore. 1995. *Developmental psychobiology: An interdisciplinary science*. Cambridge: MIT Press.

Moliere, J.-B. P. (trans. C. P. Pergolizzi) 1999. The bourgeois gentleman. In *Moliere: Four plays*, ed. A. Caso. Brookline Village, Mass.: Branden Pub. Co.

Perry, B. D. 1997. Incubated in terror: Neurodevelopmental factors in the "Cycle of Violence." In *Children in a violent society*, ed. J. D. Osofsky, 124–49. New York: Guilford Press.

Sroufe, L. A., and B. Egeland. 1991. Illustrations of person-environment interaction from a longitudinal study. In *Conceptualization and measurement of organism-environment interaction*, ed T. Wachs and R. Plomin, 68–84. Washington, D.C.: American Psychological Association.

Tramo, M. J., W. C. Loftus, C. E. Thomas, R. L. Green, L. A. Motrt, and M. S. Gazzaniga. 1994. The surface area of human cerebral cortex and its gross morphological subdivisions. Unpublished manuscript. Davis: University of California.

4

Back to the Future
in Teacher Education*

By *Charles R. Coble*

Teacher education must change. The manner in which we have recruited, pre-pared, and supported teachers in the past, and too often in the present, is no longer sufficient. Society has changed, schools have changed, and so must teacher prepara-tion. This challenge is not to engage in bashing schools of education. Indeed, some of the strongest proponents of change have been faculty members and deans of edu-cation. All too frequently, our teacher education programs have suffered from a lack of institutional support or failed political leadership.

During the past 20 years, research on teaching and learning has come of age. So much more is known now about how students learn, how they can be taught to learn, and how people can learn to teach. More recently, it has become clear that research on teaching and wisdom of practice constructed by accomplished teachers have changed. We now have rigorous standards that connect theoretical knowledge with practical experience. It is time to put this new knowledge into practice.

The most critical factor related to student success is the quality of the classroom teacher. Students are entitled to teachers who know their subjects, understand the needs of individual learners, and possess the skills required to make learning come alive. *What Matters Most: Teaching for America's Future,* a report from the National Commission on Teaching and America's Future (NCTAF 1996) on education in the United States, identified several barriers to achieving the goal of putting knowledge-able and skilled teachers into every classroom:

• To overcome barriers of low expectations for student performance and unen-forced standards for teachers, NCTAF recommended ways to get serious about stan-dards for both students and teachers.

• To overcome major flaws in teacher preparation, NCTAF recommended ways

---

* Parts of this chapter were adapted for a presentation to the Southern Regional Postsecondary Education Fo-rum by North Carolina Governor James B. Hunt Jr. and University of North Carolina President Molly Corbett Broad.

to reinvent teacher preparation and professional development.

• To overcome inadequacies in induction for beginning teachers, NCTAF recommended ways to recruit and support qualified teachers in every classroom.

• To overcome shortcomings in professional development and weak rewards for knowledge and skill, NCTAF recommended specific new ways to encourage and reward teacher knowledge and skill.

• To overcome organizational barriers, NCTAF recommended ways to restructure schools for student and teacher success.

The NCTAF report spotlighted some of the state and national problems associated with the preparation and development of teachers. Many U.S. colleges and universities have historical roots as teacher colleges; yet teacher education in those institutions and elsewhere in higher education has not enjoyed strong support for the past half century, as documented by the Holmes Group (1995). An ambitious ten-year alliance of 100 major U.S. research universities, the Holmes Group, initiated in 1987, was unable to enhance the public image of teacher education significantly. As chronicled in *The Rise and Stall of Teacher Education Reform* (Fullan, Galluzzo, Morris, and Watson 1998), the group attempted to achieve for teachers and teacher education what Abraham Flexner (1910) accomplished for doctors and medical education earlier in this century. Though it launched some important changes, the Holmes Group initiative stalled before it could genuinely reform teacher education—and public perception.

As a matter of public policy, we must recognize that teacher education is the intersection of public schools and higher education. It is either the glue that holds them together or a wedge that separates them. The great policy engine that literally transformed the United States after World War II was the G. I. Bill. This policy helped shift the war-related economy to a more domestic, consumer-based economy by encouraging and making possible access to college for hundreds of thousands of average people. Yet the G. I. Bill also affected state policy. After all, the states had to allocate funds not only to build classrooms and laboratories but to hire faculty to meet the rapid demand for a college education.

Unfortunately, the G. I. Bill had an unintended downside for teacher education. It transformed many teacher colleges into more comprehensive institutions that offered a much broader array of academic and professional programs. Many colleges closed down their teaching laboratory schools to help fund expansion as well as new programs. Schools of education became "cash cows" to help finance the transformation of state teacher colleges into multipurpose colleges or research universities. Higher education attracted a larger and more diverse student body, but the connections between the university and the school—the connection between research and practice—was sacrificed in the process.

Even at traditional liberal arts colleges and universities, teacher education declined as a priority as emphasis shifted to expanding other programs and creating new ones. Successful programs in teacher preparation require effective integration of coursework in schools of education with coursework in liberal arts disciplines comprising the area of concentration. That cohesive connection between teacher preparation and liberal arts colleges was weakened.

Some critics of schools of education and teacher education suggest the gap is now too large and the needed changes too great to revive the essential connection. They believe the most viable solutions lie in simply closing schools of education. These same forces further advocate conversion of "government schools" (that is, public schools) from a "monopoly" system into a free-market, voucher-supported, dispersed nonsystem. Such schools would be free to employ anyone as a teacher, regardless of credentials, as long as the person produced the state's minimum student-achievement standards (Thomas B. Fordham Foundation 1999).

This vision of dispersed control in education is appealing to U.S. citizens. As a society, we have deep-seated traditions of individualism and individual liberties. The U.S. Constitution and Bill of Rights helped ensure that we would be citizens in the "land of the free." However, we also have a long tradition emanating from our heritage of equality, a concern that extends beyond the individual to the total community. This Jeffersonian tradition would have us be concerned for the least of us. It is a tradition that applies some reasonable constraints on individual liberties to ensure "justice for all," another key part of our founding documents.

Out of this dual tradition of individualism and community, we deferred to each state the right to establish a system of public education, as each wished and as each has done. It is the right of states to do so, because no provision was made for public education in the Constitution or Bill of Rights. Decision makers and citizens within each state must consider and debate the purposes of public education and craft policies to support those purposes.

From a state policy perspective, there are at least two primary purposes of public education: (1) to advance the ability of individuals to contribute to their own economic well-being and that of society; and (2) to develop the knowledge and ability (and hopefully the willingness) of those individuals to lead responsible lives and to contribute to the civic well-being of our democratic society. If public schools have public purposes, then so do programs that prepare teachers. Such programs, approved by states, must be held rigorously accountable for producing teachers committed to helping students and schools achieve both the economic and democratic purposes of public education. Teacher-preparation programs must be guided by the same dualism enshrined in the Constitution and Bill of Rights: They must produce teachers with the knowledge and skills to help *each* student achieve high standards, and they must prepare teachers committed to having *all* students achieve those high standards. The needs of the individual and the needs of the democratic society will both be served well if teachers of ability can be recruited, prepared, inducted, and supported for careers in public education.

There are now some practical and strategic reasons why the political and institutional support for teacher education must change. According to U.S. Secretary of Education Richard Riley (1999), the United States will need 2 million-plus new teachers during the next decade. California, Texas, North Carolina, and other states with growing populations already are experiencing deep shortages of licensed teachers. Moreover, some of their legislative "quick fixes" tilt too far in addressing quantity without equal concern for quality (Waters 1999). Emergency certificates and other approaches may help fix the quantity problem temporarily, but they may make the quality problem worse.

We do not just need more teachers; we need more high-quality teachers. Such teachers possess knowledge about *what* they are teaching; they are skilled in *how* to teach children of different backgrounds and abilities; and they are deeply committed to those *whom* they are teaching. These are the teachers that parents want and will pay more to get, and they certainly are the teachers our children and grandchildren deserve. Our colleges and universities can help bring the finest teachers into classrooms. To produce a world-class teaching force, however, greater focus must be placed on improving teacher education.

TEACHER EDUCATION PARTNERSHIPS

Substantive linkages between higher education and public schools have failed to mature beyond rudimentary transactions. Building university-school partnerships, however, is increasingly viewed as an essential strategy for the comprehensive reform of teacher education. This strategy is premised on Goodlad's (in Bracey 1991, 13) conclusion that "any teacher education program created or conducted without the collaboration of surrounding schools is defective." Goodlad and others promote the concept of "partner schools" as a necessary structure for teacher preparation.

Partnership schools are conceptually similar to the relationship teaching hospitals have to medical schools. Those familiar with the history of teacher education in the United States know that college and university "laboratory schools" devoted to teacher preparation once flourished. Over time, however, lab schools became increasingly dissimilar from regular public schools as they became more selective in admission policies and accessed greater resources. Teachers whose preservice and student teaching experiences largely took place in lab schools were unprepared for the diversity of students and lack of resources in regular schools. This reality, in combination with G. I. Bill effects, led to the closing of lab schools across the United States following World War II.

The growing movement for schools of education to establish relationships with partner schools is not simply an attempt to revive the old university lab schools. An important distinction between them exists: lab schools served a more selective population of students; partner schools function as regular public schools, each of which enrolls students from the community served. Teachers, administrators, and students are assigned by the school(s) rather than the university. This fact alone better ensures that preservice teachers are exposed to the diversity and "real world" of today's public schools.

What makes partner schools different from other public schools is the formal relationship established with the university to support teacher preparation. In this way, partner schools are similar to Japan's "attached schools." Attached schools are Japanese public schools that have a special relationship with a university or a college teacher education program. Teachers in Japan's attached schools are expected (and supported) to assist in the development of future teachers. University faculty members and preservice students routinely observe teachers. They engage in joint lesson-plan development and careful analysis of demonstration teaching. Teachers are, thus, viewed as essential co-partners with university faculty in preparing new teachers. Japan has some concerns, though, with its teacher-preparation programs. Beginning teachers report major gaps between preservice preparation and classroom realities (West, Jarchow, and Quisenberry 1996). Still, only about one-half of them secure teaching positions, meaning only the best-prepared teachers are employed generally. Despite its shortcomings, Japan's attached school model merits further research.

EVIDENCE OF PROGRESS

Significant efforts are under way in the United States to reform teacher preparation. Bringing colleges and universities in closer collaboration is paramount. Leading these efforts is the Holmes Group (1995). Though failing to achieve all that was initially conceived, the group nevertheless conceptualized and energized teacher educators around the idea of the Professional Development School as the site for teacher preparation and development.

The Holmes Partnership, which has evolved out of the Holmes Group, offers promise in supporting universities and schools engaged in collaborative teacher education. The partnership has formally adopted six goals:

1. high-quality professional preparation;
2. simultaneous renewal (of schools and teacher education);
3. equity, diversity, and cultural competence;
4. scholarly inquiry and programs of research;
5. faculty development; and
6. policy initiation.

Moreover, the Holmes initiative is reaching out to establish partnerships with other groups involved in teacher education reform. The partnership is committed to quality networks, working relationships, and inclusive governance structures to advance reform (Fullan et al. 1998).

Other significant national initiatives are under way to build partnerships between universities and schools, including James Comer's School Development Program, Henry Levin's Accelerated Schools Project, Theodore Sizer's Coalition of Essential Schools, and Robert Slavin's Success for All Schools (Holmes Group 1995). These initiatives have offered some exciting opportunities for higher education faculty to become directly involved in school reform and for incorporating some of the best practices in schools directly into teacher preparation.

One of the most successful national initiatives in teacher education reform is the National Network for Educational Renewal, which currently consists of 14 school-university partnerships in as many states (Osguthorpe, Harris, Harris, and Black 1995). The network is guided by 19 postulates, which founder John Goodlad (1990, 54–64), director of the Center for Educational Renewal at the University of Washington, has described as conditions necessary for effective teacher education:

> *Postulate One.* Programs for the education of the nation's educators must be viewed by institutions offering them as a major responsibility to society and be adequately supported and promoted and vigorously advanced by the institution's top leadership.

Postulate Two. Programs for the education of educators must enjoy parity with other campus programs as a legitimate college or university commitment and field of study and service, worthy of rewards for faculty geared to the nature of the field.

Postulate Three. Programs for the education of educators must be autonomous and secure in their borders, with clear organizational identity, constancy of budget and personnel, and decision-making authority similar to that enjoyed by the major professional schools.

Postulate Four. There must exist a clearly identifiable group of academic and clinical faculty members for whom teacher education is the top priority; the group must be responsible and accountable for selecting students and monitoring their progress, planning and maintaining the full scope of the curriculum, continuously evaluating and improving programs, and facilitating the entry of graduates into teaching careers.

Postulate Five. The responsible group of academic and clinical faculty members described above must have a comprehensive understanding of the aims of education and the role of schools in our society and be fully committed to selecting and preparing teachers to assume the full range of educational responsibilities required.

Postulate Six. The responsible group of academic and clinical faculty members must seek out and select for a predetermined number of student places in the program those candidates who reveal an initial commitment to the moral, ethical, and enculturating responsibilities to be assumed.

Postulate Seven. Programs for the education of educators, whether elementary or secondary, must carry the responsibility to ensure that all candidates progressing through them possess or acquire the literacy and critical-thinking abilities associated with the concept of an educated person.

Postulate Eight. Programs for the education of educators must provide extensive opportunities for future teachers to move beyond being students of organized knowledge to become teachers who inquire into both knowledge and its teaching.

Postulate Nine. Programs for the education of educators must be characterized by a socialization process through which candidates transcend their self-oriented student preoccupations to become more other-oriented in identifying with a culture of teaching.

Postulate Ten. Programs for the education of educators must be characterized in all respects by the conditions for learning that future teachers are to establish in their own schools and classrooms.

Postulate Eleven. Programs for the education of educators must be conducted in such a way that future teachers inquire into the nature of teaching and schooling and assume that they will do so as a natural aspect of their careers.

Postulate Twelve. Programs for the education of educators must involve future teachers in the issues and dilemmas that emerge out of the never-ending tension between the rights and interests of individual parents and special-interest groups, on one hand, and the role of schools in transcending parochialism, on the other.

Postulate Thirteen. Programs for the education of educators must be infused with understanding of and commitment to the moral obligation of teachers to ensure equitable access to and engagement in the best possible K-12 education for *all* children and youths.

Postulate Fourteen. Programs for the education of educators must involve future teachers not only in understanding schools as they are but in alternatives, the assumptions underlying alternatives, and how to effect needed changes in school organization, pupil grouping, curriculum, and more.

Postulate Fifteen. Programs for the education of educators must assure for each candidate the availability of a wide array of laboratory settings for the observation, hands-on experiences, and exemplary schools for internships and residencies; they must admit no more students to their programs than can be assured these quality experiences.

Postulate Sixteen. Programs for the education of educators must engage future teachers in the problems and dilemmas arising out of the inevitable conflicts and incongruities between what works or is accepted in practice and the research and theory supporting other options.

> *Even in these early years of the change process, much has been learned by both university and public school educators.*

Postulate Seventeen. Programs for educating educators must establish linkages with graduates for purposes of both evaluating and revising these programs and easing the critical early years of transition into teaching.

Postulate Eighteen. Programs for the education of educators, in order to be vital and renewing, must be free from curricular specifications by licensing agencies and restrained only by enlightened professionally driven requirements for accreditation.

Postulate Nineteen. Programs for the education of educators must be protected from the vagaries of supply and demand by state policies that allow neither backdoor "emergency" programs nor temporary teaching licenses.

The final two postulates are beyond the immediate control of the universities. They can only be achieved within high-quality, productive teacher education partnerships.

Few university-school partnerships align closely with Goodlad's postulates or on a scale that allows access to "lessons learned." One initiative that does hold promise, though, is the University-School Teacher Education Partnerships, under way within 15 teacher education programs in the constituent institutions of the University of

North Carolina. The partnerships are supported by $1.8 million in new funding allocated by the North Carolina General Assembly in 1996. Operationally, they are guided by five goals (Deans' Council on Teacher Education 1996):

1. Increased time for preservice teachers to experience earlier, longer, and more intensive field-based placements in the public schools, connected to methods classes and clinical teachers at school sites.

2. Jointly crafted professional-development programs for teachers, administrators, and others in the public schools and universities.

3. Increased communication between public schools and higher education for the purpose of sharing and disseminating best practices.

4. Generation and application of research and new knowledge about teaching and learning.

5. Joint involvement of university and school personnel in curriculum planning and program development.

The University-School Teacher Education Partnerships are still young, and much more has been slated to be accomplished. However, even in these early years of the change process, much has been learned by both university and public school educators. Following are some of the key lessons learned (Coble in press):

Partnerships are beneficial.

- Partnerships can produce beneficial results that are only possible through collaboration.

- Partnerships can bring professional enrichment and renewal to participants in the public schools and the universities.

Thoughtful selection of partnership participants is an important first step.

- Involve both university and public school faculty in the selection of partnership sites to ensure specific teacher-preparation areas of study.

- Encourage "mutual selection" in teacher-intern matching to help ensure compatible pairings and increase the likelihood of successful learning experiences.

- Allow clinical teacher self-nominations to help ensure that clinical teachers are internally motivated rather than externally pressured to participate in the partnerships.

It is important to take time up-front to lay a foundation for teamwork.

- Build relationships among key participants at the beginning to help build trust and establish ties for open communication.

- Clarify goals, roles, and strategies for implementation (for example, which teaching model to use) to help avoid future confusion and conflict.

- Schedule a half- or full-day planning retreat for participants focused on mission, vision, and goals—a relatively quick and effective way to begin to accomplish partnership objectives.

All stakeholder groups should be involved at appropriate points throughout program development and implementation.

• Give all stakeholder groups opportunities to contribute ideas, communicate their interests, and ask questions before decisions that affect them are made.

• When planning, involve individuals who will be instrumental in later efforts.

• Form student cohorts and assign interns during the development phase.

• Have interns participate in the preparation for the opening of school and the first week of fall classes.

Cultural differences between partners must be acknowledged and addressed.

• Every organization has its own unique culture. Building mutual understanding of differences (for example, priorities and reward systems) can strengthen partnerships.

• Partnerships must create value for all parties. For schools, value may mean improved student performance. For universities, value may mean advances in research.

• Though university faculties have traditionally held primary responsibility for teacher preparation, these partnerships require shared ownership of this responsibility.

The scope of activities undertaken must be realistic with respect to available resources.

• Prioritize goals.

• Begin with a relatively simple focus. Trying to do too many things at one time can dilute the overall effectiveness of the partnership.

• Use regional technology plans to help universities and school districts make the most effective use of instructional technology resources and forge better communication as well.

Failure to plan ahead can hinder success and result in disappointment over unmet timelines.

• Secure long-term financing to help bring stability to partnerships. Periodically communicate the partnership benefits to those footing the bill and to those who influence the funding agencies to help keep these programs within their budgets.

• Because unforeseen difficulties always arise during implementation, allow extra time when giving promise dates for the achievement of specific milestones.

• Secure the time of preservice teachers, teachers, and university faculty members well in advance (for example, one year prior) to ensure that they will have adequate time available to devote to the partnerships.

Training is necessary prior to implementation.

• Once planning is completed, all participants should meet again to discuss how the partnership would be implemented.

• Participants need to know how their individual efforts are important to the overall success of the partnership.

• Effective, school-appropriate methods of training clinical teachers and university supervisors must be provided.

Evaluate, document, and communicate program performance.

• Measurements of program effectiveness are necessary to support funding requests.

• Evaluation of the effectiveness of partnership activities must be routinely conducted. Individual responsibilities for evaluation and documentation must be clearly communicated and consistently reviewed.

• Participants must share successes and lessons learned.

BRINGING DOWN THE SACRED COWS

Some long-held "sacred cows" must be sacrificed if teacher education is to be transformed and if partner schools are to take hold and flourish in U.S. higher education. Four of these sacred cows involve: (1) teachers and schools as co-partners; (2) tenure and promotion of faculty engaged in teacher preparation; (3) schools of education as cash cows; and (4) top leadership of universities embracing teacher preparation.

Teachers and Schools as Co-Partners

One of the most important perspectives that colleges and universities committed to teacher preparation must embrace is teachers and schools as co-partners. The more common post–World War II tradition of simply "using" public schools and teachers as sites for student teaching leaves teachers and school administrators feeling very much like junior partners.

If higher education intends to play a continuing role in the initial professional preparation of teachers (and administrators) in the future, faculty members at these institutions must fully embrace school-based professionals as senior partners in the process. Otherwise, the pedagogical preparation of future teachers will be handled directly by the schools or through other arrangements, such as private business partnerships. This practice already is under way in some states via lateral entry and alternative licensure programs to recruit working adults and liberal arts graduates into teaching (Feistritzer and Chester 1998). In such arrangements, colleges and universities are being relegated to only the academic-content preparation of future teachers. This method also seems to be the ideological preference for some individuals and groups (Thomas B. Fordham Foundation 1999).

Trends toward bypassing pedagogical preparation in higher education will have far-reaching consequences for U.S. education. By disengaging from preservice teacher preparation, higher education will have forfeited more than the opportunity to influence the preparation of teachers—it will have lost any legitimacy in the debate over the future and purposes of public elementary and secondary education. Given the many reactionary forces at work nationally to "re-purpose" U.S. public education, losing the critical perspective and democratizing influence of higher education would be a loss for the nation.

Tenure and Promotion of Faculty

A second sacred cow that must change involves policies guiding tenure and promotion of faculty members engaged in teacher preparation. Developing reward structures that promote rather than deter university faculty involvement in field-based teacher preparation and with partner schools is critical. Without codified promotion and tenure standards that support university faculty engagement in the schools, faculty members will, for self-preserving reasons, avoid extending themselves to the public schools in the substantive ways necessary to produce high-quality teachers.

The mimicking of arts and sciences promotion and tenure standards by professional schools in higher education fuels the disconnection between professional schools and practitioners. The effect of the disconnection is more pronounced in the overregulated "semiprofession" of public school teaching in which teachers have little control over their profession or in selecting their "clients," unlike other professions, such as law and medicine.

In his book *Scholarship Reconsidered,* Boyer (1990) offered a broader view of scholarship that would more fully enfranchise the scholarship of teacher educators in field-based teacher preparation. His more inclusive model defines areas of discovery, integration, application, and teaching as legitimate domains of scholarship.

The study of pedagogical practice and its relationship to increased student motivation and learning in real settings is a legitimate domain of inquiry for teacher educators. The ability to isolate discrete and often subtle interactions between teachers and students and then teach such interactions to prospective teachers is a form of scholarship undervalued in the academic reward structure. Currently, higher education faculty members are rewarded more for publishing papers about *how* to prepare effective teachers than for *applying* that knowledge and actually preparing effective teachers. This critical distinction, of course, is not confined to teacher education alone; it is true in other university-based professional schools, which adds to general criticism of higher education (Patton 1998/99).

Programs may be rewarded or sanctioned if they do not meet state or national accreditation standards, but individual faculty members are immune from those rewards or consequences, because programs are rarely, if ever, closed down. Likewise, the success (or failure) of individual faculty members in producing good teachers is seldom acknowledged.

Schools of Education as Cash Cows

Institutions serious about teacher preparation must stop using schools of education as cash cows for the university. Partner schools that support the fluid interaction of university faculty members and students engaged in clinical work and requisite professional development cannot be supported by impoverished conditions. Institutional funding formulas must recognize the intensive clinical and technology-rich nature of effective teacher preparation. Teacher education programs must have clinical and tenure-track faculty members in close relationships with public schools to ensure quality settings that include effective supervision and the necessary program and staff development.

The very best knowledge and use of technology must also be deployed in teacher education partnerships. Recent studies document the "glass ceiling" higher education is placing on new teachers' use of technology by not preparing preservice teachers in the use of computer-based high-tech equipment (Moursund 1999).

Simply put, teacher education can no longer be conducted "on the cheap." Funding for teacher preparation will need to match more closely funding provided to quality nursing programs, which also provide for clinical faculty and for technology-rich environments.

Leadership Embracing Teacher Preparation

The fourth sacred cow is that high-quality teacher education cannot develop at institutions where campus leaders hold it in low esteem. Top university leadership must embrace teacher preparation. Preparing teachers with the knowledge and skills to teach all students to reach high standards must be seen as one of the most important missions of the university. Teacher preparation must be envisioned as a university-wide function. Liberal arts faculty members must see their critical role in helping students develop a coherent understanding of their disciplines. It is insufficient simply to provide a series of discipline-based course requirements that students must pass to become licensed to teach a subject. All students, but particularly those studying to become teachers, must also understand the broader nature of the discipline and how to teach it to younger people at appropriate levels.

Arts and sciences faculty members can facilitate the success of all students, including those preparing to teach, by modeling more active problem-based learning. A university deeply committed to preparing the most knowledgeable and skilled teachers possible must find ways to encourage arts and sciences faculty members to follow students into their student teaching, assisting them, when necessary, to alter their content delivery and to clear up misconceptions that appear.

COMMIT OR CLOSE

Not all colleges and universities currently engaged in teacher preparation will be willing to give up these sacred cows and embrace teacher preparation as a central mission of the institution. It would be better for the profession if such institutions would close their teacher education programs. This action would be a far more laudable position than maintaining a second-class teacher education program. Some of these institutions may instead choose to develop an alternative strategy of keeping teacher-preparation programs, employing a cadre of experienced non-tenure-track faculty members and practitioners to engage in the important work of preparing teachers.

Individual institutions may have a choice about their commitment to prepare high-quality teachers for the future. When considering their choice, however, they also should consider the interlocking nature of public schools and higher education. The "seed corn" for higher education comes from public schools. It is in the enlightened self-interest of all teacher colleges and universities to prepare a new generation of teachers to be the best they possibly can be for the nation's public schools.

REFERENCES

Boyer, E. L. 1990. *Scholarship reconsidered: Priorities of the professoriate*. Princeton, N.J.: Carnegie Foundation for the Advancement of Teaching.

Brandt, R. 1991. On teacher education: A conversation with John Goodlad. *Educational Leadership* 49(3):11–13.

Coble, C. R. In press. *Reforming teacher education: Going to scale.* Towson, Md.: Metropolitan Universities Press.

Deans' Council on Teacher Education. 1996. A proposal to establish university-school teacher education partnerships in North Carolina. Chapel Hill: University of North Carolina.

Flexner, A. 1910. *The Flexner report on medical education in the United States and Canada.* Washington, D.C.: Carnegie Foundation for the Advancement of Teaching.

Feistritzer, C. E., and D. T. Chester. 1998. *Alternative teacher certification: A state-by-state analysis 1998–99.* Washington, D.C.: National Center for Education Information.

Fullan, M., G. Galluzzo, P. Morris, and N. Watson. 1998. *The rise & stall of teacher education reform.* Washington, D.C.: American Association of Colleges for Teacher Education.

Goodlad, J. I. 1990. *Teachers for our nation's schools.* San Francisco: Jossey-Bass.

Holmes Group. 1995. *Tomorrow's schools of education: Principles for the design for Professional Development Schools.* East Lansing, Mich.: HG.

Moursund, D. 1999. *Project-based learning using information technology.* Eugene, Ore.: International Society for Technology in Education.

National Commission on Teaching & America's Future. 1996. *What matters most: Teaching for America's future.* New York: NCTAF.

Osguthorpe, R. T., R. C. Harris, M. F. Harris, and S. Black. 1995. *Partner schools: Centers for educational renewal.* San Francisco: Jossey-Bass.

Patton, P. E. 1998/99. *Transforming postsecondary education for the 21st century.* Denver: Education Commission of the States.

Riley, R. W. 1999. Partnerships for a quality teacher workforce. A speech presented at the Southern Regional Postsecondary Education Forum, Atlanta, 13 April.

Thomas B. Fordham Foundation. 1999. The teachers we need and how to get more of them. Unpublished paper, 22 April. Washington, D.C.: TBFF.

Waters, M. J. 1999. NC Senate Bill 1124: The lowest standard in the nation for teacher certification? Unpublished paper, 5 April. Chapel Hill: University of North Carolina.

West, B. B., E. Jarchow, and N. L. Quisenberry. 1996. Teacher education research in international settings. In *Handbook of research on teacher education*, 2d ed., ed. J. Sikula, T. J. Buttery, and E. Guyton, 1047–1107. New York: Macmillan.

5

Multicultural Citizenship Education*

By *James A. Banks*

An important goal of multicultural education in the United States is to educate citizens who can participate in the workforce and take action in the civic community to help the nation actualize its democratic ideals. These ideals, including justice, equality, and freedom, are set forth in the Declaration of Independence, the Constitution, and the Bill of Rights. Democratic societies are works-in-progress that require citizens to be committed to democratic ideals, keenly aware of the gap between ideals and realities, and willing and able to take thoughtful action to make democratic ideals a reality.

MULTICULTURAL CITIZENSHIP IN THE NEW MILLENNIUM

Citizenship education must be changed in substantial ways to prepare citizens to function effectively in the 21st century. Citizens in the new century will need the knowledge, attitudes, and skills required to function in their cultural communities, beyond their cultural borders, and in the construction of a national civic culture that embodies and exemplifies democratic values.

In the past, citizenship education embraced an assimilationist ideology. Its aim was to educate students so they would fit into a mythical Anglo-Saxon Protestant conception of the "good citizen." Conformity was the goal of this conception. One of its aims was to eradicate the cultures and languages of students from diverse ethnic, cultural, racial, and language groups. Indeed, many students lost their first cultures, languages, and ethnic identities as a consequence of this assimilationist conception of citizenship education. Many also experienced social and political estrangement within the national civic culture, and some became alienated from family and community.

---

* This chapter is based in part on James A. Banks, "Multicultural Education in the New Century," *The School Administrator* 56(6), May 1990, pages 8–10. Used with permission of the American Association of School Administrators.

In addition, minorities often became marginal members of their cultural communities as well as marginal citizens, because they could function effectively neither within their cultural communities nor within the national civic culture. Even when they acquired the language and culture of the mainstream, they were denied structural inclusion and full participation in the civic culture due to their racial characteristics. They experienced cultural assimilation but were denied structural inclusion in mainstream social, political, economic, and cultural institutions (Gordon 1964).

Citizenship education must be transformed in the new century because of the deepening ethnic texture in the United States. The increasing ethnic, racial, cultural, and language diversity requires that educators reconceptualize citizenship education and educate citizens who can maintain attachments to their cultural communities as well as participate effectively in creating an overarching, shared national civic culture. The national civic culture should actualize U.S. democratic values stated in the founding documents.

Cultural and ethnic communities must be respected and given legitimacy not only because they provide safe spaces and empowerment for ethnic, cultural, and language groups on society's margins but also because they enrich the nation and its culture. The kind of citizenship education needed for the 21st century has been called "cultural citizenship" by Flores and Benmayor (1997) and "multicultural citizenship" by Kymlicka (1995). This type of citizenship recognizes and legitimizes the right and need for citizens to maintain commitments both to their cultural communities and to the national civic culture. Only when the national civic culture is transformed in ways that reflect and give voice to diverse ethnic, racial, and language communities will it be viewed as legitimate by all its citizens. Only then can its citizens develop clarified commitments to the commonwealth and its ideals.

MULTICULTURAL EDUCATION AND MULTICULTURAL CITIZENSHIP

Critics have misrepresented multicultural education, arguing that it is divisive and suggesting it will Balkanize the nation (Schlesinger 1991). Yet multicultural education is designed to help unify our nation and to actualize its ideal of *e pluribus unum*—"out of many, one" (Banks 1997). The claim that multicultural education will divide the nation assumes that it is now united. However, our nation is deeply divided along racial, ethnic, and social-class lines.

During the past two decades, the racial and ethnic divide has widened within the United States. Wilson (1996) has described in poignant detail how low-income African Americans in the inner city are isolated from middle-class African Americans and European Americans. Orfield, Eaton, and the Harvard Project on School Desegregation (1996) have indicated that school desegregation is being "dismantled" and that racial and ethnic segregation is increasing within our nation's schools. The nation seems to have lost its will to desegregate its schools and communities racially.

The new wave of nativism within the nation is also an indication that racial tension and divisions are increasing. Targets of the new nativism include bilingual education, affirmative action, and multicultural education. Much of this nativism originates in California, perhaps because it receives a larger percentage of the nation's immigrants than any other state. The number of immigrants entering the United

States today is the largest since the turn of the last century. More than 600,000 legal immigrants enter each year, most from nations in Asia and Latin America.

If current demographic trends continue, by the year 2020 approximately 46 percent of students will be of non-European descent. Many of the current students enter our schools speaking a language other than English. In 1990, about 14 percent of school-age youth lived in homes in which the primary language was not English (U.S. Bureau of the Census 1998).

Social class marks another important division. The United States has the largest percentage of poverty among Western nations. The number of people living in poverty in the United States in 1997 was 35.6 million (U.S. Bureau of the Census 1998). In 1990, approximately one in five U.S. children lived below the official government poverty line. Single families headed by women is the largest and fastest growing type of poor family (Blank 1997). The gap between the rich and the poor is widening. In 1992, the top 20 percent of U.S. households received 11 times as much income as the bottom 2 percent.

The large number of immigrants entering the United States each year, the increasing percentage of school-age youth who speak a first language other than English, and the widening gap between the rich and poor present challenges and opportunities for educating effective citizens in the new century. Educators must find ways to actualize the opportunities that racial, ethnic, and language diversity provides while creating new ways to minimize problems. All groups within our nation have values, perspectives, and languages that can help solve some of the nation's intractable problems and humanize the lives of all of its citizens. During World War II, the lives of many U.S. soldiers were saved because the Navajo language was used in a secret code that perplexed military leaders in Japan. The code contributed to the victory of the Allies in the South Pacific and advances in the Korean Conflict and Vietnam War.

Multicultural theorists assume we cannot unite the nation around its democratic ideals by forcing people from different racial, ethnic, and cultural groups to leave their cultures and languages at the schoolhouse door (J. A. Banks and Banks 1995). An important principle of a pluralistic democratic society is that citizens will voluntarily participate in the commonwealth and that their participation will enrich the nation-state. When citizens participate in society and bring their cultural strengths to the national civic culture, both they and the nation are enriched. As Flores and Benmayor (1997, 13) noted, "Agency is critical to the concept of cultural citizenship; it reflects the active role of Latinos and other groups in claiming rights." Kymlicka (1995, 6) commented that a nation-state that actualizes multicultural citizenship incorporates both universal and specific cultural rights: "A comprehensive theory of justice in a multicultural state will include both universal rights, assigned to individuals regardless of group membership, and certain group-differentiated rights or 'special status' for minority cultures."

TRANSFORMING THE CENTER BUT MAINTAINING THE MARGINS

We can create an inclusive, democratic, and civic national community only when we change the center to make it more inclusive and reflective of our nation's diver sity. This action will require bringing people and groups on the margins of society into the center. When groups on the margins of society begin to participate in the center, the center must change in fundamental ways. One important change is that groups with power must share it; equal-status relationships must be established between powerful and marginalized groups. Racial and ethnic harmony will not occur unless equal-status relationships are established and power is shared (Allport 1954).

Major problems occur in school and university communities when marginalized groups such as African Americans and Latinos are recruited and invited to participate in mainstream activities but the people in power remain unwilling to make changes to accommodate the cultural, educational, and other needs of these groups. When African Americans and Latinos enroll in predominantly European-American schools, oftentimes the curriculum, staff, and community representations remain predominantly European American and mainstream. This kind of situation results in ethnic conflict and misunderstanding. Minority groups in these situations often experience a sense of alienation and rejection. Consequently, they try to create safe and empowering microcultural communities within mainstream institutions that will respond to their alienation and satisfy their cultural needs for representation and inclusion. These kinds of microcultural communities often evoke negative responses from mainstream European Americans, leading them to ask questions such as, "Why are all the Black kids sitting together in the cafeteria?" In her thoughtful book with that question as its title, Tatum (1997) described the cultural and psychological needs that African-American students are trying to satisfy when they create microcultural communities within predominantly Europeon-American mainstream schools, colleges, and universities.

> *The cultural symbols and representations of diverse groups must be incorporated into the school community and into the curriculum if students from diverse groups are to feel included.*

When marginalized groups begin to participate in the mainstream, the relationship between the mainstream society and the margins should be a dynamic one. Within a society that reflects multicultural citizenship, people are able to participate both in the mainstream society and in their cultural communities on the margins. Marginalized communities should have the right to exist and, indeed, should be protected by the state so they can prosper. The margins are "sites of possibilities" (hooks 1984), because they enable their members to find safe spaces and experience empowerment. They also serve as a conscience for the nation-state.

The margins also enable individuals to satisfy some of their fundamental psychological needs left unfilled in a modernized nation-state. Apter (1977) described modernized societies as "thin" and primordial societies as "thick." He argued that modernized societies leave some of the fundamental psychological needs of individuals unfulfilled. These are the kinds of psychological and cultural needs that Latino and African-American students are trying to satisfy when they sit together in the cafeteria and create special clubs and groups within the school community. The cultural symbols and representations of diverse groups must be incorporated into the school community and into the curriculum if students from diverse groups are to feel included. Structural inclusion of diverse groups and their cultural symbols into a reconstructed mainstream will reduce the likelihood that marginalized groups will create cultural-specific institutions and symbols. The mainstream must be reconstructed to reflect the diverse cultural, ethnic, and language groups within it.

The margins are also sites of possibilities because people in the margins have called upon the United States to live up to the democratic ideals set forth in the nation's founding documents. These groups have served as the U.S. conscience. Okihiro (1994) noted that it was groups in the margins that called upon the United States to live up to its democratic ideals when they were challenged by events such as slavery and the Middle Passage, Indian Removal in the 1830s, the internment of Japanese Americans during World War II, and the segregation and apartheid in the South that lasted from the 1890s to the civil rights movement of the 1960s. People in the margins, such as African-American and European-American abolitionists, American Indians, and African-American civil-rights leaders, challenged events that violated U.S. ideals and consequently helped keep the nation more free and just for all citizens. As Foner (1998, xx–xxi) noted, it was not the founding fathers who extended the idea of freedom in the United States but groups on the margins of society:

> *The authors of the notion of freedom as a universal birthright, a truly human ideal, were not so much the founding fathers, who created a nation dedicated to liberty but resting in large measure on slavery, but abolitionists who sought to extend the blessings of liberty to encompass blacks, slave and free; women who seized upon the rhetoric of democratic freedom to demand the right to vote; and immigrant groups who insisted that nativity and culture ought not to form boundaries of exclusion.*

Schools should be model communities that mirror the kind of democratic society and multicultural citizenship we envision. In democratic schools, the following occurs: the curriculum reflects the cultures of the diverse groups within society; the languages and dialects that students speak remain respected and valued; cooperation rather than competition is fostered among students; and students from diverse racial, ethnic, and social-class groups experience equal status.

CITIZENSHIP EDUCATION AND THE DIMENSIONS OF MULTICULTURAL EDUCATION

To implement an education that promotes multicultural citizenship, multicultural education must be broadly conceptualized. Too often, multicultural education is conceptualized narrowly to mean adding content about diverse groups to the curriculum or expanding the canon taught in schools. For multicultural education to be implemented in ways that will help actualize effective citizenship education, improve race relations, and increase the academic achievement of students from diverse groups, it must be conceptualized broadly. Furthermore, attention must be paid to the research accumulated during the past two decades (J. A. Banks and Banks 1995).

I have conceptualized multicultural education as consisting of five dimensions: (1) content integration, (2) the knowledge-construction process, (3) prejudice reduction, (4) an equity pedagogy, and (5) an empowering school culture and social structure (Banks 1999). Each of these dimensions must receive attention to implement multicultural education in a powerful way and to promote multicultural citizenship education for the new millennium. Following are brief definitions of each of these dimensions.

Content integration addresses the extent to which teachers use examples and content from a variety of cultures and groups to illustrate key concepts, generalizations, and issues within their subject areas or disciplines.

The knowledge-construction process refers to the extent to which teachers help students understand, investigate, and determine how biases, frames of reference, and perspectives within a discipline influence the ways in which knowledge is constructed (Banks 1996). Students also learn how to build knowledge themselves in this dimension.

Prejudice reduction describes lessons and activities used by teachers to help students develop positive attitudes toward different racial, ethnic, and cultural groups. Research indicates that children come to school with many negative attitudes toward and misconceptions about different racial and ethnic groups (Phinney and Rotheram 1987). Research also indicates that lessons, units, and teaching materials that include content about different racial and ethnic groups can help students develop more positive intergroup attitudes if certain conditions exist in the teaching situation (Banks 1995). These conditions include positive images of ethnic groups in teaching materials and the use of multicultural teaching materials in a consistent and sequential way.

An equity pedagogy exists when teachers modify their teaching in ways that will facilitate the academic achievement of students from diverse racial, cultural, and social-class groups (C. A. M. Banks and Banks 1995). Research indicates that the academic achievement of African-American and Mexican-American students is increased when cooperative teaching activities and strategies, rather than competitive ones, are used in instruction (Aronson and Gonzalez 1988). Cooperative learning activities also help all students, including middle-class European-American students, develop more positive racial attitudes. To attain these positive outcomes, however, cooperative learning activities must have several important characteristics (Cohen 1986). The students from different racial and ethnic groups must feel they have equal status in intergroup interactions; teachers and administrators must value and support cross-racial interactions; and students from different racial groups must work together to pursue common goals (Allport 1954).

An empowering school culture and social structure promotes gender, racial, and social-class equality. To implement this dimension, all members of the professional and support staff must participate in examining and restructuring the culture and organization of the school. A teacher cannot implement this dimension alone but must work collaboratively with the principal and with other teachers to create an empowering school culture for all groups of students.

RESEARCH IN MULTICULTURAL EDUCATION

Educators should become familiar with research evidence regarding the effects of multicultural education and not be distracted by its critics, who disregard or distort this significant body of research. Research indicates that students come to school with many stereotypes, misconceptions, and negative attitudes toward outside racial and ethnic groups (Stephan 1999). Research also indicates that the use of multicultural textbooks, other teaching materials, and cooperative teaching strategies can help students develop more positive racial attitudes and perceptions (Banks 1995). This research also indicates that these kinds of materials and teaching strategies can result in students choosing more friends from outside racial, ethnic, and cultural groups.

Research indicates that teachers can increase the classroom participation and academic achievement of students from different ethnic groups by modifying instruction so that it draws upon their cultural strengths. In her study on the Warm Spring Indian Reservation, Philips (1983) noted that American Indian students participated more actively in class discussions when teachers used group-oriented participation structures consistent with their community cultures. Au (1980) and Tharp (1989), working in the Kamehameha Early Education Program, found that both student participation and standardized achievement-test scores increased when they incorporated teaching strategies consistent with the cultures of Native Hawaiian students and used the children's experiences in reading instruction.

Studies summarized by Darling-Hammond (1995) have indicated that the academic achievement of minority students and students from low-income families increases when they have high-quality teachers who are experts in their areas of content specialization, pedagogy, and child development. In her summary, Darling-Hammond cited a significant study by Dreeben (1987), who reported that, when African-American students received high-quality instruction, their reading achievement was as high as that of European-American students. The quality of instruction, not the race of the students, was the significant variable.

THE FUTURE

Educators should recognize that the goals of multicultural education are highly consistent with those of the nation's schools: to develop thoughtful citizens who can function effectively in the world of work and in the civic community. Ways must be found for schools to recognize and respect the cultures and languages of students from diverse groups while, at the same time, working to develop an overarching national culture toward which all groups will have allegiance. This can best be done by bringing groups on the margins of society into the center; educating students who have the knowledge, skills, and values needed to rethink and change the center so that it is more inclusive; and incorporating the research and theory in multicultural education into school reform.

Rethinking and re-imaging the United States in ways that will make it more just and equitable will enrich us all. As Martin Luther King Jr. once said, "We must learn to live together as brothers or perish together as fools."

REFERENCES

Allport, G. W. 1954. *The nature of prejudice*. Cambridge, Mass.: Addison-Wesley.

Apter, D. E. 1977. Political life and cultural pluralism. In *Pluralism in a democratic society*, ed. M. M. Tumin and W. Plotch, 58–91. New York: Praeger.

Aronson, E., and A. Gonzalez. 1988. Desegregation, jigsaw, and the Mexican-American experience. In *Eliminating racism: Profiles in controversy*, ed. P. A. Katz and D. A. Taylor, 301–14. New York: Plenum.

Au, K. 1980. Participation structures in a reading lesson with Hawaiian children. *Anthropology and Education Quarterly* 11(2): 91–115.

Banks, C. A. M., and J. A. Banks. 1995. Equity pedagogy: An essential component of multicultural education. *Theory into Practice* 34(3): 52–58.

Banks, J. A. 1995. Multicultural education: Its effects on students' racial and gender role attitudes. In *Handbook of research on multicultural education*, ed. J. A. Banks and C. A. M. Banks, 617–27. New York: Macmillan.

Banks, J. A., ed. 1996. *Multicultural education, transformative knowledge, and action: Historical and contemporary perspectives*. New York: Teachers College Press.

Banks, J. A. 1997. *Educating citizens in a multicultural society*. New York: Teachers College Press.

Banks, J. A. 1999. *An introduction to multicultural education*, 2d ed. Boston: Allyn and Bacon.

Banks, J. A., and C. A. M. Banks, eds. 1995. *Handbook of research on multicultural education*. New York: Macmillan.

Blank, R. M. 1997. *It takes a nation: A new agenda for fighting poverty*. New York: Russell Sage Foundation.

Cohen, E. G. 1986. *Designing groupwork: Strategies for the heterogeneous classroom*. New York: Teachers College Press.

Darling-Hammond, L. 1995. Inequality and access to knowledge. In *Handbook of research on multicultural education*, ed. J. A. Banks and C. A. M. Banks, 465–83. New York: Macmillan.

Dreeben, R. 1987. Closing the divide: What teachers and administrators can do to help Black students reach their reading potential. *American Educator* 11(4): 28–35.

Flores, W. V., and R. Benmayor. 1997. Constructing cultural citizenship. In *Latino cultural citizenship*, ed. W. V. Flores and R. Benmayor, 1–23. Boston: Beacon Press.

Foner, E. 1998. *The story of American freedom*. New York: Norton.

Gordon, M. M. 1964. *Assimilation in American life: The role of race, religion, and national origins*. New York: Oxford University Press.

hooks, b. 1984. *Feminist theory: From margin to center*. Boston: South End Press.

Kymlicka, W. 1995. *Multicultural citizenship: A liberal theory of minority rights*. New York: Oxford University Press.

Okihiro, G. Y. 1994. *Margins and mainstreams: Asians in American history and culture*. Seattle: University of Washington Press.

Orfield, G., S. E. Eaton, and the Harvard Project on School Desegregation. 1996. *Dismantling desegregation: The quiet reversal of Brown v. Board of Education*. New York: New Press.

Philips, S. U. 1983. *The invisible culture: Communication in classroom and community on the Warm Springs Indian Reservation*. Prospect Heights, Ill.: Waveland Press.

Phinney, J. S., and M. J. Rotheram, eds. 1987. *Children's ethnic socialization: Pluralism and development*. Beverly Hills, Calif.: Sage Publications.

Schlesinger, A. M., Jr. 1991. *The disuniting of America: Reflections on a multicultural society*. Knoxville, Tenn.: Whittle Direct Books.

Stephan, W. 1999. *Reducing prejudice and stereotyping in schools*. New York: Teachers College Press.

Tatum, B. D. 1997. *Why are all the Black kids sitting in the cafeteria? And other conversations about race*. New York: Basic Books.

Tharp, R. G. 1989. Culturally compatible education: A formula for designing effective classrooms. In *What do anthropologists have to say about dropouts?* ed. H. T. Treuba, G. Spindler, and L. Spindler, 51–66. New York: Falmer.

U. S. Bureau of the Census. 1998. *Statistical abstract of the United States: 1998*, 118th ed. Washington, D.C.: U. S. Government Printing Office.

Wilson, W. J. 1996. *When work disappears: The world of the new urban poor*. New York: Knopf.

6

The Politics of National Education Standards

By *R. Freeman Butts*

As the 1990s draw to a close, we can look back on how public education has become a top-priority political issue across the United States, albeit a highly divisive one. Sociopolitical controversies have often focused on teaching practices: bilingualism versus immersion for immigrant children, evolution versus creationism in science classes, drill exercises versus creative thinking in mathematics, phonics versus whole language in reading, and state or national standards as the basis for assessment. Religious disputes have also become common, including calls for organized prayer and Bible reading in public schools and publicly funded vouchers to send children to private and religious schools.

These rancorous, politicized debates put at risk the very idea of public education as the foundation of democratic citizenship. Ironically, these debates are pulling U.S. society apart at a time when education for democratic citizenship is receiving an enthusiastic welcome in many parts of the world, especially in newly independent states of the former Soviet bloc.

The United States was a self-proclaimed newly independent state 220 years ago. While the United States' Revolutionary War was raging up and down Virginia at the close of the 18th century, Thomas Jefferson was looking ahead. Campaigning for establishing public schools as foundations for building a cohesive civic society, Jefferson envisioned them free from religious control yet honoring the diverse values of an increasingly pluralistic people. The civic glue was to be a public system of universal, free, common schools whose basic purpose was to prepare all citizens for commitment to democratic values in a constitutional republic. Jefferson was the first to propose a state law that would vest the very existence of a free republican government in a state-sponsored system of public education, extending from primary schools through a state university. He did this in 1779 as a legislator in the House of Delegates of the newly independent state of Virginia—just three years after he wrote the U.S. Declaration of Independence.

Jefferson believed the core of primary education should be the study of history and the curriculum should be civic-centered rather than kinship- or religious-centered. Virginians, however, were not ready to adopt a system of public education at the time. In 1779, Jefferson also proposed a bill to protect religious freedoms by prohibiting the use of taxes to support religious teachers of Protestant denominations in Virginia. He lost that battle. In 1786, James Madison engineered the passage of Jefferson's Statute for Religious Freedom against the determined opposition of the Christian coalition of the day—just before he went to Philadelphia to draw up the U.S. Constitution to strengthen the Federal Government.

Madison, nurtured by Jefferson, thus was prepared to frame the first two complementary clauses of the First Amendment of the Constitution, which stated, "Congress shall pass no law respecting an establishment of religion or prohibiting the free exercise thereof." Jefferson and Madison agreed that an assessment or tax for religious worship or the teaching of religion of any kind was the essence of "an establishment of religion." President Jefferson, in his inaugural address of 1801, declared that "the essential principles of our government" were set forth in the Constitution and the U.S. Bill of Rights and should be taught as "the creed of our political faith, the text of civic instruction." These principles included equal rights, exact justice, freedom of religion, freedom of the press, and freedom of the person.

In fact, many patriots campaigned for a *national* system of public schools that would serve similar civic ends. In 1796, the American Philosophical Society, of which Jefferson was president, launched an essay contest on "the best system of liberal education adapted to the genius of the government of the United States." The two winners were Jeffersonian Democratic Republicans Samuel Harrison Smith and Samuel Knox. Strongly favoring public education in the new states, they argued that there should be a national system of public educational institutions devoted to the public good, liberty, and equality under federal auspices.

The logic of those young Jeffersonians was impeccable. If state public education systems were the proper seedbeds for the newly independent states in the 1770s and 1780s—and if those states, after a decade of separate independence, saw the necessity of a stronger federal union—then there should be a federal public education system to nourish and support the new national political community embodied in the Constitution. Impeccable logic perhaps, but it was unpersuasive politics for the 1790s—as it continued to be into the 1990s.

Let's indulge in a little historical whimsy. What if Jeffersonian educators and political leaders had somehow managed to produce a set of national standards for teaching civics and government based on Jefferson's "text of civic instruction" and then persuaded all state schools to accept it voluntarily? What if they had produced successive generations of trained teachers who could teach those ideas and instill those ideals in schoolchildren in the South as well as the North for the next 50 years? Might the nation have avoided a Civil War? After all, in less than 50 years, reform of schools in Germany and Japan helped to replace totalitarian teachings with democratic ones after World War II.

In the wake of the Cold War, significant international efforts are being made to strengthen a new democratic civic education and civic culture to speed the shift from communism in the newly independent states of the former Soviet Union, Central and Eastern Asia, and other parts of the world. One of the most significant of these efforts is called CIVITAS: An International Civic Education Exchange Program.

"Civitas," a word easily recognized outside of the United States, is a seldom used English word linked to the Latin *civis* (citizen) and *civilitas* (civility). It has two related meanings: (1) a political community or government, especially as found in a republic, and (2) the kind of citizenship required in a republic. In this chapter, the shorthand phrase, "education for civitas," is used to include the civics lessons that all students must learn to achieve and maintain a constitutional democracy and become democratic citizens. Both of these meanings are especially urgent for educational goals as we look toward the next century.

The civic knowledge and civic values foundational to constitutional democracy are neatly summed up in *CIVITAS: A Framework for Civic Education* (Quigley and Bahmueller 1991), the predecessor to the Center for Civic Education's (1994) *National Standards for Civics and Government*. These volumes in civic education are prime examples of the more general effort to develop national education standards as a major means of educational reform in the 1980s and '90s. The volumes argue that civics and government should be core studies required of all students at all school levels.

Perhaps most important for educators, teaching civic knowledge and values can help counteract competing trends in U.S. society that threaten the very idea of public education as a foundation of democracy. Cynicism, apathy, and distrust of government and all its progeny suggest a growing demand to rely more on the "free market" as the principal provider of U.S. education. To counteract privatizing campaigns, the greatest imperative for federal, state, and local education policies is to enable students to achieve national standards of educational proficiency in the core studies. Strengthening and accelerating the bipartisan efforts undertaken since the 1989 Charlottesville Education Summit in Virginia remain a top priority.

THE POLITICS OF MISTRUST

For some years, U.S. opinion polls and scholarly studies have been documenting alienation, cynicism, apathy, frustration, anger, and a generally "foul mood" among citizens about their government. For example, soon after the 1994 congressional elections marking the Republican Party "revolution," Daniel Yankelovich (1995, 6), chairman of Public Agenda, commented: "My fear is that . . . the present mood will harden into class warfare, generational warfare, exacerbated racial tensions, polarization and political extremism, demagoguery, and instability as we careen from one oversimplistic solution to another."

This distrust is explained by a number of factors, first of which is the "knowledge gap." Many people just do not know much about government or politics—nor do they care. The less knowledgeable people are, of course, the less likely they will vote and participate in public affairs. Not surprisingly, various surveys also confirm growing cynicism about politics and government among U.S. high school and college students as well as among adults. What should the curriculum of schools be doing about this pervasive political alienation?

One of the most wide-ranging answers to this question is a report called "Breaking Ranks," sponsored by the Carnegie Foundation for the Advancement of Teaching and the National Association of Secondary School Principals (1996). Gene Maeroff (1996, 60), principal author of the report, has called apathy and anonymity the twin scourges of modern post-adolescence. The study documents the ways the larger society, "teeming with cynicism over authority, government, and almost all of life's institutional dimensions," stokes similar feelings among youth, saying, in effect, "Responsibility to community is for chumps." Nevertheless, Maeroff (1996, 60) argued that schools must struggle "to persuade teenagers of the merits of learning and to inculcate within them an appreciation of civic virtue." He emphasized relating academic pursuits to young people's experiences and connecting curriculum content to real-life applications of knowledge and skills. To fuse this connection, he suggested requiring students to meet performance standards aligned with assessment of what is taught.

Thus, "Breaking Ranks" recommended that all high schools "advocate and model" a set of core values, rebutting the misguided notion that high schools should straddle questions of values by remaining neutral. There can be no neutrality when it comes to weapons, drugs, and violence. The report recommended "nurturing a feeling for the common good" by requiring students to participate in service learning. These proposals for educational reform are in tandem with ideas proposed in *CIVITAS* and the *National Standards for Civics and Government*.

Skepticism in the educational profession and in the public, however, remain about such "requirements" for values teaching, mainly on the grounds that schools cannot do much about core civic values or should not try to counteract the intrusion of social problems into the classroom. The government, the argument goes, has no business taking sides on matters of values. On the contrary, the effort to solve this problem is being made on several fronts.

THE POLITICS OF VIRTUE

One of the more popular demands for schools to combat social ills is to teach "character education" and "moral values." The pleas for teaching virtue now range across the political and intellectual spectrum from conservative to centrist to liberal. At one extreme, Christian Coalition activists deplore the absence of traditional, religious-based morality in schools and demand prayer, Bible reading, and creationism teachings as cures. Centrists and liberals argue for a more generalized character education, without the explicit stress on religion.

Current U.S. President Bill Clinton and his wife, Hillary Rodham-Clinton, have addressed educational themes regarding moral imperatives, better instruction in civics and government, access to religious expression, promotion of community service, and uniforms in schools to help develop a sense of community in young people. Communitarians under the leadership of Amitai Etzioni have sponsored White House conferences on "Character Education for a Democratic, Civil Society." A bipartisan National Commission on Civic Renewal (1998) headed by former Secretary of Education William Bennett and former Senator Sam Nunn emphasized the need for greater participation by citizens in local community groups, along with character education and service learning. Other schemes emphasizing character education have received public and professional attention in recent years. The key difference, though, is that many of these programs stress teaching *moral* virtues based on religion, rather than *civic* virtues based on the values of democratic citizenship.

Virtue and character have also appeared in scholarly academic volumes across a wide spectrum of political outlooks (Glendon and Blankenhorn 1995; Elshtain 1995; Galston 1991; Eberly 1995; Fukuyama 1995; Carter 1996). Little is being said about the role public education should play in shaping the values of our common citizenship. A great deal, however, is said about the moral education provided by "civil society"—those voluntary associations praised by de Tocqueville that lie between government and the individual, stemming from religious, socioeconomic, or charitable motivations. More rewarding for the study of civitas is research sponsored by the American Historical Association and the American Political Science Association (1983–87) during the dozen or so years leading up to the bicentennial of the Constitution and the Bill of Rights. Much of this scholarship flowed into curriculum materials produced by the civic education movement of the 1970s and 1980s (Gutmann 1987; Ketcham 1987; Barber 1992; Sandel 1996; Butts 1980; 1988; 1989).

On the eve of the 21st century, as we debate the role of government in national culture, let us consider: Shall we be guided by the politics of mistrust, which will lead to a free market approach limiting government in education, strengthening private education, and perhaps dismantling public schools? Or shall we be guided by a philosophy of civic virtue that believes a republican form of government and public education play a formative role in developing citizenship virtue? Will a free market in education or national educational standards lead us to better civic virtue as in the fundamental principles and values of civitas?

THE FREE-MARKET APPROACH TO EDUCATIONAL REFORM

On one side, the free-market approach argues that standards for school conduct and curriculum should rely chiefly on parental rights, parental choice supported by vouchers or tax-free savings accounts, privatization of public schools, or charter schools. On the other side is the view that public, professional, and scholarly bodies should define common standards that all students in all schools are expected to meet.

The historic civic purpose of public education in our constitutional democracy can be threatened by extreme free-market approaches to educational reform, including: efforts to pass laws or constitutional amendments to make "parental rights," rather than preparation for citizenship, the cornerstone of public school policy; encouraging parental choice through vouchers, enabling children to attend private and religious schools at public expense; and extending contracts to private for-profit agencies to run public schools. Moreover, it remains unclear if popular campaigns for charter schools will promote civic values of public education as a nourisher of common good. Following is an examination.

Parental Rights

Since the 1994 Republican revolution, parental rights in education have gained new popularity. Bills or proposed constitutional amendments introduced in Congress and in a majority of states permit parents to be the prime or sole judges of what schools should teach children. These proposals, however, contradict the 1925 U.S. Supreme Court decision in *Pierce v. Society of Sisters* that parents have a duty to send their children to schools that teach good citizenship. Under *Pierce*, states cannot require children to attend public schools and parents remain free to send their children to private and religious schools; however, education for civitas must remain a top priority in all schools and for all parties: government, schools, parents, and students.

Vouchers

Another approach to the free market in education involves "vouchers," often called "scholarships," enabling parents to use public funds to send their children to private and religious schools. This movement has gained enormous vitality, stoked primarily by religious and politically conservative organizations and Republican leaders. At the root of vouchers, but often suppressed in the rhetoric, is the constitutional principle of separation of church and state. A critical moment arose in June 1998, when the Wisconsin Supreme Court ruled that the state could provide public funds for economically disadvantaged children to attend religious schools in Milwaukee on the grounds that such a policy does not violate the establishment clause of the Constitution's First Amendment. When this decision reaches the U.S. Supreme Court, the opportunity will be given to Justices Rehnquist, Scalia, Thomas, and others to reinterpret Jefferson and Madison.

The effect of vouchers in the long run would undermine the very idea of a common school designed to prepare all students for their roles as citizens in a democratic republic. I say this not only from my studies of history during the past 50 years but also from my direct experience in California during the past 20 years (Butts 1950; 1985; 1997).

Privatization

Little or nothing can be found about education for civitas in projects by non-profit organizations advocating "restructuring and reinventing schools" or by profit-making organizations (like the Edison Project) advocating "educational alternatives" designed to bring better business practices into management of public schools and make money for private stockholders. All such privatizing projects must guarantee that the high duty of citizenship and the obligation for public good will be learned by the teachers, students, proprietors, promoters, administrators, and overseers of the project.

Charter Schools

A fourth variation on the free-market approach is the charter school movement, which has rapidly expanded from one school in one state in 1992 to some 800 schools in 29 states in 1998. Charter schools may turn out to be more accepted than any other effort to loosen up or do away with our public education systems. Proponents for charter schools say little about education for civitas, except for occasional references to "service learning" or "community experience." Civic education should al ways be a required part of the public's contract with charter schools as well as any other so-called school reform effort. Whatever political resolution we reach entering the 21st century, requirements for civitas education should not be weakened.

In general, the politicizing and partisanship of educational reform became the mode in elections and political debates of the late 1990s. Republicans made much of parental rights and of reducing the federal financial role in education. Some desired movement toward a full free market for private and religious efforts in education, yet supported by federal and state funds in the form of charter schools and vouchers for private and religious schools.

Democrats maintained support for public education but moved toward parental rights by supporting parental choice among public schools and by expanding support for charter schools. Whether large numbers of Democrats would begin to support vouchers for inner-city scholarships for poor children remains to be seen. Polls in Milwaukee and elsewhere found that some inner-city African Americans favored choice programs to help them escape from deteriorating public schools.

Contrarieties appeared on both sides. To oversimplify: Many Republicans in Congress and the states wanted the government to play a minimal role in education by removing regulations requiring affirmative action for minorities, thereby freeing states, localities, and parents to follow their own desires in schooling children. They also wanted the government to be "activist" by promoting private virtue through prayer, inserting creationism in public school curricula, and providing public funds for private and religious schools. Many Democrats wanted the government to protect individual rights and, thus, prohibit religious teachings in public schools. They also promoted government "activism" regarding civic virtue and good citizenship through civitas and through affirmative action to ensure equality of opportunity for all children.

THE URGENCY OF NATIONAL STANDARDS IN EDUCATION FOR CIVITAS

Free-market projects in educational reform should be funded voluntarily by private agencies of civil society rather than by federal, state, or local public funds via taxation. Public funds are better used to bolster and improve public education to achieve its historic, primary goal—a universal, free, common education for civitas. The *National Standards for Civics and Government*, and its predecessor volume, *CIVITAS*, provide a sound 21st-century rationale for this task. They could be powerful antidotes for our current sour mood of "anti-politics." They could be positive aids to "recivilizing" our political understanding and discourse.

When the new national standards for U.S. history and English came under withering criticism from politicians, publicists, and educators alike, the very idea of national standards in general was endangered. In contrast, that kind of criticism has not been leveled at the *National Standards for Civics and Government*. They have been almost universally lauded and approved, including support from former Chief Justice Warren Burger, U.S. Senators Claiborne Bell and Mark Hatfield, the National Conference of State Legislatures, and a variety of religious, civic, and educational organizations.

The civics standards were prepared by the nonprofit, nonpartisan Center for Civic

Education through an extensive and intensive consensus-building process involving some 3,000 individuals and organizations. More than 150 open hearings and public discussions were held, allowing for expression of a broad range of political views. More than 1,000 specific written suggestions were received from informed and knowledgeable commentators.

Since their unveiling at the U.S. Supreme Court in September 1991—at the invitation of former Chief Justice Warren Burger—the *National Standards for Civics and Government* recall U.S. education to its historic civic mission in ways that will enable citizens to cope with the modern world of the 21st century. They, in effect, provide us with a new edition of a "text of civic instruction," designed to achieve national education goals for all students in all schools. To paraphrase Jefferson at the onset of the 19th century, what other hope is there for Republicans and Democrats to become "brethren of the same principle" in the 21st century? In a democracy, a healthy electorate is the only sure cure for ailing politicians and government. That is why the electorate needs a reinvigorating and reenergizing civic education.

Civics standards set forth what all citizens must know to become rationally committed to constitutional democracy in the United States. They are organized around five fundamental questions:

At a time when political democracy is vital to the whole world, the U.S. national-standards movement must not be derailed.

1. What is government, and what should it do?
2. What are the basic values and principles of U.S. democracy?
3. How does the government established by the Constitution embody the values and principles of U.S. democracy?
4. What is the relationship of the United States to other nations and to world affairs?
5. What are the roles of citizens in U.S. democracy?

In March 1996, when the Governing Board of the National Assessment of Educational Progress unanimously adopted a framework for its 1998 nationwide tests in civics, it voted to use the civics standards as guidelines. During the same time, the International Association for the Evaluation of Educational Achievement adapted them for its 1998 assessment of civic education in 25 countries.

For civics and government, we are well on the way to defining "world-class standards" proposed by the Excellence Commission appointed by Secretary of Education Terrell Bell under President Ronald Reagan in 1983, by the first summit of governors under President Bush in 1989, and by the second summit of governors and business leaders in 1996. At a time when political democracy is vital to the whole world, the U.S. national-standards movement must not be derailed.

"Bureaucrats" in Washington devised neither the civics standards nor the companion volume. Both were formulated by scholarly consensus regarding core civic values and principles that should be taught in all schools, public and private. They are exemplary, voluntary guidelines for civic education conducted by states, local districts, teachers, and parents. They are quietly achieving the widely desired purposes of national standards without the divisive debates that erupted over history and English standards.

CIVITAS was developed by scholars in political science, constitutional law, and education. Its National Review Council of civic leaders was chaired by the late Ernest Boyer, president of the Carnegie Foundation for the Advancement of Teaching. It drew the consensus of a 60-member Teachers Advisory Committee drawn from all 50 states. Every topic in *CIVITAS* presents a conceptual or philosophical perspective, a historical perspective, and a contemporary perspective.

The three major topics for study were based on a consensus of scholarly and citizen judgment: (1) civic virtue, (2) civic participation, and (3) civic knowledge and skills. Moreover, familiar principles and structures of U.S. government are addressed, including "popular sovereignty," "rule of law," "separation of powers," "checks and balances," "separation of church and state," "civilian control of the military," and "federalism." Every one of these dusty and dull textbook topics has become the subject of current bitter debate over the role of government in national life.

The most distinctive aspect of *CIVITAS*, which makes it so different from most civics textbooks and curriculum frameworks, is its emphasis on the fundamental civic values of constitutional democracy. The "Seven Icons of Civic Virtue" that constitute the core of the civitas lessons that U.S. citizens must learn include:

I. The Public Good

The first icon of a democratic constitutional government and, thus, of education for civitas derives from the classical republican tradition that obligated citizens to subordinate their private interests to the public good to form a more perfect union, ensure domestic tranquility, provide for the common defense, and promote the general welfare. Drawing upon this classical republican tradition of politics, the founders of the Republic used the term "civic virtue" to mean that good citizenship requires private interests to be secondary to the common good. The founders also drew upon 17th- and 18th-century liberal tradition, viewing the chief end of government to be the prime protector of the individual rights of citizens in a constitutional democracy. *CIVITAS* argues that both the classical republican tradition and the 18th-century liberal view of citizenship belong in the spectrum of national civic values and that both have a balanced place in the scholarly curriculum of education for civic virtue in the future.

II. Freedom of Individual Rights

The second icon of democratic government and of education for civitas seeks to secure the blessings of liberty and to act as prime protector of the liberal tradition of individual rights, as proclaimed by the Declaration of Independence and guaranteed by the Constitution and Bill of Rights: life, liberty, property, and the pursuit of happiness. There are two kinds of individual rights. First, freedom of the person and of private action involves the right, the opportunity, and the ability of every person to live a life of dignity and security and to seek self-fulfillment as an individual and as a member of a chosen group without arbitrary constraint by others. Second, freedom of the mind and of intellectual inquiry involves the right, the opportunity, and the ability of every person to speak, read, think, believe, express, learn, and teach without arbitrary constraint or coercion by others.

III. Justice

A third icon establishes justice in such way that all persons are treated fairly in the distribution of benefits and burdens of society and in the correction of wrongs and injuries. Justice defines the moral basis of conduct in a democratic well-ordered society. The basic idea of justice is that which is fair. It includes, but is not limited to, the civil and criminal "justice system." All people should be treated fairly in the distribution of the benefits and burdens of society and the correction of wrongs and injuries. Justice also defines the moral basis of a democratic society: what must govern the conduct of persons in their relations to one another if the society is to be self-sufficient and well-ordered. Justice establishes the claims of what is publicly right and is prior to the claims of what is privately good as defined by different individuals or by different groups in conformity with their own particular desires. A just social system sets the boundaries within which individuals and groups may develop their own distinctive pluralistic aims and desires.

IV. Equality

A fourth icon is the nation's historic creed of equality, which decrees that all persons be treated by government and by education in such way that they have equal rights and opportunities to develop themselves to the fullest extent possible, politically, legally, socially, and economically. The idea of equality not only runs through the historic national creed of value claims in a democratic political community but also now permeates international covenants of human rights from the United Nations Declaration of Human Rights of 1945 to the Women's Conference in Beijng of 1995. Jefferson's Declaration of Independence that "all men are created equal" must now be taken to mean that "all persons should be treated as though they are equal" in their claims to the other democratic civic values. Though the physical or mental condition of all persons at birth may not be equal, they should all have equal rights to develop themselves to the fullest extent possible.

V. Diversity

Respect for social and cultural diversity is another one of the glories of the U.S. political system. In *People of Paradox*, Michael Kammen (1973, 85) made a useful distinction between an "unstable pluralism" and a "stable pluralism." A stable pluralism is based upon a strong underpinning of political legitimacy "best insured by the rule of law—law made within a framework of an explicit constitution." Kammen added that "stable pluralism in a democracy also requires a strong and lasting inventory of psychological legitimacy: understanding, acceptance, and pervasive confidence in the composite system necessary to make it run smoothly rather than by fits and starts." By contrast, an unstable pluralism occurs when cleavages in a society are so strong that they threaten the very authority of the polity itself. This happens when each racial, ethnic, religious, or regional group forms its own political party, militia, or faction, "each sect its own school, and each dogmatist his own ideology." The vicious conflicts in the states of the former Yugoslavia and Soviet Union, along with those in the Middle East and Africa, issue global warnings of the dangers of unstable pluralism.

VI. Truth

A sixth icon holds that public knowledge must be reliable and valid to maintain trust in democratic government itself. The reliability and validity of public knowledge are major requirements in a democracy. Trust in the veracity of government constitutes an essential bond between those who govern and those who are governed. The First Amendment not only protects freedom of expression for the individual but also ensures freedom for public and political discussion as a fundamental protection of constitutional government itself. These freedoms require untrammeled access to knowledge that is true, valid, and reliable. That is where knowledge of civics comes in—to help citizens in the process of "winnowing and sifting" the significant truth from the "plausible falsehood" and the "beguiling half truth" so dear to the rough and tumble of the political process in an open society. Call to mind the role of truth-telling in the investigations of the White House, from Watergate to Irangate to Monicagate, as well as charges leveled against past House speakers.

VII. Patriotism

A seventh icon of education for civitas promotes patriotism, loyalty, and love of country. Any defensible conception of citizenship and civic virtue must take account of the extraordinary dynamic force that patriotic sentiments play in national life. In its best sense, patriotism binds the diverse segments of U.S. society into an integral democratic polity. In its worst sense, it inflames a nationalistic chauvinism, setting one group against another in rival efforts to prove who are the true patriots. Fifty years ago, historian Merle Curti in his pathfinding book *The Roots of American Loyalty* (1968) defined patriotism as "love of country, pride in it, and readiness to make sacrifices for what is consideed its best interest." He echoed the expectation that public education from kindergarten through the state university should be a prime element in forming the "character of citizenship." Too often, the voice of sacrifice, apart from military service, stands mute. Notice the positive responses U.S. General Colin Powell received when he called for a sense of duty, discipline, and obligation as the essence of civic virtue.

Schools alone cannot instill the necessary values of personal obligation and responsibility when other major social institutions concentrate on promoting their private interests. Though most people believe schools must play a major role in developing a humane patriotism, they periodically disagree on whether compulsory salutes to the flag in school should be required or whether a constitutional amendment should be passed declaring that desecration of the flag be punishable by fine or imprisonment.

In regard to these Seven Icons of Civic Virtue, there remains an urgency to agree upon national education standards, especially for education in civitas. These standards can provide a common framework of civic education, whether they be compulsory-public, voluntary-public, charter-public, secular-private, religious-private, or whatever combination the political process may produce in the states and the nation in coming years.

The 1996 Education Summit in Palisades, New York, called by state governors and business leaders, reaffirmed support for high academic standards but insisted they be drawn at state and local levels, thus departing from earlier summits that stressed common national standards. Instead of a bipartisan national council to approve state standards, as provided for in Goals 2000, the 1996 summit agreed to establish a nongovernmental clearinghouse (called Achieve) to spread information and assist states in their efforts. This decision clearly implied that academic standards should be the business of states and localities rather than the federal government.

Throughout 1997 and 1998, the prospective role of national standards and voluntary national assessment tests was debated. By and large, the initial role of the federal government as envisioned by the governors and the Democratic Congress before 1994 was gradually reduced. Even President Clinton's later proposal to strengthen standards in reading and mathematics through voluntary national tests was vigorously challenged. Educators themselves were divided over the advisability of national examinations, a debate succinctly described by Sara Mosle (1996, 45):

> *Education is a campaign issue without a focus. The school reform that really matters is not vouchers or charter schools or breaking the unions or wiring the classrooms. It's a curriculum set in Washington and monitored in every town and city through testing. . . . Resistence to testing comes from both liberal and conservative quarters. Progressive educators worry that a national curriculum would lead to more rote exercises, unimaginative teaching, and a greater reliance on standardized tests, which they see as biased against poor and minority-group children. And conservatives, who you might think would cozy up to standards, are deeply suspicious of any sort of outside meddling in their neighborhood schools. Several districts, for instance, have turned down federal funds offered under Goals 2000 rather than cede any perceived control of their schools to the Federal Government.*

Mosle has come down on the side of the current movement for national standards, which emphasizes equal opportunity as well as widespread achievement—goals upon which conservatives and liberals alike could agree. She cited Diane Ravitch, C. D. Hirsch, and Al Shanker as leading advocates of standards. Mosle (1996, 47) insightfully argued, "Standards advocates like Shanker have essentially offered a trade-off with more progressive-minded educators: standards for charter schools. It's a deal that those on both the left and right can accept." She also had it right when she noted, "Choice makes no sense without standards."

Standards in education for civitas are fully as important as those in English, mathematics, history, and science. At the very least, education for civitas should be a core requirement that runs throughout the K–12 school curriculum, the preservice preparation of teachers, and the continuing professional development of all teachers. In the new millennium, teachers must reach and teach an increasingly diverse student population and must promote the cohesive values and principles underlying our common citizenship, no matter what their specialized field of teaching (Butts 1993).

National and state groups now at work to improve the licensing and assessment of teachers and the accrediting of institutions should require study of the civic foundations of education as part of the common preparation for all teachers. Only in this way will all teachers be enabled to prepare every child for "Student Achievement and Citizenship" as proclaimed in Goal 3 of Goals 2000. Only in this way will lasting success in educational reform be achieved; only then will reforms in teacher education connect with certification and accreditation.

In a society increasingly divided by those who preach religiously based moral values and those who prefer secular-based moral values, all teachers must learn about, as well as exemplify, civic-based moral values. This divisiveness has shown itself specifically in the widespread controversies over U.S. history standards. The history standards have given us *pluribus*, and the civics standards have given us *unum*. Somehow, together, history and civics must be endowed with the necessary time and scholarly quality that will enable the Republic safely to survive.

EDUCATION FOR CIVITAS A SEAMLESS WEB

Civic learning must be a seamless web throughout primary and secondary schools, continuing through liberal arts colleges and schools of education. All teachers, not merely those teachers who specialize in teaching history, geography, civics, government, or social studies, need better grounding in the challenging knowledge set forth in the *National Standards for Civics and Government* and in *CIVITAS*. This general idea was broached at the Hoover Institution Seminar on "Civic Learning in the Education of the Teaching Profession," which I chaired at Stanford University in November 1984, just a week after the election of President Reagan (Jones 1985; Butts 1983). It was attended by 60 educators from 32 different colleges and universities and co-sponsored by ten preeminent organizations devoted to the scholarly arts and sciences and professional education. The idea of a core of civic foundations of education did not get very far, however, following that election—and the results of recent elections at federal, state, and local levels have often reflected a general protest against government itself and support for promises to reduce and limit government.

We now have a window of opportunity to change the widespread perception that civics is the most boring of school subjects. Instead, it could become one of the most important and "challenging" subjects in the K–12 curriculum, as well as in the liberal arts, preservice teacher education, and professional-development programs for inservice teachers. Consider how the study and discussion of civics courses could take on new life as a result of the political debates of the 1990s leading up to the elections of 2000. High school and college students should be studying a new kind of civics that deals in a candid, lively, and scholarly way with the fundamental issues underlying the past and the future of constitutional democracy.

The *National Standards for Civics and Government* have come at just the right time to bridge the gap between communities and schoolrooms. In the long run, one cannot succeed without the other. If the voluntary community activities praised so highly by de Tocqueville in U.S. civil society of the 19th century are genuinely to promote the democratic values and principles of constitutional democracy, they must be linked with and cultivated by (1) the civic knowledge and values that students acquire in schools through *CIVITAS* and the *National Civics Standards* and (2) the civic knowledge and values that teachers acquire in their liberal arts and professional education. Though educational issues are the hottest of political buttons, it is time for all citizens to collaborate in supporting scholarly, nonpartisan programs to educate students and the public about civitas.

No matter which partisan candidates win in any one year's election and no matter what role privatization may come to play in educational reform, we must achieve the goal of nationwide standards in education for civitas to combat the politics of mistrust and promote the values of civic virtue. This goal requires the joint efforts of schools and universities, government at all levels, the media, business and labor, and the voluntary efforts of the civic-minded agencies of society. To this end, we also must mobilize university scholars of related academic disciplines to work closely with professional educators in the schools and colleges of education. We also need the support of the major players of all those community and national organizations devoted to public education and the public good.

There are ominous signs ahead for public education and for the role of the federal government in education, which includes suspicion toward government itself. In coming years, we must thread our way through the minefields set for public education and for teacher education by extremists on the right as well as extremists on the left of the political spectrum. The religious right has mounted a national campaign to elect conservative majorities on local school boards, in state legislatures, and in Congress. Political and partisan campaigns to authorize public funds to provide vouchers for parents to send their children to private and sectarian religious schools are being mounted in more than half the states and in both houses of Congress. Extending vouchers and parental choice to religiously controlled schools will intensify controversies over the separation of church and state. Combining a push for national standards along with heightened legal and political warfare over religion in education creates a complicated no-win situation for public education. If extreme parental choice and vouchers should win the campaign for educational reform, national standards will be imperiled; it could even mean the end of public education as we know it.

The battle lines over U.S. education are drawn. Public education must not shrink from its historic educational goal of cultivating civic virtue. The idea of civic virtue as a prime value of public education was virtually laughed out of the nation's classrooms and campuses during the collegiate generations of the 1960s and '70s, and thus is seldom addressed in teacher education programs of the 1980s and '90s. The revival of civic learning throughout the educational system, along with a volunteering mood in favor of service learning and professional training for public service, will provide a more hospitable climate for professional educators to deal with the values of civic virtue.

On this note, I hope that the new enterprises of education for democratic civitas on both the domestic and international fronts can succeed in their own terms and in support of one another. For, above all, the success of democracy in any country of the world rests in the long run on the success of educating youth for democratic civitas in its schools, in its higher educational institutions, and in its education of teachers. I applaud the many organizations that are supporting these tasks. Now, more than ever, we need good education that is, in its very nature, *public*.

REFERENCES

American Historical Association and American Political Science Association. 1983–87. *This Constitution*. A serial. Washington, D.C.: Project '87.

Barber, B. 1992. *An aristocracy for everyone: The politics of education and the future of America*. New York: Ballantine.

Butts, R. F. 1950. *The American tradition in religion and education*. Boston: Beacon Press.

Butts, R. F. 1980. *The revival of civic learning: A rationale for citizenship education in American schools*. Bloomington, Ind.: Phi Delta Kappa Educational Foundation.

Butts, R. F. 1983. The civic education of the American teacher. *Journal of Teacher Education* 34(6): 48–49.

Butts, R. F. 1985. *Religion, education, and the First Amendment: The appeal to history*. Washington, D.C.: People for the American Way.

Butts, R. F. 1988. *The morality of democratic citizenship: Goals for civic education in the Republic's third century*. Calabasas, Calif.: Center for Civic Education.

Butts, R. F. 1989. *The civic mission in educational reform: Perspectives for the public and the profession*. Stanford, Calif.: Hoover Institution Press.

Butts, R. F. 1993. The time is now for framing the civic foundations of teacher education. *Journal of Teacher Education* 44(6): 325–34.

Butts, R. F. 1997. Education for civitas: The lessons Americans must learn. In *Working Paper in Education*, 19–21. Stanford, Calif.: Hanna Collection on the Role of Education in Society, Hoover Institution.

Carter, S. J. 1996. *The culture of disbelief*. New York: Basic Books.

Center for Civic Education. 1994. *National standards for civics and government*. Calabasas, Calif.: CCE.

Curti, M. 1968. *The roots of American loyalty*. New York: Atheneum.

Eberly, D., ed. 1995. *The content of America's character: Recovering civic virtue*. Lanham, Md.: Madison Books.

Elshtain, J. B. 1995. *Democracy on trial*. New York: Basic Books.

Fukuyama, F. 1995. *Trust: The social virtues and the creation of prosperity*. New York: Free Press.

Galston, W. 1991. *Liberal purposes: Goods, virtues, and diversity in the liberal state*. New York: Cambridge University Press.

Glendon, M. A., and D. Blankenhorn, eds. 1995. *Seedbeds of virtue: Sources of competence, character, and citizenship in American society*. Lanham, Md.: Madison Books.

Gutmann, A. 1987. *Democratic education*. Princeton, N.J.: Princeton University Press.

Jones, A. H., ed. 1985. *Civic learning for teachers: Capstone for educational reform*. Ann Arbor, Mich.: Prakken.

Kammen, M. 1973. *People of paradox: An inquiry concerning the origins of American civilization*. New York: Vintage.

Ketcham, R. 1987. *Individualism and public life: A modern dilemma*. New York: Basil Blackwell.

Maeroff, G. I. 1996. Apathy and anonymity. *Education Week* 15(24): 60, 46.

Mosle, S. 1996. The answer is national standards. *New York Times Magazine* 15(4): 45–47, 68–69.

National Association of Secondary School Principals and the Carnegie Foundation for the Advancement of Teaching. 1996. *Breaking ranks*. Reston, Va.: NASSP.

National Commission on Civic Renewal. 1998. A nation of spectators. Available at: *www.puaf.umdedu/civicrenewal*.

Quigley, C. N., and C. F. Bahmueller. 1991. *CIVITAS: A framework for civic education*. Calabasas, Calif.: Center for Civic Education.

Sandel, M. J. 1996. *Democracy's discontent: America in search of a public philosophy*. Cambridge, Mass. Harvard University Press.

Yankelovich, D. 1995. Three destructive trends. *The Kettering Review* (fall): 6–15.

7

Assessment: Past Practices, Future Expectations

By *Tracie Y. Hargrove*

Assessment and evaluation are essential to student growth. The implications of enriching our methods for assessing student growth are enormous. Assessment has the potential to dictate what is taught and drive the methodologies that make learning an exciting and worthwhile endeavor.

An examination of trends in current assessment practice reveals that standardized testing and high-stakes accountability are on the rise in the United States. These trends are not surprising given the nature of today's society. As Caudell (1997) stated, "Ours is an age when personal computers and golden arches are the defining artifacts of culture. Fast and cheap have their place, even in education."

Though many states are content with the speed and economy that come with large-scale, standardized assessments, others seek more than just a ranking and sorting of students. As we enter the 21st century, it is important to reflect on assessment and evaluation of the past, as well as state designs currently in place, to ensure best practice for the future.

Assessment in the Early 20th Century: A Look to the Past

Assessment and evaluation have been part of teaching and learning for centuries. Though assessment may be older than evaluation, both have been used to inform the educational process. The ancient Greeks used assessments as formative, rather than evaluative, tools. Students demonstrated what they had learned, and teachers used the information to inform future instruction. It was not until around 1850 that grading became part of the culture of schooling. Around 1850, students were grouped together regardless of age and background in the renowned "one-room schoolhouse." As communities grew and attendance became mandatory, schools began to group students in grades according to their age. As students progressed through the grades, the curriculum became more challenging and built upon what was previously taught.

It was not until the late 1800s that schools began to issue progress evaluations. Schools participated in an early form of "outcome-based education" in which students progressed to the next level only after completing requirements in the previous level. Assessment consisted of a skills checklist, which delineated what students had mastered. By the early 1900s, the high school was beginning to report progress in the form of percentages as a way to verify that students had mastered the skills in a specific grade level. Elementary schools of this era continued to use written descriptions to document learning.

In the 1910s, the reliability of percentage grading was questioned. A study conducted by Starch and Elliott found that English teachers, when scoring papers on a zero-to-100 scale, gave the same paper—the same student work—grades ranging from 50 to 97. Factors such as neatness, spelling, and punctuation were stressed by some teachers, while others focused on the content of the paper. In response to critics who claimed that good writing is highly subjective and cannot be scored appropriately using a percentage scale, Starch and Elliott repeated their study with geometry papers. They found the spread in scores to be even greater, ranging from 28 to 95 (Kirschenbaum, Napier, and Simon 1971).

In the 1930s, teachers employed "grading on the curve" in an effort to decrease subjectivity in grading. This method of ranking students ensured a more even distribution of scores. Some educators even specified the number of students to be assigned each grade so as to produce a perfect bell-shaped curve—hence, the moniker "bell curve."

As the debate over assessment and evaluation continued, many schools abandoned formal grading practices altogether and returned to written descriptions of student achievement. Others moved to a pass/fail form of grading, which took away the graduated nature of describing student progress. Some went so far as to promote only students who demonstrated mastery at a particular level (Kirschenbaum, et al. 1971).

ASSESSMENT IN THE LATE 20TH CENTURY: A LOOK TO THE FUTURE

Providing a framework for reform efforts in the latter part of the 20th century, the 1989 Charlottesville Education Summit, made up of all 50 state governors and then-President George Bush, met in Virginia to determine how best to prepare all U.S. students to meet the challenges of the 21st century. The summit resulted in the adoption of six National Education Goals to be reached by the year 2000 (National Education Goals Panel 1996). With the enactment of the Goals 2000: Educate America Act in March 1994, the U.S. Congress added two additional goals on top of the summit's original six. Indeed, Goals 2000 represented a consensus of direction in pubic education from the highest level. These goals are as follows (U.S. Department of Education 1996):

1. All children in the United States will start school ready to learn.

2. The high school graduation rate will increase to at least 90 percent.

3. All students will leave grades 4, 8, and 12 having demonstrated competency over challenging subject matter, including English, mathematics, science, foreign languages, civics and government, economics, the arts, history, and geography—and

every school in the nation will ensure that all students learn to use their minds well, so they may be prepared for responsible citizenship, further learning, and productive employment in our modern economy.

4. The nation's teaching force will have access to programs for the continued improvement of their professional skills and the opportunity to acquire the knowledge and skills needed to instruct and prepare all students for the next century.

5. U.S. students will be first in the world in science and mathematics achievement.

6. Every adult citizen will be literate and will possess the knowledge and skills necessary to compete in a global economy and exercise the rights and responsibilities of citizenship.

7. Every school in the United States will be free of drugs, violence, and the unauthorized presence of firearms and alcohol, and will offer a disciplined environment conducive to learning.

8. Every school will promote partnerships that will increase parental involvement and participation in promoting the social, emotional, and academic growth of children.

The National Education Goals Panel was established to oversee the achievement of these goals. The panel's first report, issued in 1991, indicated the need for national assessment activities for goals 1, 3, 4, and 5 to collect centralized information on the nation as a whole (National Education Goals Panel 1996). President Bush presented a proposal for a set of voluntary national tests developed for goals 4, 8, and 12 (U.S. Department of Education 1991). There was, however, very little support at the national level in terms of new monies or new programs. The focus of school reform now shifted to the state level. By December 1998, it was clear that the projected goals would not be met by the beginning of the year 2000.

Public opinion about schools remained divided along two lines: (1) nationally, perceptions were negative; (2) locally, perceptions of *local* schools were relatively positive. Elam, Rose, and Gallup (1993) reported on perceptions of the nation's schools. Only 19 percent of respondents gave public schools "A" or "B" grades; 21 percent gave them "D" or "F" grades. When the same people rated their local schools, 44 percent gave "A" or "B" grades, and only 14 percent gave them "D" or "F" grades. Interestingly, when parents were asked about the specific school serving their children, 72 percent gave the school "A" or "B" grades, and just 7 percent gave grades of "D" or "F."

Great emphasis has been placed on statewide testing as a means of determining academic-achievement status. By 1991, most states had instituted systems for statewide educational assessment. During the 1994–95 school year, only seven U.S. states did not conduct any assessment in kindergarten through fifth grade (Bond and Braskamp 1996). Of the 43 states with testing programs, 16 had programs that primarily focused on the "three R's"—reading (including language arts), writing, and arithmetic.

In 1999, 48 states administer statewide exams, with Nebraska and Iowa excluded. By 2000, 49 states will administer their own statewide tests (National Education Association 1999). Only one state, Illinois, did not have an assessment program intended to improve curriculum and instruction. Others, including North Carolina, use assessment testing as part of the accountability portion of educational reform efforts. Though nearly 85 percent of states use multiple-choice exams for statewide assessments, most combine other forms of performance assessment.

During the 1993–94 school year, 38 states assessed writing, 25 states used other performance assessments, and seven states required portfolios. By 1996, Kentucky and Maine had abandoned multiple-choice testing altogether in favor of alternative-assessment strategies (Bond and Braskamp 1996). Standardized tests, however, remain the rule of the day. This situation is maintained by three factors: cost, purpose, and scoring.

A study by the U.S. General Accounting Office (1993) predicted that a national multiple-choice achievement test would cost about $40 million, while a slightly longer test with short performance-based questions would cost $210 million. According to a 1993 estimate, statewide performance assessment would cost $35 to $70 per student. Standardized multiple-choice tests can cost as little as $1 to $2 per student. Another question is whether such added expense will produce significant, meaningful results. States committed to performance-based assessment seek information on student mastery of the complex skills missed by multiple-choice items.

To assess complex skills, evaluators must be trained. To assess the complexity of desired findings—how well students can create, think, and analyze—each performance must be compared against a desired criterion, a scoring rubric. How well this works depends on how well evaluators understand the skill being assessed and how consistently the criteria are applied. We must, of course, then ask ourselves whether the test measures what it is supposed to measure (Caudell 1997).

In 43 states, improving instruction was the most common purpose for assessment; 41 states used this information for performance reporting. Other purposes include program evaluation (37 states), student diagnosis (26 states), high school graduation (17 states) and school accreditation (12 states). In almost half of the schools, stakes are high, including funding gains and losses, loss of accreditation, warnings, and eventual takeover of schools (Caudell 1997).

At the state level, Kentucky, Tennessee, Texas, and North Carolina were among the first states to implement comprehensive and far-reaching accountability plans. They set the tone and the format for efforts to follow.

The Kentucky Plan

In June 1989, the Kentucky State Supreme Court upheld a lower court's decision that the commonwealth of Kentucky did not provide an equitable and efficient system of education, declared Kentucky's educational system to be unconstitutional, and directed the General Assembly to establish a new system of common schools and set minimal compliance standards. In March 1990, the Kentucky Legislature passed the Kentucky Education Reform Act (KERA). The act restructured processes in curriculum, school governance, and school finance. It created a new Kentucky Department of Education (KDE) and replaced the elected State Superintendent of Schools with an appointed Commissioner of Education. In addition, KERA established a statewide school accountability system based on student performance, supported by a system of rewards, sanctions, and assistance.

In 1992, assessments were administered to all 4th-, 8th-, and 12th-grade students, including writing portfolios, on-demand performance tasks, open-ended questions, and multiple-choice items. The results were used to develop "baseline" data for each school in the state (Millman 1997). In 1994, KDE voted to discontinue the use of multiple-choice items as part of the accountability system.

The Kentucky Instructional Results Information System (KIRIS), which drove accountability efforts in Kentucky until 1998, had the following components: (1) school-based accountability; (2) schools judged on progress against their own baseline data; (3) accountability scores based on a performance-based test of academic achievement as well as measures of attendance, dropout rate, and successful transition to adult life; (4) substantial financial rewards for exceeding accountability goals; (5) state-provided assistance for those schools with declining test scores; and (6) provisions for "state takeover" of schools that show significant score declines (Millman 1997). In the first four years of the KIRIS program, scores showed steep gains. KDE awarded approximately $50 million to schools that posted large score gains. Kentucky educators were elated (KDE 1999).

Standardized tests remain the rule of the day. This situation is maintained by three factors: cost, purpose, and scoring.

During this period, KIRIS scores were reported in terms of four levels: "novice," "apprentice," "proficient," and "distinguished," and arbitrarily assigned scores of 1, 40, 100, and 140. Regardless of their starting point, at the end of 20 years all schools were expected to reach a mean score of 100, equivalent to all students performing at the proficient level. To meet this goal, a typical school in Kentucky would have to show an improvement of two standard deviations per 20 years, or 0.2 per year. To receive cash awards, increases had to be larger. A mean increase of two standard deviations meant that 50 percent of all students in 2012 would have to exceed the performance exceeded by only 2 percent of students in 1992 (KDE 1999).

A RAND Corporation (1999) study compared KIRIS scores for 1992 through 1996 and postulated that gains on KIRIS instruments should be reflected substantially on other tests. A comparison of KIRIS scores and scores from administrations of the National Assessment of Educational Progress (NAEP) for the period were important, because KIRIS is designed to measure much of the same content and skills.

While fourth-graders' KIRIS scores increased by 0.75 standard deviations in two years, NAEP scores remained unchanged. In math, Kentucky scores demonstrated an increase comparable to national trends. Gains on KIRIS were 3.6 times larger than NAEP score increases in the fourth grade and 4.1 times larger in the eighth grade. The study also found that KIRIS increases were not reflected in high school students' American College Test (ACT) scores. The difference in performance on KIRIS and

ACT math tests was 0.7 standard deviations. The difference in reading scores was about 0.4 standard deviations. In science, ACT scores increased slightly, by 0.1 standard deviations, but KIRIS scores increased about five times as much. According to RAND Corporation (1999) researchers, the results suggested "an appreciable inflation of gains on KIRIS outcomes." Researchers also noted a "sawtooth" pattern in which scores increased on reused items, then dropped again when new items were introduced. This outcome was most pronounced in schools with the greatest reading and mathematics gains on KIRIS. In summary, RAND Corporation (1999) researchers discussed steps to reduce score inflation:

1. Set realistic targets for improvement. If teachers are told they must make large gains, they are more likely to teach to the test.

2. Tie assessments to clear curricula. It is easy in the absence of an accompanying curriculum to use the test as a substitute curriculum framework.

3. Design instruments to minimize inflation.

4. Monitor for potential inflation of gains.

5. Discount early gains.

RAND Corporation (1999) researchers have noted that their study has implications beyond Kentucky. Other states have similar assessment programs in that they focus on aggregate gains, tie these gains to rewards, rely on tests administered in only a few grades, and set goals without regard to the distribution of performance.

In April 1998, the Kentucky Legislature replaced KIRIS with a new test. Under the new plan, reward money for schools with improving test scores would be given to schools rather than to individual teachers. Schools with declining scores would be required to develop a school improvement plan to receive state financial help. Such schools would also be assigned an assistance team. The bill would also allow parents of students attending schools with declining scores to request a transfer. These teams—composed of lawmakers, educators, parents, and national testing experts—were created to hammer out details of the new tests and rating system (KDE 1999).

In June 1998, KDE issued a request for proposals for the development of the Commonwealth Accountability Testing System (CATS) to replace KIRIS. The new CATS test is expected to have the following advantages (KDE 1999):

1. norm-referenced assessment that measures core content and gives valid, reliable results for individual students;

2. longitudinal comparisons that will provide a reliable comparison of individual student scores over several years;

3. shorter administration time—no more than two and one-half hours for each content area;

4. consistent administration for at least four years; and

5. more rapid reporting of scores, with results due by mid-September of the year the test is administered.

Some of the problems that plagued KIRIS and resulted in its demise included (KDE 1999):

1. a lack of incentive to make as much growth as possible in a biennium, because a significant advance resulted in a new goal that was higher and, if not reached, resulted in the school being designated "in-decline" or "in-crisis." Schools could have

some of the highest scores in the state and be characterized as "in-decline." Furthermore, all schools in this category received the same level of assistance;

2. the lower-performance categories were so large that a school could make considerable growth and not leave the category;

3. a student giving no response or turning in no portfolio received a zero, the same score as a student who did the work but performed poorly;

4. elementary school courses were weighted the same even though teachers and parents felt greater weight should be placed on math and reading; and

5. norm-referenced tests did not "count" in the accountability system.

The Tennessee Value-Added Accountability System

The Tennessee Education Improvement Act of 1992 contained provisions for the equitable distribution of state revenues to school systems and accountability for results at the district level, including the appointments of superintendents and the elections of school boards. Principals were required to develop and execute performance contracts. In addition, accountability included evidence of improvement in other areas: dropout rates, promotion rates, and evidence that student achievement was improving year to year (Millman 1997).

The Tennessee Value-Added Assessment System was developed by McLean and Sanders (1984) at the University of Tennessee. Their research indicated that: (1) schools and teachers differed in their effect on student learning; (2) school and teacher effects seemed consistent across time; (3) teacher effects were not influenced by the location of the school; (4) teacher effects were highly correlated to subjective reports of supervisors; and (5) student-achievement gains were not correlated with previous achievement levels. The developers placed emphasis on the advantages of the increased precision offered through longitudinal analysis.

In support of this approach, Raudenbush and Bryk (1988) stated that the substantial effects of schooling have eluded researchers because of dependence on one or two time points rather than multiple time points. Studies conducted in Tennessee's Knox County, Blount County, and Chattanooga City schools are convincing with regard to measuring the influence that school systems, schools, and teachers have on indicators of student learning.

The Texas Assessment of Academic Skills

In 1991, the Texas legislature mandated a study of Texas Public Schools to establish a statewide system for holding schools accountable for student achievement. Like other states, Texas had gone through a decade of process reforms in public education, aimed at improving administrative and instructional processes without focusing on what students were learning or what they could do. The outcomes of the study resulted in the development of one of the nation's most comprehensive school-accountability systems and, for its time, the only legislative appropriations bill to incorporate achievement outcomes in an agency-funding document (Texas State Legislative Budget Board 1994).

Senate Bill Seven, passed in May 1993 by the 73rd Legislature, was the enabling act that established the Texas public school accountability system. The genesis of the act was House Bill 246 of the 1981 legislative session. Other components were added with House Bill 72 in 1984 and Senate Bill I in 1990, such as district annual-performance reports and the implementation of academic-excellence indicators used to judge school and district performance. Senate Bill Seven required the state to (1) provide reliable measurement of student performance, (2) relate student academic outcomes to the state standards, (3) recommend actions when results deviated from expected performance, and (4) devise a method for informing the public of the schools' results (Texas State Legislative Budget Board 1994).

The implementation of the Texas Assessment of Academic Skills (TAAS) shifted the focus of assessment in Texas from minimum skills to academic skills. The criterion-referenced instrument also measures higher-order thinking skills and problem-solving ability. End-of-course tests were developed for selected high school courses (Texas Educational Agency 1999).

In November 1995, the Texas State Board of Education adopted new rules for student assessments that became part of the Texas Administrative Code Chapter 101. During the 1996–97 school year, eligible students were required to meet minimum expectations on each section of the exit-level examinations to be eligible to receive a high school diploma (Texas Educational Agency 1999).

The Academic Excellence Indicator System (AEIS) drives the emphasis on student achievement. A subset of AEIS performance measures is used to assign a rating to each public school and public school district in the state. Additionally, schools send out School Report Cards, which show the performance, staff, and financial measures at work in individual schools (Texas Educational Agency 1999).

An interesting feature of Texas reform efforts is the provision for student academic growth to be measured in terms of "required improvement" and "comparable improvement." Required improvement is defined as the progress necessary to pass intermediate and exit criteria successfully for graduation. This measurement is student-based as opposed to comparable improvement, which is a district or a school-gains index comparing similar schools but using individual required-improvement aggregated data. In Texas, schools are rated as "exemplary," "recognized," "acceptable," or "low-performing" (Cornett and Gaines 1997).

A recognized rating requires a TAAS passing rate of at least 80 percent in each subject for all students and each student group, a dropout rate of 3.5 percent or less for all students and student groups, and an attendance rate of 94 percent. To earn an exemplary rating during the 1997–98 school year, at least 90 percent of all students in a school and each student group (African American, Hispanic, European American, and economically disadvantaged) had to pass the reading, writing, and math sections of the TAAS test. A dropout rate of less than 1 percent for all students and each student group and an attendance rate of at least 94 percent are required. The 1998 ratings criteria included schools achieving a 5 percent increase for recognized and acceptable categories (Cornett and Gaines 1997).

The North Carolina ABCs of Public Education

In 1995, the North Carolina General Assembly directed the Department of Public Instruction (NCDPI) to examine the public schools under NCDPI's control to ascertain ways to improve student performance, increase local flexibility and control, and promote economy and efficiency. In response, NCDPI developed a program called the ABCs of Public Education.

The ABC program was designed to meet these goals without asking local schools to invest in new instructional programs and without requiring NCDPI to spend additional money on new tests. The plan called for school-based accountability focused on increased local control and the basic subjects of reading, writing, and math, and focused on more local control. A 1996 law gave NCDPI authority to implement the program, including authority to set student-achievement goals, revamp site-based management legislation, and revise performance-based accountability to focus on improvements in reading, writing, and mathematics (NCDPI 1997b).

The ABCs is an acronym that represents the three goals of the ABC program: accountability, basics, and control. The ABCs Accountability Model establishes growth standards for each school in the state. Schools that attain the level of growth specified by NCDPI are eligible for various incentive awards. Schools that fall short of the specified level of growth are designated low-performing and provided assistance. If this assistance, along with mandated additional staff development, does not raise schools to the appropriate level, measures may be taken to terminate contracts for both administrators and teachers.

NCDPI (1997a) has suggested that "one of the best ways to restore faith in public education is to instill a strong sense of accountability." According to NCDPI, individual schools are to be held accountable for student performance. Staff members in each school must take responsibility for the education of each student. Grades 3 through 8 and high school are tested and held accountable by the state for basic subjects. Furthermore, accountability is not limited to certain grades or positions. School boards, superintendents, supervisors, and directors are just as responsible for improvement as schoolteachers and principals. Teacher assistants have a stake in it, and NCDPI has contended that the larger community is also responsible through parental involvement on the school-improvement team. NCDPI (1997d) has even stated that its personnel must be held accountable by the General Assembly for the plan's overall success.

NCDPI has identified several facets of accountability key to the assessment model, including performance-growth standards, school-incentive awards, assistance, and intervention. Performance-growth standards set this accountability model apart from other high-stakes models. According to NCDPI, all students are not expected to perform at grade level. This model accounts for the growth of each individual by comparing the previous year's end-of-grade (EOG) test score to the current EOG test score; hence, schools are expected to make "a year's worth of growth for a year's worth of schooling" (NCDPI 1997c).

Additionally, the ABC program is based on the performance of individual schools. It is not carried out on the district level nor on the basis of individual teachers. The goal is for all schools to meet their expected growth, which is based on that school's previous growth. Some schools are anticipated to go beyond expected growth and make exemplary growth. Exemplary growth is defined as 10 percent above expected growth. Schools that do not meet the expected growth but have 50 percent or more students performing at or above grade level are classified as making adequate performance. Schools that do not meet the expected growth standard and have fewer than 50 percent of students performing at or above grade level are considered low-performing schools.

Schools are also categorized by the percentage of students performing on or above grade level. Grade-level categories include Schools of Excellence and Schools of Distinction. Schools that meet their expected growth and have at least 90 percent of their students performing at or above grade level are considered to be Schools of Excellence. Schools of Distinction are schools that have at least 80 percent of their students performing at or above grade level.

For schools having difficulty meeting growth standards, assistance teams are available to help increase student achievement. The teams can point out schools' deficiencies, make suggestions for improvement, and help with setting goals. Some low-performing schools are assigned assistance. These schools are defined as those that fell far below their growth standard established by the formula and those in which the majority of students are considered low-performing (below grade level, below proficiency). Intervention, a measure that might involve "the removal of a school principal or removing teachers who are not willing to improve their practices," is a component of the program (NCDPI 1997a).

During August 1998, school-by-school performance results for the 1997–98 school year were released. Results showed that twice as many schools reached exemplary status than in the previous year. For elementary and middle schools, 83.9 percent met either expected or exemplary growth standards. During the 1996–97 school year, only 56.7 percent of schools did as well. A total of 65.9 percent, or 1,075 schools, were exemplary, exceeding expected student-achievement growth by approximately 10 percent; 18 percent, or 307 schools, met expected growth; and 15.2 percent had adequate performance.

After the first year of the ABCs high school accountability model, 63 percent (198 schools) of high schools reached exemplary status and 19.7 percent (78 schools) reached expected gain. Results show that 12.3 percent (51 schools) demonstrated adequate performance (NCDPI 1998).

A group of schools designated as low-performing received assistance-team support during the 1997–98 school year. As a result, nearly all the schools made exemplary growth and none were identified as low-performing at the end of year. The state plans to broaden its assistance efforts to more low-performing schools through the creation of NCHELPS, a joint project of the Governor's Office, the University of North Carolina system, North Carolina Community Colleges, and the State Department of Public Instruction.

High-Stakes Accountability

High-stakes accountability programs like the ones in Kentucky, Tennessee, Texas, and North Carolina are now being implemented nationwide. A high-stakes testing program is one whose results are used to trigger actions or decisions such as passing or failing a grade, graduating or not, determining teacher or principal merit, or assuming responsibility for a failing district by a state agency (Popham 1987).

High-stakes accountability can also be defined as the implementation of sanctions attached to test results. There are two types of high-stakes accountability cited in the literature: One involves consequences for examinees, including qualifying students for promotion to the next grade level or for receipt of a high school diploma. Another type is used as an index of instructional quality and identifies consequences for educators, such as test results being published in local newspapers, determination of merit pay, or loss of tenure or position.

Madaus (in Brandt 1989) found less fault with tests themselves than with the sanctions and rewards attached to the information they provide. The director of the Center of the Study of Testing, Education and Educational Policy further remarked that high-stakes accountability based on standardized testing assures educators will find ways to deliver the testing results that administrators desire. Moreover, Madaus commented that Measurement-Driven Instruction (MDI)—that is, instruction driven by the test—is harmful, because it takes a lot of key decisions out of the hands of teachers. Popham (1987, 680), on the other hand, has labeled MDI a benefit to the instructional process, defining MDI as occurring when a "high-stakes test of educational achievement, because of the important contingencies associated with the students' performance, influences the instructional program that prepares students for the test"—contending as well that MDI can be a "potent force for educational improvement if properly conceived and implemented."

One effect of high-stakes testing has become known as the "Lake Wobegon Effect," after radio personality Garrison Keillor's fictional town in which "all the women are strong, all the men are good-looking, and all the children are above average." The Lake Wobegon Report, issued in 1987, asserted that all states reporting statewide test scores ranked above the national average (Cannell 1988). High scores were reported at a time when these same states were doing poorly on other indicators, such as graduation and literacy rates. A report of the North Carolina Education Standards and Accountability Commission (1997) has stated, "If standards are defined by content knowledge, America places at the top of the list. If, however, the ability to apply knowledge outside the classroom is the criteria, America's students fall far behind."

The inappropriate use of standardized test instruments—such as decisions made at the local level to include or exclude certain students, increase testing time, teach to the test, or align the curriculum to more closely fit the emphasis of the test—often leads to great difficulty in interpreting test data correctly. Shepard and Dougherty (1991) cited ways in which high-stakes testing affect teachers' instruction and classroom management. An unjustified amount of time may be spent preparing for the test at the expense of regular instruction. Other concerns are undue emphasis on basic skills, discouragement of classroom innovation, and lowered feelings of teacher professionalism (Archbald and Porter 1991).

Testing purposes often clash. Problems arise when states use the same program to hold schools or students accountable on the one hand and to improve instruction on the other. Flexibility and ongoing use should characterize tests used for improving instruction. Test data also should be available quickly so that instructional adjustments can be made. Accountability calls for standardization, comparability, and fairness. Standardized scoring means weeks or months can go by without scoring information.

As Caudell (1997) noted, assessment can play the role of "curricular magnets," ensuring that, in a high-stakes environment, the test gets taught and that, the higher the stakes, the more likely narrowing of the curriculum will occur. Tests, unfortunately, do not take into consideration the wide array of factors that contribute to academic success. Schools do influence instruction and the learning environment but may have little or no effect on family, maturity, or mental ability (Perrone 1991).

In 1985, Massachusetts enacted legislation requiring prospective teachers to pass a test to receive a license to teach. In October 1997, the state hired National Evaluation Systems (NES) of Amherst, Massachusetts, to custom-design a teacher test. The company was given six months to create the test before the first administration in April 1998. NES drew upon a library of questions given to teachers in other states. The cutoff score, or passing mark, had not been established at the time. This decision was left to the political arena. The state's governor, Paul Cellucci, called together members of the State Board of Education and asked them to consider higher standards than those projected earlier. "We must send a clear message that we are going to hold the line for higher standards," Cellucci said. The board voted 6-1 in favor of the higher standards—on the same day that the Interim Commissioner of Education resigned in protest.

Cellucci won reelection on a campaign that included a commitment to testing veteran teachers. Under the higher standards for prospective teachers, 49 percent failed at least one part of the test. "Politics drove the system," complained Margaret McKenna, president of Lesley College, the state's largest trainer of teachers (in Bradley 1999, 26).

In April, only 41 percent of test-takers passed—but 70 percent passed the reading test, 59 percent passed the writing test, and 51 percent passed the subject-matter test. In October, during the third round of the exam, 55 percent of first-time test takers passed the entire test. Further breakdowns of the scores show that 81 percent passed reading, 75 percent passed writing, and 68 passed their subject tests. The outcome has been a closer examination of teacher-training institutions in Massachusetts. The state education department is developing a series of initiatives aimed at prompting career interest in the profession (Bradley 1999).

Assessing the impact of standardized testing in school reform efforts, Darling-Hammond (1991, 220) stated, "Evidence now available suggests that, by and large, testing policies have not had many of the positive effects that were intended for them. Indeed, they have had many negative consequences for the quality of American schooling and for the equitable allocation of school opportunities." Lieberman (1991, 219) contended, "Testing further limits students' opportunities to learn, because it is used as a means to track and retain students—practices that have been shown to produce lower achievement, lower self-esteem, and higher dropout rates." Ample evidence shows that, while low-level skills of U.S. students have increased, higher-order skills have declined. Among the reasons: teachers learn to postpone efforts to teach thinking and reasoning until basic skills have been mastered; students in lower tracks are exposed to a limited curriculum emphasizing rote learning; and students are damaged by adherence to the limits that the tests impose (Lieberman 1991).

Assessment: Two Different Points of View

Two major points of view emerge in the literature on assessment: (1) the constructivist instructional-reform advocate, and (2) the measurement/technical-quality advocate. Certainly, the constructivist point of view and the measurement point of view are perceived as representing two ends of the assessment dichotomy. Most advocates realize the importance of both goals but view their own goal as paramount.

The constructivist perspective seems to emerge more frequently when the assessment is used for local purposes, at the classroom or school level. These situations tend to address local curricula in which the goal is for the child to master the given objective before proceeding to the next level. Individual students are given multiple opportunities to demonstrate what they know and can do. Assessment in the constructivist classroom becomes a learning experience for both the student and the teacher (North Central Regional Educational Laboratory [NCREL] 1999).

The primary goal of the constructivist approach is to change what is taught and how the curriculum gets delivered, rather than to measure performance for the sake of being held accountable. Advocates on this end of the continuum are willing to sacrifice some technical quality to realize a more meaningful assessment system. They believe that the measurement/technical group has become too focused on technical issues such as reliability and validity (NCREL 1999).

All too often, practitioners abandon good practice to incorporate strategies they believe to be "cutting edge."

Darling-Hammond (1991) suggested that educators and policy makers should focus attention on whether the assessment is real, how well it really measures the quality of schooling or teaching and its effects, and whether it improves teaching and learning. At the heart of all assessment issues is the question of whether the assessment drives best instructional practices, which in turn promote increased student learning. Darling-Hammond (1991) claimed there is a wealth of evidence to support her assertion that greater learning does not result from simply setting test-score goals and attaching sanctions to them. In fact, sanctions sometimes produce destructive side effects. She further claimed that a growing number of states believe education will improve if sanctions for students and schools are attached to standardized test scores. Finally, Darling-Hammond contended that some strategies implemented in the name of increased student achievement actually lower levels of student learning and increase dropout rates in the long run, even though test scores appear to improve.

The measurement/technical perspective seems to emerge when there are large-scale assessments at the state, district, or national level that involve high stakes (student or school accountability). Measurement/technical advocates have to be sure that tests are reliable and valid, because important consequences and decisions are attached to students' success on the test. If teachers are going to lose tenure and students are going to be denied a high school diploma, then the assessment must meet rigid technical quality criteria (NCREL 1999).

According to Millman (1997), there are four criteria for judging how well measurement/technical systems function. If accountability is going to be paramount, the evaluation should (1) be fair to the teachers and the school, (2) be comprehensive in types of learning objectives measured, (3) be competitive in relation to other methods used to evaluate teachers and schools for the sake of accountability, and (4) not cause ill effects when used correctly. Although Millman (1997, 245) highlighted the importance of the second goal, he noted that "tests that are used [for accountability purposes] cannot possibly capture entirely the richness of [the] objectives. The subject matter knowledge, the learning skills, the testing formats, and the noncognitive outcomes targeted by the reformers/educators are greater than the information accessible by testing." His comment illustrates the fact that the purpose for implementing a constructivist assessment system is distinctly different than the purpose for implementing a measurement/technical framework. This fundamental difference in purpose greatly affects the design of the assessment.

Assessment for the New Millennium: What Is Best Practice?

The best way to assess and report student achievement has been debated for years. Though multiple-choice tests have been common for reasons already mentioned, forms of authentic assessment such as portfolios are being touted as viable ways to assess what students know and can do. Measurement can range from observation of student behavior to more traditional assessments that rely on written demonstrations of student achievement. All too often, practitioners abandon good practice to incorporate strategies they believe to be "cutting edge." It does not take long to discover that there is no quick fix when developing and implementing meaningful assessment strategies. To assess student progress optimally, practitioners must incorporate a more eclectic approach, utilizing the best of all known approaches.

Naturally, numbers come to mind when one thinks of assessment and evaluation. With district and state initiatives focusing on models of accountability, many of which involve high stakes for teachers, it is understandable that teachers stay focused on preparing students for the test by quantifying their achievement. Unfortunately, most of the assessments used for such important decisions are reduced to short-answer or multiple-choice questions. Active skills, such as writing, speaking, acting, or constructing, are not part of the assessment. Instead of students actually performing targeted learning tasks through the use of performance-based assessment, they may have to choose from another person's list of answers in a multiple-choice format. With this approach, there is no way to distinguish among the student who truly understands the problem and solves it correctly, the student who understands the problem and makes a careless error, and the student who does not possess the concept at all. Even the student who has no knowledge of the subject matter being tested may produce a correct answer from time to time based simply on luck. The process by which the student solves the problem is completely discounted in these traditional methods of assessment.

In fact, most standardized assessments are limited to judging the effectiveness of schools and their teachers (Routman 1991). Teachers feel a great deal of pressure for students to perform on standardized tests. Heavy emphasis on testing drives what is taught and how instruction gets delivered. This fact would not be so problematic if standardized tests provided an in-depth, comprehensive assessment of what students really know. Unfortunately, this outcome is not true of many assessment programs.

To make assessment a meaningful tool in the learning process, teachers can incorporate new methods of measuring student progress, including the use of authentic assessment. Authentic assessment encompasses the use of portfolios, exhibitions, performances, learning logs, and experiments as measures of student progress. Anthony, Johnson, Mickelson, and Preece (1991) suggested that there are three key characteristics imperative to making authentic assessment meaningful for all learners: First, assessment should be multifaceted, including a wide repertoire of sources for making an evaluation. Second, a variety of voices should be used to arrive at the final evaluation. Third, meaningful assessment must be seen as a process and not a product. Balance must exist at the heart of each of these characteristics.

Evaluation should come from many sources, including observation of processes as well as written products. Some students may do well given the structure of a typical state writing examination in which the prompt is outlined and students know exactly how many details should be stated and how the paper should be organized. Other students, perhaps even those who are more creative, would falter under such constraints. These students may write effective essays when given the freedom to incorporate their own experiences and interests. On the other hand, students who need structure may find writing an insurmountable task when given absolute independence.

Assessment should be balanced through the collaboration of many voices. Meaningful assessment should include the voices of the student being evaluated, peers, parents, and teachers. Depending on the evaluative purpose, information from the various sources should be considered differently. Parents can provide invaluable insight into the interests and motivation of the student.

Finally, assessment should be a recursive process, continually informing the teacher of what learning should follow. Assessment should occur in an ongoing and continuous fashion, the results of which should help shape future learning experiences in the classroom.

To get at the heart of what a student can do, educators must employ a more complete approach to collecting assessment data. There is no single test, activity, or task that can accurately provide a comprehensive picture of everything a student has learned. Only a variety of measures carefully examined over a long period of time can give teachers an accurate account of what students know (Routman 1991). The recent push for authentic assessment comes from concern by some educators that traditional methods of assessment do not adequately measure how well students think or solve problems, what subjects they know in depth, or how well they are able to direct their own learning. Meaningful learning is reflective, constructive, and self-regulated (Pool and Bracey 1992).

One model that embraces the need for assessment to be multifaceted, collaborative, and ongoing was developed by Anthony et al. (1991) and discussed in detail in their book *Evaluating Literacy: A Perspective for Change*. The authors explained authentic assessment through the use of a framework they called "The Quad." Their model focused on making assessment multifaceted by categorizing four types of data that can be collected in a classroom to constitute the balance needed. The Quad can be visualized as a pie dissected into four pieces. The upper two quadrants include assessment measures that involve observation. The top left quadrant includes those items measured by observing the learning process. Process observation includes anecdotal records, interviews, and responses to reading. The top right quadrant includes those activities measured by observing children's products, such as journals, projects, and writing samples.

The bottom half of the pie is representative of more traditional types of assessments, including classroom measures and decontextualized measures. Classroom measures, the lower left-hand portion of The Quad, represent those assignments that are scored, such as worksheets designed to give students practice with a particular skill, essays, or teacher-made concept tests. The last quadrant, measures that are decontextualized, include those assessments mandated by the state or district. Examples include criterion-referenced measures or district or state standardized tests. Though decontextualized measures are usually discussed unfavorably in literature, Anthony et al. (1991) saw a place for them in a balanced assessment program.

A common misconception associated with authentic assessment is that it remains a method that abandons multiple-choice testing. Strangely enough, this belief is coupled with a fear that, just as some students perform poorly on multiple-choice tests, others will not do well on measures of authentic assessment. Multiple-choice testing is still a viable part of the evaluation process, albeit no longer the sole basis of the evaluation.

One important characteristic of The Quad is its flexibility in determining an appropriate balance. The authors recognize that balance does not mean rigidly devoting 25 percent of the assessment to each of the various portions of The Quad. Instead, balance should take the individual into account, paying particular attention to developmentally appropriate areas. For example, students in the early elementary grades might be assessed using mostly observation; in fact, it is entirely possible that state or district-mandated tests will be administered at this level. Secondary students, on the other hand, may have more classroom measures or decontextualized measures. Observation of process and product should not be ignored for these students, however, even though fewer opportunities may exist for them to demonstrate knowledge in these areas.

In their book *Best Practice: New Standards for Teaching and Learning in America's Schools*, Zemelman, Daniels, and Hyde (1993) contended that methods that do not advance learning or that do not drive meaningful curriculum should be abandoned—if policy makers are to establish more productive assessment and evaluation. Furthermore, those involved with assessment should differentiate their assessment efforts, looking at a child's growth in a wider variety of ways. According to Zemelman et al., the most valuable forms of assessment are formative—that is, they are designed with a child's development in mind and used to make instructional decisions to advance particular children. In best-practice classrooms, summative evaluation, which converts achievement into a ranked, ordinal system to compare children to one another, is used much less frequently, if at all.

Zemelman et al. (1993) delineated the characteristics of Best Practice Assessment and Evaluation across subject areas. These characteristics include:

- The purpose of most assessment is formative, not summative.
- Most evaluation is descriptive or narrative, not scored and numerical.
- Students are involved in record-keeping and in judging their own work.
- Teachers triangulate their assessments, looking at each child from several angles, by drawing on observation, conversation, artifacts, performances, etc.
- Evaluation activities are part of instruction (such as teacher-student conferences), rather than separate from it.
- Teachers spend a moderate amount of their time on evaluation and assessment, not allowing it to rule their professional lives or consume their instruction.
- Where possible, competitive grading systems are abolished or de-emphasized.
- Parent education programs help community members to understand the value of new approaches—why, for example, a portfolio or work sample actually provides far better information about student growth than an "83" or a "B" grade.

Authentic assessment is proving to be an integral part of the evaluative process. If evaluation in the 21st century is to give an accurate and complete picture of student progress, a wider variety of sources should be examined. Traditional methods of assessment used in conjunction with more authentic methodologies can lead to better evaluative decisions—decisions that become a means for authentic teaching and learning.

REFERENCES

Anthony, R. J., T. D. Johnson, N. I. Mickelson, and A. Preece. 1991. *Evaluating literacy: A perspective for change.* Portsmouth, N.H.: Heinemann.

Archbald, D. A., and A. C. Porter. 1991. A retrospective and an analysis of roles of mandated testing in education reform. Washington, D.C.: Office of Technology Assessment. ERIC ED 340 782.

Bond, L. A., and D. Braskamp. 1996. The status report of the assessment programs in the United States: State student assessment programs database school year 1994–1995. Oak Brook, Ill.: North Central Regional Educational Lab. ERIC ED 401 333.

Bradley, A. 1999. Testing teachers. *Teacher Magazine* 10(4): 26–29.

Brandt, R. 1989. On misuse of testing: A conversation with George Madaus. *Educational Leadership* 46(7): 26–29.

Cannell, J. J. 1988. Nationally normed elementary achievement testing in America's public schools: How all 50 states are above the national average. *Educational Measurement: Issues and Practice* 7(2): 5–9.

Caudell, L. S. 1997. High stakes: Innovation meets backlash as states struggle with large-scale assessment. *Northwest Education* 2(1): 26–28, 35.

Cornett, L. M., and G. Gaines. 1997. Accountability in the 1990s: Holding schools responsible for student achievement. Atlanta, Ga.: Southern Regional Education Board. ERIC ED 406 739.

Darling-Hammond, L. 1991. The implications of testing policy for quality and equality. *Phi Delta Kappan* 73(3): 220–25.

Elam, S. M., L. C. Rose, and A. M. Gallup. 1993. The 25th annual Phi Delta Kappan Gallup poll of the public's attitude toward the public schools. *Phi Delta Kappan* 75(2): 137–52.

Kentucky Department of Education. 1999. Proposed solutions: Commonwealth accountability testing system. Lexington: KDE. Available at: *http://www.kde.state.ky.us/coe/ocpg/dpg/cats/cats_model.htm.*

Kirschenbaum, H., R. W. Napier, and S. B. Simon. 1971. *Wad-ja-get? The grading game in American education.* New York: Hart Pub. Co.

Lieberman, A. 1991. Accountability: As a reform strategy. *Phi Delta Kappan* 73(3): 219–20.

McLean, R. A., and W. L. Sanders. 1984. Objective component of teacher evaluation: A feasibility study. Knoxville: University of Tennessee, College of Business Administration.

Millman, J., ed. 1997. *Grading teachers, grading schools: Is student achievement a valid evaluation measure?* Thousand Oaks, Calif.: Corwin.

National Education Association. 1999. High-stakes tests. *NEA Today* 17(6): 4–5.

National Education Goals Panel. 1996. National education goals: Building a nation of learners. Available at: *http://www.negp.gov/WEBPG10.htm.*

North Carolina Department of Public Instruction. 1997a. ABCs of public education. Raleigh: NCDPI.

North Carolina Department of Public Instruction. 1997b. Guide to the ABCs for superintendents and school boards. Raleigh: NCDPI.

North Carolina Department of Public Instruction. 1997c. Guide to the ABCs for teachers. Raleigh: NCDPI.

North Carolina Department of Public Instruction. 1997d. They're going to take over my school. Raleigh: NCDPI.

North Carolina Department of Public Instruction. 1998. News division of communications and information. Raleigh: NCDPI. Available at: *http://www.dpi.state.nc.us/news/1998_news_archive.*

North Carolina Education Standards and Accountability Commission. 1997. Expanding the ABCs to assure student performance accountability. Raleigh: NCESAC.

North Central Regional Educational Laboratory. 1999. Critical issue: Rethinking assessment and its role in supporting educational reform. Available at: *http://www.ncrel.org/sdrs/areas/issues/methods/assment/as700.htm.*

Perrone, V., ed. 1991. *Expanding student assessment.* Alexandria, Va.: Association for Supervision and Curriculum Development.

Pool, C., and G. W. Bracey. 1992. Making sense of authentic assessment: Putting research to work. *Instructor* 102(4): 40–41.

Popham, W. J. 1987. The merits of measurement-driven instruction. *Phi Delta Kappan* 68(9): 679–82.

RAND Corporation. 1999. Test-based accountability systems: Lessons of Kentucky's experiment. Santa Monica, Calif.: RAND.

Raudenbush, S. W., and A. S. Bryk. 1988. Methodological advances in analyzing the effects of schools and classrooms on student learning. In *Review of research in education*, vol. 15, ed. E. Z. Rothkopf, 423–79. Washington, D.C.: American Educational Research Association.

Routman, R. 1991. *Invitations: Changing as teachers and learners K–12.* Portsmouth, N.H.: Heinemann.

Shepard, L. A., and K. C. Dougherty. 1991. Effects of high stakes testing on instruction. Paper presented at the Annual Meeting of the American Educational Research Association, Chicago, 3–7 April. ERIC ED 337 468.

Texas Educational Agency. 1999. About the student assessment program. Austin: TEA. Available at: *http://www.tea.state.tx.us/student.assessment/about.htm.*

Texas State Legislative Budget Board. 1994. Texas public school accountability: A report card on implementation of the system. Austin: TSLB. ERIC ED 394 205.

U.S. Department of Education. 1991. America 2000: An education strategy. Washington, D.C.: USDE. ERIC ED 332 380.

U.S. Department of Education. 1996. National education goals. Washington, D.C: USDE. Available at: *http://inet.ed.gov/pubs/AchGoal4/neg.html.*

U.S. General Accounting Office. 1993. Educational achievement standards: NAGB's approach yields misleading interpretations. Washington, D.C.: USGAO. ERIC ED 359 268.

Zemelman, S., H. Daniels, and A. A. Hyde. 1993. *Best practice: New standards for teaching and learning in America's schools.* Portsmouth, N.H.: Heinemann.

8

Assessment and the English Language Arts: Present and Future Perspectives

By *William S. Palmer*
and *David K. Pugalee*

For years, educators interested in the improved teaching of the English Language Arts have sought ways to measure student growth in all the communication skills: listening, speaking, reading, writing, and viewing. Efforts to develop instruments to evaluate the individual English Language Arts have not been easy. These skills are often interactive, both in everyday usage and during instruction. For example, when teachers integrate these skills with one another, such as the use of listening and speaking activities before reading and writing activities, they do so based on certain methodological assumptions. They are assuming that, through the use of some English Language Arts skills in combination with one another, learners will improve their abilities to construct meaning. These same teachers also are assuming that, when learners read and comprehend, they do so in a similar way as when they write or compose. Most important, these teachers are assuming that meaning is not just in the text or in the head of the learner to be extracted through a series of simplistic and isolated analyses, because the reading/writing act is not a static experience. In contrast, these teachers realize that meaning is constructed in the mind of the reader/writer through the dynamic interaction among reader/writer, text, and contextual factors (Lipson and Wixon 1991).

As a result of increased emphasis on interactive processes during the teaching of the English Language Arts, we view the need for new assessment measures of student learning in the next century as one important focus for change in the English Language Arts curriculum. At present, many English Language Arts teachers have lessened their use of formal, objectively scored assessment procedures to measure student performance and achievement. As alternatives, they are using more expansive possibilities for securing individual indicators and patterns of student learning behaviors, such as interest inventories, error analysis, skill mastery, and problem-solving strategies. These assessment strategies emphasize process as part of instruction during the learning act—processes that require students to ask, clarify, and solve problems in more "real world" situations. Moreover, students, teachers, parents, and school administrators are increasingly being asked to become involved in new English Language Arts assessment designs and practices.

If all of these personnel are to assist in documenting alternative ways of measuring student learning, they will need more than collaborative support and appropriate training. They will first need an understanding of present efforts to measure student learning in the English Language Arts, efforts that attempt to measure students' processes, progress, and personal growth. Furthermore, they will need additional insights regarding the future direction of student assessment as well as regarding the development of new measures for eventual use in the 21st century.

ASSESSMENT: PRESENT PERSPECTIVES

Today we have multiple approaches to the assessment of student learning in the English Language Arts. Among these approaches are standardized tests, authentic assessment, performance-based assessment, portfolio assessment, statewide literacy tests, and national literacy exams.

Standardized Tests

Since the beginning of their development in the 1920s, standardized tests have been criticized for their shortcomings. Numerous scholars have frequently indicated that traditional standardized tests represent too narrow a view of student achievement. These objectively scored tests generally emphasize low-level and isolated skills, factual knowledge, and the memorization of procedures. Moreover, standardized tests tend to view comprehension as an aggregate of these isolated skills. Such abilities in reading, for example, may be correlated with comprehension; but, by themselves, these abilities do not necessarily constitute the flexible, high-level skills needed for generating logical arguments and the construction of sound solutions to everyday problems. Thus, all too often, the use of objectively scored tests result in little more than the teaching of isolated skills rather than the study of processes involved in problem-solving and real-world situations.

Some additional limitations of standardized tests: They evaluate students on passages much shorter than those read in classroom assignments. They do not take into account the type of reading demands different kinds of genre require, nor the coherence—or lack of it—within the reading selections used as test items. Standardized tests fail to consider how students' performances are affected by their background knowledge of the selected topics or of the purposes, goals, and strategies needed for comprehension. Finally, these tests do not consider students' attitudes and motivations toward learning.

Authentic Assessment

Teachers who evaluate authentically create environments representative of the larger literacy systems outside of classrooms. The two basic requirements of these environments are that the literacy tasks and the text both remain authentic. Authentic literacy tasks are reading, writing, and speaking tasks students could be asked to perform outside the world of school (Jett-Simpson and Leslie 1994). No longer are English Language Arts teachers simply giving tests at the end of units as the main means of assessment. Instead, teachers who are creating authentic literacy environments evaluate much learning by capturing, describing, and interpreting authentic literacy events and behaviors. In short, assessment in the English Language Arts is changing from the administration of primarily formal, objectively scored tests to the increased use of new practices that emphasize more authentic forms of measurement. A good reference for beginning, developing, and evaluating portfolios is *Portfolio Assessment in the Reading-Writing Classroom* by Tierney, Carter, and Desai (1991). In this text, the authors describe how teachers can collect and interpret representative examples of authentic learning and make observational notes on how learning is occurring in classrooms.

Much of the work in compiling literacy portfolios can be completed in collaboration with students. Jett-Simpson and Leslie (1994) called authentic assessment "ecological," because it is ongoing and integrated into instruction and learning—part of the classroom ecosystem as researched and described by Bartoli and Botel (1988). To some degree, performance-based tests are an example of authentic assessment.

Performance-Based Assessment

Tasks used in performance-based assessment are usually authentic because they require knowledge and problem-solving abilities the student may be required to use in the world beyond school. In addition, the materials used are representative of those required for real-world purposes. However, unlike authentic assessment, which is ongoing in classroom settings, performance-based assessment typically focuses on a demonstration or performance of knowledge at the end of some predetermined time period, such as at the conclusion of a unit or at the end of the year. Archbald and Newmann (1988) stated that this assessment process often results in new knowledge—students learn and produce something new, usually as a result of performance-based assessment. Though the use of projects and the processes are beneficial as end-of-year indicators of performance, assessment should be extended into ongoing curricular activities. The continuous examination of the processes and products of learning are key ingredients to authentic assessment. Furthermore, portfolio assessment lends itself to such use.

Portfolio Assessment

A portfolio system is a collection of assessments, organized in a systematic way, that provide information for noting and charting a student's literacy growth and development. In essence, a portfolio often is little more than a container, such as a file folder. However, most educators who collect and select items for literacy portfolios do so in relation to seeking answers to questions such as the following:

• How does the student's reading reflect an interactive approach to reading?

• What authentic-assessment measures are best for me to use with this particular work?

• What was the classroom context for this assessment?

• What patterns of development can I observe in this student's ongoing work?

• What are the district reading/literacy goals, and how well is this particular student meeting them?

In developing literacy portfolios, students, classroom teachers, parents, administrators, and school board representatives often work together to recommend items for inclusion in portfolios. They also identify required and optional assessments, and teachers often collect and contribute materials in their classrooms beyond those recommended by committees. Periodically, students reflect on their growth and development as readers and writers with parents and teachers, using their portfolios as a conference source and focus.

Statewide Literacy-Assessment Efforts

Many states have attempted to develop literacy-assessment measures for a wide range of differing purposes. In many statewide efforts, teachers are held accountable for teaching prescribed skills that may or may not be momentarily beneficial to all students. In the United States, we have been seduced by the notion that English Language Arts skills can be measured quantitatively through statewide use of standardized tests. State legislators and many members of the general public believe standardized tests have the capacity to identify "true" achievement levels of students—and, recently, even of teachers. Moreover, teachers' tenure often is questioned when students do not pass statewide tests. Present efforts by numerous states to push for large-scale use of standardized measures are in direct opposition to many learning theorists, researchers, and practitioners, who frequently echo one another's recommendations for greater flexibility and alternative ways of assessing student literacy.

National Reading-Assessment Trends

The National Council of Teachers of English (NCTE) and the International Reading Association (IRA) have joined forces in developing Standards for the English Language Arts. Developed by teams of teachers and teacher educators, these standards account for processes such as reading as well as major aspects of program content.

This collaborative NCTE and IRA effort attempts to provide educators with answers regarding what students of reading and the related language arts should know and be able to do as a result of ongoing instruction in grades K–12. These standards are not a disguised form of behavioral objectives, nor do they set levels of achievement to be tested at various grade levels. Rather, they are theory- and research-based content and process standards that can guide classroom instruction in both general and specific ways. Moreover, these standards, which have undergone extensive review by numerous task forces, are not intended as a mandate or as the basis for a national curriculum. Rather, NCTE and IRA hope that they will be voluntarily examined and adapted at building, local, and state levels (Suhor 1994).

ASSESSMENT: FUTURE PERSPECTIVES

Teaching and learning in the next millennium will bring about many changes. We predict the following perspectives for the assessment of instruction in the English Language Arts.

New assessment instruments for use in the English Language Arts will attempt to measure a learner's critical thinking ability. We know that recent research in cognitive psychology has described the learner as an "active constructor of knowledge." Yet we must remember what Moffett (1993) noted about the construction of meaning during communication—during use of the English Language Arts—and how all of us learn to make use of different levels of coding in communicating in order for meaning to occur. We first learn to think, to conceptualize, to put our experiences into thought. Second, we learn to verbalize, to speak, to put our thoughts into oral language. Third, we learn to read, to write—the literacy skills—to put our oral language into graphic form to be read.

What remains so significant about the acquisition of the language arts skills in Moffett's cumulative description is that thinking and speaking become prerequisites for most literacy tasks. To Moffett, thinking and speaking are the true language arts skills, and reading and writing are derived skills. Thus, thinking and speaking skills become key considerations to measure in relation to outcomes on varied reading-assessment measures.

In the future, skilled interpreters of reading-assessment measures will also need to assess different kinds and patterns of thinking and responding.

We know from Gardner's (1983) work that many of our students possess multiple ways of thinking. Students often use learning behaviors that transcend typical language patterns and math logistics, both areas to which we presently restrict most assessment measures. Some of these other ways of thinking are related to spatial, kinesthetic, social, and interpersonal reasoning, or combinations of these ways of knowing. Thus, in the future, skilled interpreters of reading-assessment measures will also need to assess different kinds and patterns of thinking and responding, and in direct relation to additional processes and products related to specific reading acts.

The use of standardized tests will continue. Though we will have changing views of the assessment of literacy skills in the future, standardized tests will still be used to document some student achievement. There are many forms of standardized measures. Based on the responses of the standardized or normative samples within many of these tests, raw scores will be converted into a variety of derived scores designed to measure relative standing. For example, grade and age equivalents will continue to be derived from the average scores earned by students in the normative sample at a particular grade or age level. Other types of derived scores will be percentile ranks and standard scores. These scores will be used to track past and present progress as well as chart future trends in reading assessment. Whether or not we like it, many standardized test scores will continue to be used for accountability as well as political purposes in our society of ever-increasing polarized ideological beliefs.

Standardized tests will be used with greater caution and primarily as general estimates of various reading aspects, followed by more in-depth, instructionally valid, informal measures. However, educators will continue to explore present standardized reading tests and revise them in relation to issues such as efficiency, equity, and bias. Furthermore, educators will give greater scrutiny to the unfair use of standardized tests.

Authentic-assessment measures will include a greater emphasis on bibliotherapy. "I have been reading and keeping a notebook of thoughts and questions, and sometimes just garbage, since I was about nine," said Madeleine L'Engle, author of *Walking on Water* (1982, 11). "They are both, for me, my own psychiatrist's couch." The use of reading and writing for therapeutic value will increase in the 21st century. Humankind has pondered the personal meaning of life for centuries, and the therapeutic or personal recreational value of reading and writing is not a novel idea. In fact, the relationship between reading, writing, and the psyche is an ancient one.

Aristotle, for example, wrote about the healing power of poetry. To Aristotle, the poet was physician to the psyche, and the writing of poetry cleansed the soul through the process of catharsis. Similarly, in this past century, Sigmund Freud wrote about the projective powers of reading and writing in which a reader and writer undergo catharsis through the tapping of feelings. Likewise, Carl Jung believed that some books become classics because they connect with something deep inside the reader. Jung's insights led, in part, to the bibliotherapy movement of the 1940s. Humanists such as Abraham Maslow wrote that one way to reach the top hierarchy of self-actualization is through the use of reading and writing.

From all present indications, our current citizenry is reading with great interest and introspection books such as Thomas Moore's *Care of the Soul* (1992) and James Redfield's *The Celestine Prophesy* (1993). In the 21st century, we will have more leisure time to ponder the worth of life and the dimension of our souls. Many of us will turn more to reflective thought in reading and writing, making use of both for increased personal, bibliotherapeutic value. Our future world will be much more complex than today and, though we may have more leisure, we will need to know how to sift and sort through multiple problem-solving strategies as well as explore the human condition.

In *The Courage to Teach* (1999), Palmer reminded us that all-too-objective approaches to teaching and measuring student learning in schools is not enough. Learning, teaching, and assessment cannot be reduced to just technique. We must consider teaching, learning, and assessment in relation to teacher identity and integrity. When we do, we project the condition of our souls onto our students, almost like holding up mirrors to our souls. If we have the courage not to run away from what we see in the mirror, we gain self-knowledge and our students will soon join us in these inward quests. This increased focus on learning, teaching, and living "with soul" is presently becoming a powerful and pivotal force for inclusion, expansion, and refinement—not only in the field of the English Language Arts but within all curricula.

In relation to making use of bibliotherapy and teaching with soul, the English Language Arts will include a greater use of narrative inquiry. Narrative inquiry is the study of how humans make meaning of experience by endlessly telling, reading, and writing stories. Many teachers have found that rich, compelling stories with a universal theme are ideal for containing and organizing parts of the English Language Arts curriculum. They note that readers and writers interact with stories and, if given the opportunity, develop inquiries and resolutions from their texts. Furthermore, their stories frequently lead to questions across the curriculum in other disciplines so that their stories become transdisciplinary.

Many English Language Arts teachers have developed story-based, constructivist perspectives in the development of narrative curriculum. Consequently, an English Language Arts curriculum suited to prepare students for the 21st century should have as its foundation a set of broad goals for understanding and assessing student learning and performance—namely, helping students to think critically, creatively, and reflectively when making decisions and solving problems (Connelly and Clandinin 1988; Lauritzen and Jaeger 1997; Temple and Gillet 1989; Witherell and Noddings 1991).

Performance-based reading assessment will include strategies to measure reading within and across disciplines. There will be a more interdisciplinary focus to teaching of English Language Arts. Many state assessment-development teams have studied English Language Arts skills in relation to teaching different content areas. This meshing of reading skills with specialized content, such as mathematics, will continue into the next millennium.

Palmer and Pugalee (1997) described how mathematical literacy involves the ability both to comprehend and process math language to interpret and solve problem situations. The conclusion to this study underscored the significance of using informal reading inventories in math to identify student difficulties with processing and comprehending math-text language. Thus, this practice can provide teachers with information central to improving students' performance in solving word problems. The study identified these student reading difficulties: (1) lack of notional discrimination ability with the use of calculators, particularly with dollar signs, percent signs, and zeros; (2) lack of ability to represent word problems algebraically; and (3) lack of ability to read and solve word problems with multiple tasks.

Portfolio-assessment efforts will include greater parental involvement. There is some parental involvement today in literacy assessment of students. However, there will be even more in the future. Parents can provide insights into students' literacy behaviors at home, help educators assess reading progress when students appear to have certain skills yet actually may not, or offer help when students cannot master certain skills yet have the ability to do so (Brice 1997).

Parent and teacher conferences will be centered more around portfolios. This focus will communicate students' developmental progress, growth in independent reading, development of attitudes and interests, and ability to use reading and writing for a variety of purposes.

Reading-assessment efforts at state levels will become more extensive. Many statewide literacy-assessment movements will pattern themselves after those from the early 1990s that were exemplified by the state of California. When assessment efforts began to take shape, attempts were made to develop an integrated test, one that would ask students to read, write, and discuss in ways worthwhile and valid for them. More recently in California, developmental teacher teams have worked diligently to select passages to use in reading-assessment efforts. Moreover, they have sought to understand more fully student-interpretation processes and develop sound scoring criteria for assessing reading responses.

Another goal was to get students to reflect upon different prompts and to begin assessing their understanding of it. Next came several questions that assessed students' levels of comprehension—their abilities to evaluate, analyze, and appreciate a text; their abilities to make connections between what they read and other literature, learning, and experiences. This California statewide team effort earned the respect and support of teachers. It set high expectations for students and provided educators with strategies and insights to help teachers and students meet expectations (Dudley 1997).

The demand will increase for electronic reading and new assessment instruments to measure nonlinear forms of print. Our society in the 21st century will demand that most of us read electronic text, presently called "hypertext." Hypertext, a term coined in the 1960s, refers to a form of electronic text, a radically new information technology, and a mode of publication. As Nelson (1981) explained, "By 'hypertext' I mean nonsequential writing—text that branches and allows choices on an interactive screen. As popularly conceived, this is a series of text chunks connected by links which offer readers different pathways."

Hypermedia extends the notion of hypertext by including visual information, sound, animation, and other forms of data. Because hypertext links a passage of verbal discourse to images, maps, diagrams, and sound from other verbal passages, it can expand the notion of text beyond the solely verbal. Electronic links connect parallel or contrasting texts, thereby creating text that can be experienced as nonlinear, multilinear, and multisequential. Though some conventional reading habits will still be required with the use of electronic print, new rules and new experiences of a nondirectional kind will become necessary—what Landow (1992) called the learning of "the new electronic literacies." Our young children are now being called the Digital Generation. They will grow up in schools and in a society that make prominent use of electronic literacies from wide and varied sources.

New electronic literacies will also include expanded viewing of television and films by both students and adults. We will continue to watch TV and films, but with even greater opportunities than presently available. Students, of course, already watch a lot of TV, averaging some 6,000 hours by the time they finish kindergarten (Trelease 1989). Time spent watching TV could, of course, be spent reading. However, Teasley and Wilder (1997) have argued that it is more a matter of *the way* students view movies and TV at present—in passive, trance-like states—than the amount of time they spend watching.

Teasley and Wilder (1997) have developed strategies that call for students to attend carefully while they are viewing—to notice details of auditory and visual images, to talk with one another about what they noticed, to develop hypotheses and make predictions, to form opinions and evaluations, and to communicate their ideas. When students and adults engage with film and video in these active ways, they will develop many of the same skills we value in our reading-literature-literacy curriculum. Both sources of learning—print and visual media—can assist students in becoming lifelong learners.

One major objective for our present and future generation of educators, then, is to determine what best can be learned from print, what best can be learned from electronic print and nonprint media, and what best can be learned through powerful combinations of these literacy resources (Palmer 1998).

Toward the Future

As educators, one of the most significant events we presently witness and must address is our changing student population. It is becoming more diverse, more multicultural; in many states, our minority students are becoming the majority. No longer are classes filled with a majority of the once-typical European-American, middle-class, English-speaking culture. Data suggests unequivocally that culturally and linguistically diverse students, once a minority in our classrooms, are fast becoming a significant proportion of the school-age population (Gonzalez 1990).

This dramatic shift in complexion, native language, and culture will render future classrooms unrecognizable to those of past generations. Clearly, a number of new and sound instructional strategies and assessment measures will be needed. Thus, new instructional techniques and assessment measures will be needed in the English Language Arts to bridge language gaps across the curriculum; to evaluate skills in oral-language acquisition, usage, and development; to foster the mastery of a sound foundation in literacy skills; to instruct students in recognizing and using text organization, structure, and vocabulary in various situations; and to encourage students to transfer these classroom skills to real-life situations. By applying such teaching techniques, educators may enable culturally and linguistically diverse students to make important gains in language production, skill acquisition and use, and, therefore, self-esteem.

As a result, partly due to our growing diverse and linguistically different student populations, one major challenge to all educators in the 21st century will be to develop assessment measures that consider abundant interactions among varied readers, texts, and contexts. The payoff for educators and our society will be monumental. Our citizenry of the next millennium will gain many enriching and beneficial outcomes, because the individual contributions all our students are capable of bringing into our classrooms, schools, homes, and lives are as great as the next century itself.

References

Archbald, D. A., and F. M. Newmann. 1988. *Beyond standardized testing: Assessing authentic academic achievement in the secondary school.* Reston, Va.: National Association of Secondary School Principals.

Bartoli, J,. and M. Botel. 1988. *Reading/learning disabilities: An ecological approach.* New York: Teachers College Press.

Brice, R. 1997. Personal conference. Chapel Hill: University of North Carolina.

Connelly, E. M., and D. J. Clandinin. 1988. *Teachers as curriculum planners: Narratives of experience.* New York: Teachers College Press.

Dudley, M. 1997. The rise and fall of a statewide assessment system. *English Journal* 86(1): 15–20.

Gardner, H. 1983. *Frames of mind: The theory of multiple intelligences.* New York: Basic Books.

Gonzalez, R. D. 1990. When minority becomes majority: The changing face of classrooms. In *English Journal* 79(1): 16–23.

Jett-Simpson, M., and L. Leslie. 1994. *Ecological assessment.* Schofield: Wisconsin State Reading Association.

Landow, G. P. 1992. *Hypertext: The convergence of contemporary critical theory and technology.* Baltimore: Johns Hopkins University Press.

Lauritzen, C., and M. Jaeger. 1997. *Integrating learning through story: The narrative curriculum.* Albany, N.Y.: Delmar Publishers.

L'Engle, M. 1982. *Walking on water: Reflections on faith and art.* New York: Banton Books.

Lipson, M., and K. W. Wixon. 1991. *Assessment and instruction of reading disability: An interactive approach.* New York: HarperCollins.

Moffett, J. 1993. *Teaching the universe of discourse,* 4th ed. Boston: Houghton Mifflin.

Moore, T. 1992. *Care of the soul.* New York: HarperCollins.

Nelson, T. H. 1981. *Literary machines.* Swarthmore, Pa.: T. H. Nelson.

Palmer, P. J. 1999. *The courage to teach: Exploring the inner landscapes of a teaching life.* San Francisco: Jossey-Bass.

Palmer, W. S. 1998. Challenge to change in teacher involvement. In *The challenge of change: Assessment in the 21st century,* ed. R. Reising, 61–72. Greensboro: North Carolina Association for Supervision and Curriculum Development.

Palmer, W. S., and D. K. Pugalee. 1997. Mathematical literacy: A study of student performance in solving algebraic word problems. Paper presented at the Research Council for Diagnostic and Prescriptive Mathematics, Oklahoma City, 9 February.

Redfield, J. 1993. *The celestine prophesy: An adventure.* New York: Warner Books.

Suhor, C. 1994. National standards in English: What are they? Where does NCTE stand? *English Journal* 83(7): 25–27.

Teasley, A. B., and A. Wilder. 1997. *Reel conversations: Reading films with young adults.* Portsmouth, N.H.: Boynton/Cook.

Temple, C., and J. W. Gillet. 1989. *Language arts: Learning processes and teaching practices,* 2d ed. Glenwood, Ill.: Scott, Foresman.

Tierney, R., M. Carter, and L. Desai. 1991. *Portfolio assessment in the reading-writing classroom.* Norwood, Mass.: Christopher-Gordon.

Trelease, J. 1989. *The new read-aloud handbook.* New York: Viking Penguin.

Witherell, C., and N. Noddings, eds. 1991. *Stories lives tell: Narrative and dialogue in education.* New York: Teachers College Press.

9

Educating Young Children in Mathematics, Science, and Technology

By *David Elkind*

Any intellectually responsible program to instruct young children in mathematics, science, and technology must overcome at least three, seemingly insurmountable, obstacles. First, we must address our adult inability to discover, either through reflection or analysis, the means by which children acquire science and technology concepts. Second, we must consider the fact that young children think differently and do not organize their world along the same lines as older children and adults. Finally, we must acknowledge that young children have their own curriculum priorities and construct their own math, science, and technology concepts. These concepts, while age appropriate, may appear wrong from an adult perspective.

OBSTACLES TO EFFECTIVE EARLY CHILDHOOD EDUCATION

Effective learning can occur only when teachers make connections with their students. We must, however, consider each of these obstacles before turning to a few suggestions as to how they can be best overcome.

Deconstructing Math, Science, and Technology Concepts

Math, science, and technology are abstract mental constructions far removed from the immediate, here-and-now world of the young child. As adults, we cannot retrace the steps we took in attaining these concepts, inasmuch as they are part of our intellectual unconscious and unavailable to retrospective analysis. A simple thought experiment illustrates this first obstacle.

Imagine you are teaching a five-year-old to ride a small, two-wheeled bicycle. What is the most important concept the child has to learn to succeed at this skill? Most adults will answer "balance." The child has to learn to keep his or her weight centered on the seat. If you actually attempt to teach a child to ride a two-wheeled bicycle, however, the problem turns out to be quite different. What you observe is that the child either focuses on pumping the pedals and forgets to steer or focuses on steering and forgets to pump. In fact, balance is attained when children coordinate pumping with steering. Once attaining that balance, however, they are no longer aware of how they accomplished it—they just do it.

This simple illustration makes a very powerful point: If we want to teach young children math, science, and technology, we cannot start from some reflective analysis of the task; rather, we must actually observe children attempting to learn the task. This concept was one of Piaget's (1950) most important insights—and one that must not be forgotten.

To make this insight concrete, consider Piaget's (1952) investigations regarding the parallel between a child's spontaneous construction of number and the three types of scales used in psychological measurement. In psychological research, we distinguish among nominal, ordinal, and interval scales of measurement. We speak of "nominal number" when we use a number as a name—for example, the number on a football jersey. Nominal numbers have no numerical value or meaning. We speak of "ordinal number" to designate rank—for example, numbers used to describe a figure skater's performance. A rating of "5.6" given one skater is better than a rating of "5.4" given to a second, but there is no exact measure of how much better the one skater is than the other. That is, there are no units of skating skill or artistic presentation. We speak of "interval number" to reflect equal units or intervals. It is only interval numbers that justify the operations of arithmetic and higher mathematics. This fact is often neglected, however, and many psychological measurements, such as IQ (rank), get treated as interval numbers.

The distinction between nominal, ordinal, and interval scales dates from the early days of psychology as a science and its attempts to employ quantitative methods. Interestingly, as Piaget (1952) has shown, children employ first nominal, then ordinal, and finally interval scales in their spontaneous attainment of measurement concepts. Inasmuch as nominal number is essentially a label, young children can use it as soon as they are able to use names, usually by age two or three. Then, by the age of three or four, children are able to order blocks (or other size-graded materials) according to size, and thus demonstrate the ability to construct ordinal scales and employ numbers in an ordinal sense. However, only when children attain what Piaget termed "concrete operations," at ages five to seven, can they construct units and employ interval scales.

The way in which a child constructs a unit remains instructive and illustrates how different this process is than what one might conclude on the basis of an introspective or logical analysis of the task. Piaget (1952) demonstrated that, to construct the concept of a unit, a child must coordinate the ideas of "sameness" and "difference." To understand a unit, a child must grasp the idea that, for example, the number "3" is both like every other number (its cardinal meaning) but also different from every other number (its ordinal meaning), in that "3" comes after "2" and before "4." It is only at this stage that the child can perform true arithmetic operations. In short, the only way to understand how children learn a concept is to observe them in the process of acquiring it.

Understanding Young Children's Transductive Thinking

Young children think differently than do older children and adults, the second obstacle to overcome for teaching them math, science, and technology. Inhelder and Piaget (1958) discovered, among other important insights, that young children think "transductively," from object to object and from event to event, rather than inductively or deductively. All concepts and ideas are at the same level. For example, a child who asks, "If I eat spaghetti, will I become Italian?" is thinking transductively—joining concepts at two very different levels of abstraction. Transductive thinking is age-appropriate and not something to be overcome or extinguished.

Transductive thinking accounts for a number of thought characteristics in preschool children. Young children often exhibit "animism" and ascribe life to any object that moves. Again, this characteristic arises from the joining of concrete and abstract conceptions as if they were on the same level. Young children also give evidence of "purposivism," the idea that every event and object has a purpose of goal, as well as evidence of "phenomenalistic causality," the idea that when two things occur together, one causes the other.

The Fundamental Curriculum

The third obstacle to the effective math, science, and technology education of young children is that preschoolers have their own curriculum goals. As adults, we tend to assume children are born with all of the concepts they display upon entering first grade. This assumption results from the fact that adults have few memories of their first years of life. Recall memory requires a space/time framework that young children have yet to achieve. Children do not have a good sense of clock time until the age of seven or eight, and a true understanding of calendar time comes even later than that. In the same way, young children only acquire a sense of map and geographical space in the later elementary grades. Without a space/time conception, there is no framework to order and store memories. As adults, when we try to remember what we learned as preschoolers, we start where we should be ending.

What we learn as young children, despite not remembering it, might be called "fundamental curriculum"—that is, our knowledge of things, their sensory properties, their spatial relations, and their temporal sequencing (Elkind 1987). Put more concretely, to operate successfully in the world, young children must learn concepts such as "light," "heavy," "behind," "in front," "inside," "outside," "top," "bottom," "night," "day," "before," "after," and much, much more. None of these ideas is inborn; each must be constructed using a great deal of time and effort. Indeed, young children have their own curriculum priorities.

Perhaps Froebel (1904, 43), the creator of kindergarten, put it best when he wrote that young children must "learn the language of forms before they learn the language of words." Even without explicit instruction, young children are acquiring significant elementary and adaptive math, science, and technology knowledge and skills.

IMPLICATIONS FOR MATH, SCIENCE, AND TECHNOLOGICAL EDUCATION

The obstacles to math, science, and technological education have a number of practical implications for educating children in these domains, only a few of which can be described here. These implications include: (1) the importance of observing young children learning; (2) the need to recognize the limits of instruction; and (3) the value of employing capacity-linked and socially derived motivation.

Observing Young Children Learning

In a nursery school recently, a group of children gathered around a computer that one child was operating. They worked together and made suggestions to the child at the keyboard, who seemed to appreciate their help. The teacher, however, intervened and suggested that they take turns and let the child at the keyboard have his turn without the other children bothering him. This reaction is good example of how a well-intentioned teacher nonetheless ignored the necessity of observing children before making an instructional decision. The children were working cooperatively and not fighting or competing to be at the keyboard. This method may be the way young children approach technology—they may find it less intimidating in a group project. At the very least, it is a possibility that should be investigated.

The world of technology, particularly computers, is a new one. The obstacle to the most effective instruction using technology is the same. We must observe how children themselves deal with technology. To be sure, some initial instruction is required and certain limits must be set; but we also need to be careful observers of the choices the children make for themselves.

In another nursery school recently, a child at a computer chose an animated reading program, which she obviously was enjoying. The teacher, however, encouraged her to use a more advanced, strictly word-oriented program. In such situations, we must respect children's choices. We really do not know what types of programs are most effective for young children without careful observation and study.

Recognizing the Limits of Young Children's Learning

Transductive thinking is concrete and unilevel. Math, science, and technology, on the other hand, have concepts at many different levels of abstraction. For some disciplines, even the lowest levels of abstraction are beyond the abilities of young children. The failure to recognize and accept this fact was the fundamental error in Bruner's (1962, 12) assertion that, "You can teach any child any subject at any age in an intellectually responsible way." There is simply no way to teach a preschooler algebra without so concretizing the concepts as to beg the question of whether they are indeed algebraic. Understanding algebra requires a learner to have acquired already what Inhelder and Piaget (1958) called "formal operations"—operations that enable a young person to deal with second-symbol systems. In algebra, a letter stands for another symbol (a number). Young children are unable to deal with second-symbol systems.

A more concrete example may help amplify the point and provide a practical guideline. Early childhood is a question-asking period, but how one answers has to reflect the child's level of thinking. If a child asks, for example, "Why does the sun shine?" he or she will be lost if you begin to explain the relation between heat and light. The young child is asking not for a scientific explanation but for a purposive one. If we answer, "To keep us warm and make the grass grow," we respond to the true intent of the child's question. Such answers are not really "wrong" per se, and they accomplish the important goal of encouraging further questioning and a wonderful sense of being understood.

Alternatively, one can always turn the question around and ask what the child thinks. Many of the young child's questions are partly rhetorical, in the sense that he or she has thought about them and may have his or her own answers. Moreover, the child is most happy to share these insights with us. If we accept these answers without challenging them, we get insight into the child's thinking and communicate that we are interested in his or her ideas, not in right or wrong answers. In so doing, we are not reinforcing wrong answers so much as promoting the child's sense of self-confidence and security in expressing ideas.

There *are* limits to what one can effectively teach young children in the fields of math, science, and technology. There are, however, no limits to young children's curiosity and imagination if we support and encourage their own ways of thinking.

Motivation in Math, Science, and Technology Education

Young children, as noted earlier, have their own curriculum priorities. They also have their own motivations for assigning these priorities. Everyone who has ever worked with youngsters usually remarks about children's seemingly innate eagerness for exploring and learning. The origins of this motivation, however, are a matter of dispute. Some argue that children are intrinsically motivated to learn, and it is rigid, constraining schooling that dulls their avid striving to learn about their world. In contrast, Piaget (1950) suggested that the spontaneous motivation we observe is actually a byproduct of developing mental abilities. When a child's abilities are maturing, he or she spontaneously seeks out stimuli to nourish them. For example, children will often ask adults to give them numbers to add or subtract once they are able to use these operations.

> *It is not that the school deadens motivation; rather, the spontaneous motivation associated with developing mental structures dissipates.*

If we accept this relation of motivation to developing operations, it means that, once the operations are fully acquired, the motivation will be lost. Indeed, this course of motivation is what seems to happen during the early grades of school. It is not that the school deadens motivation; rather, the spontaneous motivation associated with developing mental structures dissipates. Taking the place of spontaneous motivation is social motivation. Parents who are curious, who read newspapers, magazines, and books, and who talk about world events encourage their children to do likewise. Children, in turn, believe that following parental examples will please their parents and warrant their continued love and protection. In early childhood education, as in later education, parental modeling is all important. Involving parents is a vital part of effective early education.

Before leaving the subject of motivation, it is important to distinguish between capacity and learning. Currently, there is a growing body of knowledge about brain growth and a number of facile extrapolations to early childhood education. As Bruer (1997) has recently made clear, such extrapolations are quite premature and reflect a failure to appreciate the complexities and intricacies of brain growth. Even if the young brain is growing rapidly, that does not tell us what type and how much stimulation is most conducive to productive learning. As Healy (1990, 43) noted:

> Unproven technologies . . . may offer lively visions, but they can also be detrimental to the development of the young plastic brain. The cerebral cortex is a wondrously well-buffered mechanism that can withstand a good bit of well-intentioned bungling. Yet there is a point at which fundamental neural substrates for reasoning may be jeopardized for children who lack proper physical, intellectual, and emotional nurturance. Childhood—and the brain—have their own imperatives. In development, missed opportunities may be difficult to recapture.

In addition to inappropriateness, there is also the issue of the relation of motivation to capacity. A case in point is the young child's great facility for learning foreign languages. It is generally accepted that the early years are the time to acquire a second language. Children who learn a second language early often speak without accent and with the rhythm and intonation of a native speaker. This unquestioned capacity of young children to learn a second language has prompted some parents and schools to provide second-language learning at kindergarten and first-grade levels. Young children are being instructed in languages from French to Japanese. Much of this instruction is wasted time and effort.

Learning a foreign language requires more than capacity; it requires motivation. If a child has parents or grandparents who speak a foreign language, the child has plenty of motivation to learn that language. Yet there is no such motivation if the child is just given lessons in the language. He or she does not need it for anything and cannot use it for anything. Even with the capacity to learn a foreign language, without the motivation, that capacity will not be realized. It is not unlike the natural athlete who lacks the competitive zeal to succeed in a sport. Another individual, with less native ability but with more ambition, may succeed where the native athlete failed. It is when motivation and capacity work together that we find the most successful results.

ACTIONS FOR THE NEXT MILLENNIUM

This chapter has addressed three major obstacles to effective math, science, and technology instruction in early childhood. These obstacles are not insurmountable but must be addressed to engage in meaningful and effective math, science, and technology education in early childhood.

A few strategies for overcoming these roadblocks were suggested. To overcome the barrier of understanding how children learn, we have to *observe* children learning. To surmount the barrier of a child's limited transductive thinking, we must *en-*

courage their unlimited imagination and curiosity. Finally, we must *engage* children's spontaneous motivation. We also must help instill social motivation by involving parents in ways that encourage their modeling of reading, question asking, and knowledge gathering. Early childhood is a most important period for math, science, and technology education—but only if we adapt such instruction to the unique needs, interests, and abilities of young children.

REFERENCES

Bruer, J. T. 1997. Education and the brain: A bridge too far. *Educational Researcher* 26(8): 4–16.

Bruner, J. S. 1962. *The process of education.* Cambridge, Mass.: Harvard University Press.

Elkind, D. 1987. *Miseducation: Preschoolers at risk.* New York: Knopf.

Froebel, F. (trans. J. Jarvis) 1904. *Pedagogics of the kindergarten.* New York: D. Appleton & Co.

Healy, J. M. 1990. *Endangered minds: Why our children don't think.* New York: Simon and Schuster.

Inhelder, B., and J. Piaget. (trans. A. Parsons and S. Milgram) 1958. *The growth of logical thinking from childhood to adolescence: An essay on the construction of formal operational structures.* New York: Basic Books.

Piaget, J. (trans. C. Gattegno and F. M. Hodgson) 1952. *The child's conception of number.* London, England: Routledge & K. Paul.

Piaget, J. (trans. M. Piercy and D. E. Berlyne) 1950. *The psychology of intelligence.* London, England: Routledge & K. Paul.

10

Mathematics in the Next Century

By *Hunter Ballew*

The attainment of higher-order thinking by young people in mathematics classes is the most critical challenge faced by the mathematics education community in the coming millennium. By helping the young learner absorb mathematical facts and algorithms, we do a necessary service to our students. However, absorbing material, while necessary, stops short of the ultimate goal in mathematics education. To be successful, we must get the mind fully absorbed in higher-order thinking. Unless the mind of the student is absorbed in the work, mathematics will not be learned, except perhaps by those few who learn it in spite of our teaching.

WHAT IS HIGHER-ORDER THINKING?

In *The Marvelous Land of Oz* (Baum 1904, 37), Jack Pumpkin-head remarked, "That is a very interesting history, and I understand it perfectly—all but the explanation." Higher-order thinking means you understand the explanation, and that you can form the explanation in your own words. For example, higher-order thinking enables you to apply your understanding of percent to an analysis of the data in Figure 10.1 on page 113, taken from a local newspaper. It also explains why the 300 percent figure has to be an error.

Higher-order thinking requires power that allows reasoning that goes beyond memorization and beyond the application of a learned set of rules—that is, beyond but not in place of memorization. According to the National Council of Teachers of Mathematics (NCTM 1989, 5), mathematical power "denotes an individual's abilities to explore, conjecture and reason logically, as well as the ability to use a variety of mathematical methods effectively to solve nonroutine problems." Higher-order thinking might involve the application of learned knowledge to new situations, or it might involve making judgments based on facts and then supporting these judgments with data and reasoning.

Gagné and Briggs's (1979, 72) concept of "cognitive thinking" can be closely related to higher-order thinking: "A cognitive strategy is an internally organized skill that selects and guides the internal processes involved in defining and solving novel problems." An "intellectual skill" is the ability to apply a step-by-step process to something, like the solution of a given quadratic equation. A cognitive strategy is more than this. A cognitive strategy means not merely doing more examples using the same formula but actually applying a method to a situation new to the learner. This strategy is a form of higher-order thinking that, in turn, provides the learner with the power needed to solve problems and to go beyond the data given and into territory new to the learner.

Higher-order thinking is also closely related to Skemp's (1987) concept of "relational understanding" as opposed to "instrumental understanding." Instrumental understanding is rule oriented—knowing what to do by learning and applying a set of rules, or an algorithm, to solve a problem or answer a question. Effective application of algorithms is a necessary skill in learning mathematics, but it is not enough to enable the learner to deal with new situations. Relational understanding, on the other hand, means knowing both what to do and why. Relational understanding may take longer to learn, but it also may be longer lasting than instrumental understanding. Like Gagné and Briggs's cognitive strategies, relational understanding gives lasting power to the learner.

SCHOOL MATHEMATICS

Higher-order thinking, cognitive strategy, and relational understanding are learning principles that have been known for some time (as the dates in this chapter's reference section can attest). These principles simply have not been applied widely enough in our schools. That is why a plea must be made to find ways to incorporate them in our teaching and learning in the new millennium.

"Schoolmath" has been coined to describe the material presently taught in the schools under the name of mathematics (Fowler 1994). The thought associated with this word is that the mathematics taught in the schools is good, but schoolmath stops short of what we really need for our young people. We need schoolmath, but we need more. We need something better, something more interesting to students "in their learning years" and something that will be more valuable to them in their future learning and in their years beyond school. The differences between the activities and outcomes of schoolmath and higher-order thinking are illustrated through line-by-line

Figure 10.1: Crimes over two years in one locality

Crimes	1992	1993	+/-%
Homicide	0	3	+300%
Robbery	27	29	+7.4%
Rape/Sexual Assault	8	4	-50%
Break-Ins	315	180	-42.9%

comparisons in Figure 10.2 on page 115. All of these activities are not necessarily things you would actually do in school; rather, they are used here to illustrate the differences between schoolmath and schoolmath plus higher-order thinking.

The direction we need to take as educators is indicated by the National Research Council (NRC 1989, 10) in the book *Everybody Counts: A Report to the Nation on the Future of Mathematics Education*:

> *Some adults blame the "new math" for their fears, having become con-*
> *vinced of their own mathematical ineptitude by instruction steeped in pre-*
> *mature abstraction. Others have been made apprehensive by a teacher's rigid*
> *view of mathematics as a string of procedures to be memorized, where right*
> *answers count more than right thinking. Either extreme—mindless abstrac-*
> *tion or mindless calculation—yields mindless mathematics.*

The Relation of Cognitive Strategies to Higher-Order Thinking

How can we avoid "mindless mathematics" and help young people develop higher-order thinking skills? The best way is to find the time, over a period of each school year, to go beyond the mandatory learning of facts, such as the multiplication table, and beyond the ability to apply algorithms, such as how to solve quadratic equations. This change would mean allotting time each school year to develop cognitive strategies. A cognitive strategy cannot be developed on a single occasion but must be developed over long periods of time. Furthermore, as Gagné and Briggs (1979, 72) observed, "A cognitive strategy is an internally organized skill that selects and guides the internal processes involved in defining and solving novel problems."

Cognitive strategies probably cannot be taught directly. Instead, the best hope for helping young people develop cognitive strategies, and therefore higher-order thinking skills, is for the teacher to provide favorable conditions for their development. There is no guaranteed way to be certain that students will develop cognitive strategies. The best method, however, is to challenge students on frequent occasions with novel problems. This practice means the problem is new to the student engaged in searching for the solution. It requires a combination of time invested by the teacher and genuine effort supplied by the student. Higher-order thinking requires a collaborative effort by teacher and student over a long period of time. Consequently, such an investment of time and effort probably will require that fewer topics be covered in a given school year's time.

The Role of Discourse in Developing Higher-Order Thinking

Yogi Berra is said to have quipped, "You can't think and hit at the same time." Yet in mathematics, unlike baseball, you *must* think and do mathematics at the same time if you want to go beyond schoolmath. Moreover, students must think while they read and think while participating in discourse. Discourse helps promote thinking by contrasting one person's ideas or concepts with those of another. NCTM (1991, 1) takes the position that elementary and secondary teachers of mathematics should orchestrate "classroom discourse in ways that promote the investigation and growth of mathematical ideas." NCTM (1991, 35) recommends that this orchestration be accomplished by:

• posing questions and tasks that elicit, engage, and challenge each student's thinking;

• listening carefully to students' ideas;

• asking students to clarify and justify their ideas orally and in writing;

• deciding what to do in depth from among the ideas that students bring up during a discussion;

• deciding when and how to attach mathematical notation and language to students' ideas;

• deciding when to provide information, when to clarify an issue, when to model, when to lead, and when to let a student struggle with a difficulty; and

• monitoring students' participation in discussions and deciding when and how to encourage each student to participate.

Discourse in the classroom pulls together concepts, ideas, conclusions, definitions, interpretations, and examples, thus enabling students to think about what they are learning. This practice, in turn, empowers students to correct and expand their understanding of concepts in the curriculum. Furthermore, discourse enables students to test their understanding against the thoughts of other students and the teacher as well as against what they read and hear in and out of school.

Successful discourse, with the result of higher-order thinking, requires an environment in which all persons and comments are respected. Students must feel secure in the knowledge that it is perfectly all right to express an incomplete or vague thought. The idea is that, by expressing such thoughts and gauging the reaction from others, the thought might be clarified or even changed. This process is precisely what learning entails. Discourse in small groups can help students develop the confidence to express their thoughts and questions without fear of ridicule.

Figure 10.2. Comparing Schoolmath with Higher-Order Thinking

Schoolmath	Higher-Order Thinking
Doing mathematics	**Thinking** mathematically
Following instructions	**Creating** instructions
Applying routines	**Developing** routines
Knowing what to do	**Finding** what to do
Common sense	**Uncommon** sense
Repetitive procedures	**Innovative** procedures
Reading a map	**Constructing** a map
Taking a shortcut	**Taking** the scenic route
Picking corn	**Plowing** new ground

WHAT ARE THE DETERRENTS TO THE DEVELOPMENT OF HIGHER-ORDER THINKING SKILLS?

The NRC (1989, 75) has reported, "Parental and legislative pressures in the past few years, driven largely by frustration over declining test scores, have led to many rash actions." Two of these actions are:

(1) increased use of standardized tests—where there is very little understanding of what the tests contain or what they are capable of testing; and

(2) increased use of test scores, especially for teacher and school accountability—where there is little recognition that the tests reflect only a small part of curricular objectives.

The NRC (1989, 69) further warned, "What is tested is what gets taught." Teachers teach for the "End of Grade" tests and "End of Course" tests. And who can blame them? Teachers are being held accountable for the test scores of their students. Now, there is nothing wrong with the concept of accountability, especially in regard to public funds. Rather, what causes problems is the *application* of accountability to test results that do not measure what is most important. Under the laudable banner of accountability, higher-order thinking and the resulting valuable and lasting learning get lost. As the NRC (1989, 69) noted, "Because assessment is so pervasive and has such powerful impact on the lives of both students and teachers, it is very important that assessment practice align properly both with the purpose of the test and with curricular objectives."

The weight applied to results of End of Grade tests and End of Course tests, as well as standardized tests, almost certainly precludes the attainment of higher-order thinking skills. Again, this goal is the most important challenge facing mathematics education in the coming millennium.

WHAT DIRECTION FOR HIGHER-ORDER THINKING?

The connections among the concept of higher-order thinking, Gagné and Briggs's cognitive strategies, and Skemp's relational understanding have been clearly demonstrated. This connection shows us the way mathematics teaching can be improved in the coming millennium. This proposed way of teaching is to keep the basic facts and algorithms at the heart of the mathematics curriculum as we have in the past but, at the same time, absolutely *insist* on having these facts and algorithms lead students on to the rich ground of higher-order thinking. Though I acknowledge that this concept may not be terribly new, it is nonetheless key to student success; still, it has not been widely attempted in the mathematics classroom. Consider this NRC (1989, 57) summation:

> *Despite daily homework, for most students and most teachers mathematics continues to be primarily a passive activity: teachers prescribe; students transcribe. Students simply do not retain for long what they learn by imitation from lectures, worksheets, or routine homework. Presentation and repetition help students do well on standardized tests and lower-order skills, but they are generally ineffective as teaching strategies for long-term learning, for higher-order thinking, and for versatile problem solving.*

If we want students to think, we must do these two things: (1) provide time for students to do the thinking; and (2) give the students something to think about, not solely something to remember. Above all, remember that memorizing facts and algorithms is not unimportant; on the contrary, facts and algorithms are necessary. Yet they are not sufficient for the attainment of higher-order thinking skills.

REFERENCES

Baum, L. F. 1904. *The marvelous land of Oz.* New York: William Morrow & Co.

Fowler, D. 1994. What society means by mathematics. *Focus: The Newsletter of the Mathematics Association of America* 14(2): 12–13.

Gagné, R. M., and L. J. Briggs. 1979. *Principles of instructional design,* 2d ed. New York: Holt, Rinehart, and Winston.

National Council of Teachers of Mathematics. 1989. *Curriculum and evaluation standards for school mathematics.* Reston, Va.: NCTM.

National Council of Teachers of Mathematics. 1991. *Professional standards for teaching mathematics.* Reston, Va.: NCTM.

National Research Council. 1989. *Everybody counts: A report to the nation on the future of mathematics education.* Washington, D.C.: National Academy Press.

Skemp, R. R. 1987. *The psychology of learning mathematics,* expanded American ed. Hillsdale, N.J.: L. Erlbaum Associates.

11

Teaching Media Literacy: An Urgent Task for Social Studies Educators

By *Xue Lan Rong*

Among the many challenges facing educators in the United States, competently and creatively enabling our students to develop media literacy ranks foremost. Media literacy, especially electronic-media literacy, is becoming a skill vital for our young citizens' effective functioning. Why is it important for public school students in the United States to become media literate? The vast media culture that surrounds us suggests teachers are beginning to face a generation of students overwhelmingly versed in using computers and other changing technology.

We are living in a media-saturated culture (Potter 1998). Cable television provides more than 40 channels, offering some 1,000 hours of television per day. Hollywood studios release about 350 film vehicles each year. People who live in large cities can access about 50 radio stations; residents of modest-sized towns can tune in at least a dozen. We have a choice of daily and weekly newspapers, more than 10,000 magazines, and 1,000 new book titles *every week*. Most of us have computers or can easily find one to use, enabling entire multimedia facilities and thousands of programs and games to be presented at our fingertips. The Internet provides us with more than 12,000 electronic-information services, offering almost everything imaginable. We can communicate point-to-point through e-mail, get together with others in chat rooms for interactive conversations, exchange information on bulletin boards, share software, undertake electronic publishing, participate in clubs and contests, and buy almost any product or service. Every year, the amount of information rapidly expands as new technological channels come on-line and place more messages in front of us.

The presence of media in our daily lives greatly influences the way children live and learn—it therefore must change the ways teachers think and work. A frequent topic of discussion among educators is how television and other technological mass media have accelerated a decrease in reading literacy, a decline in motivation in for-mal school learning, and an increase in shortened attention spans. Furthermore, some pundits and popular analysts have suggested that TV and other media foster a value system among our youth that may be at odds with a healthy maturation process, creating an uncritical consumerist mentality and nurturing some delusional expec-tations with regard to relationships and life in general (Robins 1995).

In the midst of these concerns expressed by educators, parents, and the general public, many argue that educators have failed to acknowledge the important influ-ence of media literacy in children's learning, in their daily lives, and in their long-term growth (Martorella 1996). Young people are given little guidance regarding how to read, interpret, and critically evaluate media images and information—even though they are exposed to more and more media messages all the time. They are, thus, left in a visually vulnerable situation, easily influenced and manipulated by mass-media messages (Considine 1987). Educators have voiced concerns such as these for more than a decade. They have noticed that classroom teachers are lacking in technologi-cal training and skills, while too many schools simply lack facilities to aid them in their instruction. Many have called for change, strongly advocating that public schools and educators position themselves to influence the direction and content of media studies, and in a manner that is media-savvy and non-reactionary (Robins 1995).

MEDIA LITERACY

There are two major types of media: First, there are various forms of electronic media, such as broadcast, cable, and satellite TV, as well as compact discs, radio, movies, and the Internet. Second, there are various forms of printed media, such as books, newspapers, and magazines. The electronic dimension of media literacy is increasingly important. The widespread use of rapidly developing electronic media and the accompanying lack of expertise among educators suggest that issues related to critical analysis and consumption of this form of media are moving in different directions.

Electronic-media literacy for teachers and students must be emphasized for three reasons:

1. The study of electronic media may appear to be an inconsequential subject area in social studies, but it actually represents one the most motivational approaches to engaging students in the acquisition of new knowledge, not to mention some of the most potent socializing forces in our culture (Godin 1993).

2. The influence and effects of electronic media on our children are overwhelm-ing in terms of extent, frequency, and depth. Yet the attention, understanding, and experience necessary to teach on this topic remain at a minimum among social stud-ies educators. In fact, many educators believe that critical analysis of screen media is at least as, if not more, important as understanding the printed word.

3. The social sciences teach about social knowledge and critical-thinking skills. Abilities like knowing, identifying, and evaluating sources of social studies informa-tion are considered more important in social studies classrooms than in classrooms of other subjects.

Electronic-media literacy can be understood in a broader or a narrower sense;

however, media literacy for pre-university students is usually defined as the ability to communicate competently in all media forms (Lloyd-Kolkin and Tyner 1991). It may comprise abilities in two related dimensions: (1) to operate electronic facilities and manipulate electronic technologies; and (2) to understand, interpret, analyze, and evaluate media messages. The more crucial components of media literacy for a social studies curriculum are the latter, rather than the former. Teaching media literacy within a social studies curriculum means emphasizing the ability to read media texts critically and interpret media messages effectively. Potter (1998) has argued that students with a high level of media literacy have a strong and broad understanding of the context and subtext of media messages. They actively use a set of highly developed skills to place a media message inside the context of a well-elaborated knowledge structure and, thus, can interpret any message along many different dimensions (cognitive, emotional, aesthetic, and moral). Highly literate youth have developed an understanding of the symbols, information, values, and ideas that emerge from the media messages. Moreover, they know how to sort through all the choices of meaning to select the one most useful from several points of view—cognitive, emotional, moral, and aesthetic. Hence, people who are highly media literate have greater control over the influence and effects of media messages on their own lives (Potter 1998).

MEDIA LITERACY AND SOCIAL STUDIES

No matter what curriculum aims a social studies teacher prefers—citizenship transmission, social science for pedagogical purposes, critical or reflective thinking—developing children's civic knowledge, civic skills, and civic values are considered common goals (Thornton 1995). Three central components—knowledge of civilization, democratic values, and critical-thinking skills—are among the most noted learning objectives in social studies. If students are to be taught how to become informed media consumers, the social studies curriculum is an ideal place to start.

The Importance of Media Literacy in Social Studies Classrooms

Electronic-media literacy should be included in all levels of school curricula, specifically within the social studies curriculum. Significant shifts in theories about curriculum development and instructional methodologies are introducing dramatic challenges to traditional thinking among social studies professionals. Wilson and Marsh (1995) have argued that none of these changes poses as many challenges—or as many opportunities—as the rapid development and spread of cable and direct-satellite TV and electronic-computer technologies. This blast of telecommunication with an incredible explosion of information impacts heavily upon the social sciences. Terms such as "infotainment," "infomercial," and "edutainment" indicate that the line between entertainment, commercialism, information, and education is becoming obscure (Vargas and Pyssler 1998).

Many media educators (Ornstein 1987; Potter 1998) have argued that, just as we teach students about the development of the National Aeronautics and Space Administration and other information related to space studies in science education classes, we should also teach about the development of movies, television, computers, and the Internet in social science education. Moreover, social studies educators may bear more burdens for the political, social, and economic consequences of the micro-revolution, as well as its fascinating history and geographical dispersion—an important dimension of contemporary U.S. history and world history.

Many educators believe that electronic technologies have created an impossible situation for social studies educators. Among the main reasons for this situation:

Electronic media simply plays an obsessive role in children's lives. According to Levine (1996) and Potter (1998), media saturation—in the form of billboards, movies, radio, TV, and the Internet—has reached levels scarcely imaginable just 25 years ago. Children watch about five hours of television per day. Between the ages of 2 and 11, children watch 28 to 30 hours of TV a week, and view between 300 and 1,600 advertisements every day. By the time they have graduated from high school, average children will have watched about 23,000 hours of TV and will have spent 50 percent more time in front of a TV set than in front of their teachers. Two-thirds of U.S. families have access to computers. By 1997, more than 9.5 million people were using the Internet, including more than 1 million children under age 18. The average session lasts about 68 minutes, and about two-thirds of users look for information weekly; a quarter search daily (Potter 1998). As early as 1989, 65 percent of U.S. residents used TV as their main source for news, and 44 percent used it as their only source for news (Television Information Office 1989).

Many educators have warned that excessive time spent on electronic media may cause problems for students in the classroom. They suggest that it might contribute to reading difficulties and illiteracy in social science knowledge, and that students' knowledge of geography, history, political systems, and economics is sketchy because their memory banks stay crammed with popular-culture images and "infobits." Potter (1998) reported that more students know what actors make in salaries for movies than know the name of either senator from their home state. Less than one-half of students know the population of their country, and fewer still can name the relative employment sizes of different professions. Worse, they have not developed any strategies to help them make good estimates of these things. When they do form an opinion about something in the media or in society, it rarely is rooted in information from reliable and diverse sources; instead, it is tethered only to shifting intuitive feelings generated from electronic media.

Television has influenced the socialization process of children. It is possible that time spent on the computer, especially with the Internet, may have social and psychological effects on children (Splaine 1991). Electronic media inform children about their social roles and train their perceptions. For instance, TV communicates examples of people working, families interacting, and other acts of interpersonal communication, and may precipitate prosocial or antisocial behavior. Media scholars (Alvermann 1999; Artz 1998; Delgado 1998; Gandy 1994; Goodall, Jakubowicz, and Martin 1994; McLean 1998; Vargas and Pyssler 1998) have argued that inaccurate portrayals of gender and minority roles in society are frequently communicated through the mass media.

Historically, the coverage and representation of minorities and women on television and in films have been limited and stereotypically presented; indeed, the overwhelming majority of all actors in positive roles on TV are male, European American, heterosexual, middle-class, and young adult. The lack of full and accurate representation makes it difficult for children to see a variety of role models. Though not deliberately attempting to reflect a devaluation of people in these underrepresented groups, their relative exclusion and unflattering portrayal may be considered an accurate reflection of this devaluation. Of particular concern, African-American and Hispanic children tend to watch more television, have less access to reading materials, and have less opportunity to use computers than European Americans. Thus, for members of minorities, the potential effects of televised communication are intensified, and they may have fewer chances to develop computer and print literacies (Potter 1998).

Electronic media may affect children's learning styles. Some educators have argued that long hours spent watching television can cause an increase in shortened attention spans and a decline in reading ability. Print learning appears to require more abstract thought than does learning from TV, though the use of visuals may improve student recall (Splaine 1991). Obsession with the Internet can lead to a declining enthusiasm for homework and a steady alienation from peers and reality. At the least, electronic media may promote learning styles incompatible with traditional curriculum, instruction, and classroom management.

Though some researchers have suggested that electronic media may introduce complexities to social studies curriculum and instruction, others have argued that social studies education, in particular, could benefit from primary and secondary source materials, databases, pictures, graphics, maps, lesson plans, and other resources readily available via this media outlet (Risinger 1996). Electronic media offer students a wealth of data on contemporary affairs through colorful visual images, thereby becoming powerful tools for teaching current affairs. Television programs and commercials carry more information on gender, race, self-image, values, and norms than most schools have time to offer (Godin 1993).

Some educators have argued that the most important issue here is that electronic media may be a good learning tool that presents teachers with a cognitively different and empathetic way to teach. Films and television arguably have the advantage of recreating an event or process within a realistic setting—making lessons "come alive" for students. Cognitively speaking, the greatest advantage of film and TV productions is that they combine seeing and hearing within an action setting. In addition, films can encourage students' participation and interaction within an instructional setting through eyewitness reports of unfolding events (Dynneson and Gross 1995). In this way, electronic media can help bridge the gap between the "real world" and that of the school curriculum, especially for history teachers, who are teaching about events old and/or distant.

Many media specialists have argued that multimedia technological tools already have demonstrated their potential to revolutionize learning and assist both teachers and students in performing an endless variety of complex tasks. Multimedia tools can provide instructional variety and continuous reinforcement. They can help students quickly access large amounts of information in relation to problem solving and serve as springboards to new questions and issues. They have demonstrated this capability with all ages and types of students, while simulating patience, personalized assistance, and immediate feedback (Martorella 1996).

In recent years, more teachers have begun to use computers for assisting their instruction. Dynneson and Gross (1995) have summarized the possible aids that computers can provide for teachers. For example, computers with CD-ROM drives (the ability to read compact disks) can provide encyclopedic amounts of information in databases, which can supplement instructional information using narrative and audiovisual resources on almost any social studies topic. Exceptional educational technology programs show how to weave multimedia software, CD-ROM technology, videodiscs, and Internet resources into the curriculum to enhance learning and increase student productivity. Software programs can be used to enhance instruction and promote learning in an alternative-textbook setting. Computers can be used to retain students' knowledge and skills through the use of drill-and-practice software, tutorial programs, and simulations. Computers can also be used as tools to foster critical-thinking and problem-solving skills through student use of databases, spreadsheets, and electronic-analysis networks.

Dynneson and Gross (1995) also have summarized many important implications for teachers with the introduction of electronic technology to the social studies classroom. According to at least one study, interactive technologies can help teachers act as facilitators and enable them to observe and guide more of the learning process, rather than directing it. Teachers reported that when students used computers, they assumed more responsibility for their own work, worked at their own pace, and cooperated more with one another. Students took on differentiated roles, including experts, experimenters, and observers while working with computers in groups.

As social studies educators and social scientists, it is important to highlight the powerful potential of Internet usage in social studies teaching. Social studies educators can utilize the tremendous resources of the electronic media in their curriculum planning and instruction. The Internet, serving as an information highway, provides text, pictures, sounds, and colorful graphics. It allows users to connect—or link—to thousands of resources throughout the world. The Internet as a tool for instruction in social studies is presenting students with an unprecedented opportunity to engage in one of the democratizing movements in learning: equal access to unbounded, unlimited information (Risinger 1996). To teach current affairs, public affairs, controversial issues, and historical issues and events with renewed public interest, teachers can find programs with lesson plans and supporting newspaper and magazine materials on-line as well as share materials and conduct schoolwide, local, national, and international discourse with other educators on-line.

Finally, one undeniable advantage of using electronic media is that children and teens love it. Electronic media can hold their attention, and they find media images easy to grasp. As Dynneson and Gross (1995) noted, TV programs and films colorfully, interestingly, and neatly pack large amounts of information into an easily understandable presentation. Learning for some becomes effortless. Though students sometimes encounter difficulties in conceptualizing the information, many instructors have indicated that using media examples makes learning delightful and easier to explain in complex concepts. Research has suggested that interactive media better engages the interests of students in local, national, and global issues and affairs than printed media (Wilson and Marsh 1995). Research also suggests that teen attitudes toward current affairs derive more from the mass media than from teachers, parents, or peers (Croteau and Hoybes 1997).

Teaching Electronic-Media Literacy

There has been a trend in schools to introduce media literacy into the curriculum. Media-literacy education helps students develop the ability to access, analyze, and evaluate media messages and helps them learn to produce communication in a variety of media forms. Robins (1995) has argued that, at the most superficial level, some media-study programs might use TV programs, films, music, and some computer-software programs as educational tools to supplement the principle curriculum. Less frequently, yet with a much more meaningful impact, teaching media literacy both uses the text of popular media in the classroom and applies it to teach the context and subtext (underlying aspects) of the media messages themselves. Programs of this kind in school are usually modest in nature (a several-hour unit) and delivered as a workshop rather than integrated into daily instruction and homework assignments. However, more and more educators believe that media studies should be taught in schools at all levels and that social science is the most appropriate place for such instruction. Some studies (Dynneson and Gross 1995; Hamot, Shiveley, and VanFossen 1997) suggested that a media-literacy curriculum should be incorporated, intensively and extensively, into social studies teachers' daily lesson planning.

The elements or topics to be emphasized in the study of electronic-media literacy and how to teach these topics in social studies classrooms are subject to debate. The instruction of media literacy is commonly accepted as enhancing technical understanding and/or as developing critical-thinking skills among educators. Surveys of secondary social studies educators on how they define media literacy and what aspects of media literacy they address in their classes have indicated that technical understanding was the primary category (Hamot et al. 1997). Though social studies teachers should work with school media specialists and other teachers to help students learn to produce communication in a variety of interactive electronic forms (Lloyd-Kolkin and Tyner 1991), their primary task in terms of media literacy is to help students develop an ability to analyze media messages and evaluate information sources on the Internet. Armed with these skills, students can better construct their own interpretations of those media messages and the events of the world around them.

Media-literacy curricula in social studies should aim to help students develop analytical skills to avoid becoming passive receivers of electronic communication. Several key elements should therefore be considered in curriculum design and instructional planning. Students first must understand that most media messages are outcomes of commercial and economic concerns, and these messages are constructed representations based on the perspectives of those generating the messages. According to Potter (1998), in electronic media, news reporters tell us their interpretation of what is important and who is important. Though this is true of both print and broadcast-news reporters, it seems exaggerated in the electronic media because the time limitations of TV programs are more constrictive than the space limitations of printed newspapers. Film and television producers show us their interpretations of life, living, success, happiness, and so forth. Advertisers try to convince us that we are inadequate and that only their products can help us quickly overcome our problems and fill our personal emptiness. Students need to know there are values and points of view inherently embedded in media based on how and why a particular medium is structured (Ferrington and Anderson-Inman 1996). Furthermore, students must be aware that profit is the primary—and in some cases the only—purpose for the operation of most electronic media. Ratings and ticket sales sometimes render truth and other social concerns irrelevant. The frequent appearance of sex, violence, and spectacle in electronic media is due largely to a single belief: they bring in big ratings.

Because most television programs are aimed at certain demographic groups, students (media targets themselves) must have a general knowledge of how and why these messages were constructed and delivered. This knowledge will help them understand how and why television programs and films sometimes distort reality and why they are neither "objective" nor "neutral," as many of the media industries claim—and many unsophisticated viewers believe. Media literacy should teach students to recognize the context of the messages and, thereby, to understand the subtext of them. They must be aware of the underrepresented and devalued groups in, and absent from, media messages and the current and historical inaccuracies—that is, the misrepresentation of past and present events due to bias, misinformation, and/or misinterpretation. Teaching students to understand the subtext of electronic-media language is accomplished in much the same way as teaching them to read between the lines of printed language. If students know how to "read" the electronic-media language, they will be able to negotiate the meanings of these messages more successfully rather than accepting them totally and uncritically.

If students know how to "read" the electronic-media language, they will be able to negotiate the meanings of these messages more successfully.

For example, social studies educators who teach economic, legal, and political systems (ELP) courses, U.S. government, and international studies must pay close attention to the content of political messages conveyed through TV and other mass media and to how they are conveyed (Graber 1988). There are several crucial questions social studies educators must discuss with students: What is the impact of television on the public's perception of reality? How do citizens decide what is real? What will be the effect of the use of news reenactments? What are the effects of TV on public attention to complex matters? Is there an apparent inability of the mass media to capture the complexity and contradictions of many public issues?

Moreover, teachers should discuss with their students why almost any news delivery is potentially distorted. Viewers must know that the news media reflect a distorted sense of news values held by a majority of news professionals, most of whom tend to define news from a European-American majority perspective (Ferrington and Anderson-Inman 1996; Greenberg and Brand 1998). Ratings also impact news coverage. Events such as protests, disasters, scandals, or people involved in violence (as a victim or a perpetrator) invite intense media coverage (Gans 1979). Though topic selection of this kind has been a part of the historical journalistic fabric, some of the most interesting aspects of it include which scandals get chosen to be reported, which perpetrators of violence capture attention, and what ways reports are sensationalized to frighten or titillate. Teachers must consider how the effects of distortion can be identified, understood, and, therefore, reduced through social studies education.

Along with developing an analytical skill and a critical attitude toward media messages (applying and analyzing multiple sources of information and uncovering multiple interpretation), it is also crucial that students learn to recognize and understand the context and subtext of Web sites. In addition, one goal of teaching media literacy should be to help students acquire the desire and ability to diversify the sources of their information. The absence of this goal could mean serious consequences for teaching about social and political issues and for civic participation in political and public events (such as elections).

A growing number of publications describe tactics, strategies, and specific programs for media literacy developed by media critics, interactive-technology specialists, and social studies professionals (Buckingham and Sefton-Green 1995; Dennis and Pease 1996; Lloyd-Kolkin and Tyner 1991, Potter 1998; Semali and Pailliotet 1999; Silverblatt 1995). Though they offer a variety of approaches, a broad summary of their goals and attributes can provide insight and direction for educators.

Foremost, we must teach students to become informed and conscientious consumers. Research has indicated that, before U.S. children are old enough to drive, they already have viewed an estimated 100,000 television commercials promoting the consumption of beer—commercials that link images and ideals of the intended purchaser's masculinity to the product. Teaching students to identify the interests of media industry and media-production processes can help tap their media-based perceptions and denaturalize media subtexts.

Teachers can assign students to collect examples of advertisements and then analyze them in terms of the intended audience of the TV programs or Web sites they accompany. Students can then share these examples in class. Lloyd-Kolkin and Tyner (1991) suggested the following categories of questions for class discussion:

• What persuasive appeal techniques and propaganda techniques were used by the advertiser?

• What types of viewers are likely to find this commercial appealing? Are you a member of the group the advertiser is hoping to reach?

• What is the effect of the commercial (for example, is it successful at what it intends to do)?

• How does the content of a TV program relate to the advertisements that appear during the program's commercial breaks?

If we want TV programs, films, computer-software programs, and Web sites to be used effectively, teachers must screen them to identify hidden agendas, discern bias, and examine historical inaccuracies prior to presenting them in the classroom. However, it will be more effective and more beneficial to students in the long run if teachers help students develop these same abilities to analyze media messages critically themselves.

There are several specific activities that teachers can use to help students spot bias or propaganda and to sensitize them to hidden subtexts in the electronic media used in schools and in their everyday lives:

1. Watch movies or television programs on the same topic but made by different producers at different times. Detect hidden agendas and biases and identify historical inaccuracies.

2. Listen to the debate of a controversial issue on TV that presents multiple opinions. Then, evaluate how any side of any issue can be justified if one does not approach the issue from all angles. Though this activity has been done without electronic media for centuries in public-speaking and debate classes, electronic media can make the process of debating even more observable.

3. Observe witnesses' testimony of real court cases and compare different accounts of the same event. This activity can help students understand how to separate fact from opinion and think critically about what "truth" is—whose truth it might be and what it takes to ascertain the truth and why.

4. Read eyewitness accounts of an event in printed materials after watching television accounts of the same event. Compare the similarities and differences of these two media forms to discover the nature of television's version of reality.

Because exposure to mass media is now a central means by which young people learn and internalize values, beliefs, and norms of our political system—a socialization that lays the foundation for political views later in life (Croteau and Hoybes 1997)—media literacy must help students understand how the media affect their beliefs and values. For instance, teachers can ask students to write down their thoughts or opinions about a familiar event and then instruct them to watch TV programs or movies about this event. They can help students examine whether they alter their moral positions throughout this process of viewing. The point of this exercise is not to see whether a student can hold onto his or her previous positions; instead, the point is to become aware of how this piece of media affects a person's opinion and why a person might be unable to perceive a sense of right and wrong about certain issues or events when taking a stand (Potter 1998).

Teaching media literacy also can help high school students critically examine the elements of popular-youth culture, such as music, cartoons, movies, radio programs, newspapers, magazines, computer games, on-line chat rooms, TV news, Web sites for children and teens, and more. Students can learn how those images were constructed, why those images were constructed in a certain way, what effects those images have on them, and how these effects relate to advertising and product sales. However, teachers should take precautions before getting into this territory; they should stimulate student interest in the project by embracing, not opposing, students' pop-culture interests to gain the respect and trust essential for a healthy and workable learning situation (Godin 1993; Tyner 1998).

A final way to help students gain a critical understanding of basic media-literacy concepts and master media-literacy skills is to get them experientially involved in the process (Lloyd-Kolkin and Tyner 1991). Children could learn to discern advertising intent and identify persuasive technique from role-playing. Students might assume the role of producers and create their own commercials. Children could also learn to produce interactive multimedia products, such as a television series, on-line journal pieces, compact disk projects, home-page design, and an on-line chat room. Existing software programs allow teachers and students to create and edit motion images and sounds. Though these are obviously more complicated media-literacy tasks, the basic argument is that, if citizens receive most of their information from TV and Web sites, they should be aware of how this information is constructed.

Teachers also can assign students a project to assemble media-literacy strategies (personal and group strategies) to influence other young people. The project might include: (1) a listing of the student's media exposure (time, content, sources, types of media) to develop an accurate awareness; (2) practicing literacy skills (thinking about the reality-fantasy continuum, making cross-channel comparisons) to examine opinions; and (3) focusing on usefulness and behavior change as goals (Potter 1998). Many students might be interested in evaluating relevant Web sites as to their accessibility, usefulness, content appropriateness, and accuracy. These evaluations could then be used as peer recommendations and suggestions for Internet usage and Web-site selection.

Though media literacy can be taught as a workshop or a short unit, rather than discarding part of the current curriculum, many educators have suggested including media studies within the already existing framework of history, ELP, and other courses of social study. Television programs and films are most effective when *incorporated* into a lesson rather than *used* as a lesson. However, Martorella (1996) reported resistance to classroom integration of media literacy and a reluctance to create social studies teacher–media specialist partnerships to teach media literacy in an inquiry-based learning environment.

Media Literacy and Social Studies Teachers

Today, electronic visual materials and computer technologies are influencing the traditional patterns of instruction. These new techniques and materials often require multimedia presentations as well as computer applications. Teachers also face the demanding task of keeping pace with rapid changes in subject-matter emphasis and instructional orientations by selecting materials appropriate for their instructional programs and students (Risko 1999). Subsequently, teachers are required to review, assess, select, and revise materials from within a wide range of items available for classroom instruction. Under this condition, teachers should develop a systematic means for performing these tasks to avoid costly mistakes (Dynneson and Gross 1995). This demand may raise a question: Are our teachers media literate? And how prepared are high school social science teachers to instruct students about the media and help them become informed media consumers?

No published data are available on the extent of preparation of social studies teachers to use technology and teach media literacy. Many social studies teachers identify a lack of experience and training as major barriers to the integration of computers in social studies. Teachers feel unqualified to offer such instruction, because few of them received college training and/or in-service training that included a media-studies component. Most of the texts they use are of little help in this regard. Estimation about preparation must be inferred from the general literature about preservice and in-service teacher preparation. This literature has suggested social studies teachers are among the biggest "laggards" in utilizing computers and information technology in the schools. There is a distinct generation gap between the recently graduated and early graduated in terms of computer and Internet use, yet no gap exists in terms of media critique (Ross 1988). Social studies teachers of all ages have a severe lack of training in media critique.

Besides the improper training of teachers, problems pertaining to teaching media literacy in social studies instruction are many: traditional lecture methodology; lack of proper technological support in the schools; competition with other subjects to use computers and other multimedia facilities; misuse or improper use of technology; and the overall cost of technology with the associated inequity of resources available to schools and social studies classrooms (Freiwald 1997). The reasons most often given by social studies teachers for not teaching media literacy and not using the computer in the classroom include: (1) a lack of knowledge about computers and computer software, (2) limited access to computers and the Internet, (3) a lack of expectation for the computer's use in social studies by school leaders, and (4) a lack of adequate software. Accounts from public school computer coordinators and media specialists have supported these reasons; they note less collaboration with social studies teachers than teachers of other subjects and little time preparing for social studies software, which usually trails behind that for mathematics, science, and general problem-solving classes (Ehman and Glenn 1991).

Considering the large proportion of social studies teachers who feel less than adequately trained to offer media-literacy instruction, it might be fruitful to take a team-training approach. In developing a media-literacy curriculum and teaching strategies by a collaborative effort of social studies teachers, electronic-media education specialists, media representatives, media-literacy specialists, concerned parents, and students, a multidisciplinary collaborative team could facilitate the truly needed expertise (knowledge, skills, experience, and viewpoints) for preparing social studies educators for this task.

MEDIA LITERACY, SOCIAL STUDIES, AND THE NEW MILLENNIUM

Teaching media literacy in the social studies classroom is a way to prepare reflective, competent, and concerned citizens living in a global and culturally diverse world. Educators working with parents and the community can enrich the electronic-media experience for children by encouraging a deeper and more involved experience, such as getting children to think more critically while they are watching TV or operating a computer. However, achieving higher levels of media literacy is a lifelong developmental process of building stronger and more elaborate knowledge structures by using a wide range of skills (Wilson and Marsh 1995). Therefore, teaching media literacy is not a tentative task; instead, it should be integrated fully into every segment of the social studies curriculum at all levels of school.

Concerns about media literacy have been voiced for more than a decade. Still, the United States, unlike other developed nations, has not yet established media education as a priority. Megee (1997) argued that—though television and, more recently, computers have played major roles in U.S. life for almost half a century and U.S. residents produce and consume more movies, TV, computer software, and Internet sites than people in any other country—schools in the United States teach less about who is communicating for what purpose, with what effect, and on behalf of which individuals than do schools in many other countries (Tyner 1998).

U.S. schools at all levels are in danger of experiencing a cultural lag, because the technologies they offer students increasingly lag behind what is available in the commercial, governmental, and other sectors of society (Martorella 1996). On the eve of the new millennium, the telecommunication era, one of the major challenges educators face is teaching electronic-media literacy. No matter what our personal preference is, electronic media will stay and expand, and the influence will grow forever greater. With the advent of the digital camera, virtual reality, and other new technologies, both children and adults will spend even more time on electronic media in the future. This new generation is growing up in the midst of a new kind of electronic-media "addiction," and there surely will be many new technology waves ahead. It is time for us to accept that electronic media will not only enhance but further revolutionize and even institutionalize a new approach to learning and teaching (Wilson and Marsh 1995).

Widespread media literacy is essential if all citizens are to wield power, make rational decisions, become effective change agents, and impact political and social affairs in the United States and around the world (Masterman 1985). The question is, how long will it take to convince this country's leadership, as well as its social studies educators, to become media literate themselves so we can help our young people do the same?

REFERENCES

Alvermann, D. E. 1999. A feminist critique of media representation. In *Intermediality: The teachers' handbook of critical media literacy*, ed. L. M. Semali and A. W. Palliotet, 141–54. Boulder, Colo.: Westview.

Artz, B. L. 1998. Hegemony in black and white: Interracial buddy films and the new racism. In *Cultural diversity and the U.S. media*, ed. Y. R. Kamalipour and T. Carilli, 67–78. Albany: State University of New York Press.

Buckingham, D., and J. Sefton-Green. 1995. *Cultural studies goes to school: Reading and teaching popular media*. Bristol, Pa.: Taylor & Francis.

Considine, D. M. 1987. Visual literacy and the curriculum: More to it than meets the eye. *Language Arts* 64(6): 634–40.

Croteau, D., and W. Hoybes. 1997. *Media/Society: Industries, images, and audiences*. Thousand Oaks, Calif.: Pine Forge Press.

Delgado, F. 1998. Moving beyond the screen: Hollywood and Mexican American stereotypes. In *Cultural diversity and the U.S. media*, ed. Y. R. Kamalipour and T. Carilli, 169–82. Albany: State University of New York Press.

Dennis, E. E., and E. C. Pease, eds. 1996. *Children and the media*. New Brunswick, N.J.: Transaction Publishers.

Dynneson, T. L., and R. E. Gross. 1995. *Designing effective instruction for secondary social studies*. Englewood Cliffs, N.J.: Prentice Hall.

Ehman, L. H., and A. D. Glenn. 1991. Interactive technology in social studies. In *Handbook of research on social studies teaching and learning*, ed. J. P. Shaver, 513–22. New York: Macmillian.

Ferrington, G., and L. Anderson-Inman. 1996. Media literacy: Upfront and on-line (Technology tidbits). *Journal of Adolescent & Adult Literacy* 39(8): 666–70.

Freiwald, W. D. 1997. Computer use in elementary social studies. ERIC ED 418 024.

Gandy, O. H. 1994. *Communication and race: A structural perspective.* London, England: Arnold.

Gans, H. J. 1979. *Deciding what's news: A study of CBS Evening News, NBC Nightly News, "Newsweek," and "Time."* New York: Pantheon Books.

Godin, R. 1993. Television in the English curriculum—Study advertising. *English Journal* 82(6): 77–79.

Graber, D. A. 1988. *Processing the news: How people tame the information tide,* 2d ed. New York: Longman.

Greenberg, B. S., and J. E. Brand. 1998. U.S. minorities and the news. In *Cultural diversity and the U.S. media,* ed. Y. R. Kamalipour and T. Carilli, 3–22. Albany: State University of New York Press.

Goodall, H., A. Jakubowicz, and J. Martin, eds. 1994. *Racism, ethnicity and the media.* Sydney, Australia: Allen & Unwin.

Hamot, G. E., J. M. Shiveley, and P. J. VanFossen. 1997. Media literacy in social studies teacher education: Relating meaning to practice. Paper presented at the Annual Meeting of the American Educational Research Association, Chicago, 24–28 March. ERIC ED 416 161.

Lloyd-Kolkin, D., and K. R. Tyner. 1991. *Media and you.* Englewood Cliffs, N.J.: Educational Technology Publications.

Levine, M. 1996. *Viewing violence: How media violence affects your child's and adolescent's development.* New York: Doubleday.

Masterman, L. 1985. *Teaching the media.* London, England: Routledge.

Martorella, P. H. 1996. Using technology to enhance social studies instruction. In *Teaching social studies in middle and secondary schools,* ed. P. H. Martorella, 325–57. Englewood Cliffs, N.J.: Merrill.

McLean, S. 1998. Minority representation and portrayal in modern newsprint cartoons. In *Cultural diversity and the U.S. media,* ed. Y. R. Kamalipour and T. Carilli, 23–38. Albany: State University of New York Press.

Megee, M. 1997. Media literacy: The new basic: Will the real curriculum please stand up? *Emergency Librarian* 25(2): 23-26.

Ornstein, A. C. 1987. Planning the curriculum in a world of change. *Curriculum Review* 26(3): 22–24.

Potter, W. J. 1998. *Media literacy.* Thousand Oaks, Calif.: Sage.

Risinger, F. C. 1996. Webbing the social studies. *Social Education* 60(2): 111–12.

Risko, V. J. 1999. The power and possibilities of video technology and intermediality. In *Intermediality: The teachers' handbook of critical media literacy,* ed. L. M. Semali and A. W. Palliotet, 129–40. Boulder, Colo.: Westview.

Robins, J. 1995. Project for teaching media literacy at high schools. Unpublished paper. Chapel Hill: University of North Carolina.

Ross, E. W. 1988. Survey of microcomputer use in secondary social studies classrooms. Paper presented at the Annual Meeting of the National Council for the Social Studies, Orlando, 14–18 November. ERIC ED 306 169.

Semali, L. M., and A. W. Pailliotet, eds. 1999. *Intermediality: The teachers' handbook of critical media literacy.* Boulder, Colo.: Westview.

Silverblatt, A. 1995. *Media literacy: Keys to interpreting media messages.* Westport, Conn.: Praeger.

Splaine, J. E. 1991. The mass media as an influence on social studies. In *Handbook of research on social studies teaching and learning,* ed. J. P. Shaver, 300–309. New York: Macmillian.

Television Information Office. 1989. *America's watching: Public attitudes toward television.* New York: TIO.

Thornton, S. J. 1995. The social studies near century's end: Reconsidering patterns of curriculum and instruction. *Review of Research in Education,* vol 20, ed. L. Darling-Hammond, 223–53. Washington, D.C.: American Educational Research Association.

Tyner, K. 1998. *Literacy in a digital world.* London, England: L. Erlbaum Associates.

Vargas, L., and B. D. Pyssler. 1998. Using media literacy to explore stereotypes of Mexican immigrants. *Social Education* 62(7): 407–12.

Wilson, E. K., and G. E. Marsh. 1995. Social studies and the Internet revolution. *Social Education* 59(4): 198–202.

12

Digital Technology: Transforming Schools and Improving Learning

By *David Moursund*

A Scenario from 2012

It is still raining and cloudy early in the morning when Saundri finishes her breakfast and opens her PEA (Personal Education Assistant). Clouds and rain mean the household solar energy system is not producing much power. Today is Saundri's 15th birthday, and she is looking forward to a busy and fun-filled day. She hopes the weather will improve so that a lack of electrical power will not interfere with her evening party plans.

Glancing at her PEA, Saundri notices that the wireless connectivity to the Internet is solid at one megabyte per second. The battery level indicator is at the one-third level, indicating that she has about seven hours of power. She will have to charge the batteries later in the day. She also notes that the PEA's free memory is down to 25 gigabytes. Soon she will have to do some house cleaning.

With a few voice commands, Saundri sends her previous evening's homework to her various teachers. While doing so, she thinks briefly about her mathematics teacher in London, her science teacher in Washington, D.C., and her global studies teacher in Mexico City. It would be neat to meet them face to face someday. Being in secondary school is fun, but she misses the interpersonal contacts of elementary school, where the teachers and students came together each school day.

Next, Saundri checks her computer "Inbox" and sees that she has quite a few e-mail messages, voice-phone messages, and videophone messages. Her friends and fellow students from around the world sent messages because they know it is her birthday. Plus, all of her course instructors have provided feedback on the schoolwork she turned in yesterday. Other messages are from her teammates on several school group projects.

Saundri opens some of the birthday greetings and talks to a couple of her friends. Several of her friends speak and write in languages that Saundri does not know, but her PEA provides reasonable-quality translations in real time. One message contains a gift for two free video viewings. She instructs her PEA to download Gone with the Wind, *her current all-time favorite. She will share it with her friends and family at the birthday party this evening.*

In her courses, Saundri is working on several large projects. In math and science, for example, her project is to explore situations in which math research has led to new discoveries in science and situations in which science research has led to new discoveries in math. She is one member of a four-person team collaborating on this project. Her specific task is to understand what led to the development of the math topics currently being studied in her math course. The intended audience for this team term project are students located throughout the world with an interest in both math and science. The team will publish its report as an interactive World Wide Web site, which is designed to help users learn how math and science benefit each other.

Saundri is working on another project independently. It combines global studies with health education. She is particularly interested in how various levels of education in different countries may be affecting health levels, and vice versa. This project is dear to her heart, because one of her brothers died from a disease when he was only six years old. So she decides to start her day with this project.

She begins by looking at death rates from disease among people worldwide 15–30 years of age as well as the number of school years the deceased achieved. Saundri is searching for possible correlations. This project, however, seems too complex for the correlation techniques she has studied in the past. She asks to speak to her Statistical Consultant, a computer-based "agent." After a brief conversation, the Statistical Consultant senses that Saundri is in over her head and begins to provide her with an interactive tutorial on possible statistical techniques to use in this situation. In addition, the Statistical Consultant suggests that Saundri first study data from just two countries, rather than from the whole set of 273. This method will allow her to carry out some trial-and-error experiments quickly to help her define the problem more fully.

Meanwhile, her PEA has combed its own databases and begun a Web search. It reports that its own databases contain baseline data on education in the 273 countries but that the desired health data is scattered among thousands of databases on the Web. Saundri picks two countries for her pilot study and tells her PEA how to set up the database. Her PEA indicates that this task will take a few minutes, because it will have to search 72 Web sites to get the needed data.

Rather than sit and twiddle her thumbs, the birthday girl asks to speak to her Personal Tutor. Saundri's Personal Tutor is another computer-based agent that works with her as she uses the Intelligent Computer-Assisted Learning (ICAL) materials in her PEA. The tutor immediately appears onscreen and praises her for beginning her schoolwork so early in the morning. Her Personal Tutor has complete records on what Saundri has studied, her interests, her preferred learning styles, and her areas of greatest intelligence from Howard Gardner's most recent list of ten intelligences. Saundri's Personal Tutor and the ICAL system make it possible for her to study anything she wants to study, at any time she wants to study it. The nature and level of instruction is always appropriate to her current knowledge and skills, and the best current theories of teaching and learning are always incorporated.

Later in the day, the sun shines bright and clear. Saundri plugs her PEA into the household solar energy system so it can recharge while she is out for soccer practice. She remembers to give a mental "Thank you!" to UNESCO for providing her with a full scholarship and the PEA for her secondary school education—especially because many of Saundri's friends dropped out of school at age 12.

The bus into Nairobi will be coming through Saundri's village in a few minutes, and she is looking forward to this afternoon's workout with the soccer team. However, she will have to be on time getting back to her village, because she has a music lesson just before supper.

Does Saundri's scenario from the year 2012 sound like science fiction? Or does the technology-assisted education of this 15-year-old girl from Kenya seem like a plausible picture of the future? Before answering those questions, let us examine where we have been and where we stand now in information technology (IT). Then we can make some forecasts on the costs, capabilities, and availability of IT facilities in the year 2012.

INTRODUCTION TO IT IN EDUCATION

First, it is important to understand the major differences among the three main instructional-use categories of IT, which are illustrated in figure 12.1 below. Many misunderstandings about IT in instruction can be resolved through an analysis of these three categories.

The next three sections describe these three categories as if they are separate and distinct. In many applications, these categories overlap one another. Indeed, a student is seldom engaged in a use of IT that falls purely into one of the three categories.

Computer and Information Science

Over the past 50 years, computer and information science has emerged as a major discipline of study. Many community colleges, technical institutes, colleges, and universities offer degree programs in this discipline, and a relatively high demand exists for workers with good knowledge and skills in it. A number of high schools offer an advance placement (AP) course in computer science. The course prepares

Figure 12.1

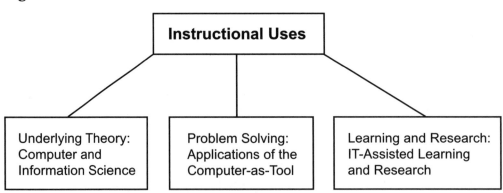

students to take an AP test; those who score well may receive college credit. This course is a balance between theory and practice in the field and includes a considerable emphasis on computer programming. Sometimes it is offered as a two-year sequence, designed to cover roughly the equivalent of a one-year university course. Only a small percentage of students take AP computer science courses in high school. The majority of K–12 students receive little or no formal instruction in this academic discipline.

This fact highlights a considerable change over the past 20 years. In the early days of microcomputer use in schools, there was an emphasis on teaching students computer programming. Gradually, that emphasis has been replaced with instruction that has students learn to use computer tools, such as word processors, spreadsheets, databases, graphics, and the Internet. Interestingly, developing interactive multimedia or spreadsheets tends to require some of the same knowledge and skills used in computer programming. Few K–12 teachers who use multimedia and spreadsheets in their classes have this insight or the computer-programming knowledge to follow up the connection. This oversight is a significant weakness in computer science instruction.

Computer-as-Tool

The computer is a useful and versatile mind tool. It can be used to help solve problems and accomplish tasks at the center of many different academic disciplines. Computer tools for education can be divided into three categories:

Generic tools. Software programs such as word processors, spreadsheets, databases, graphics, e-mail, and the Web cut across many disciplines. A student who learns to use these tools can apply them in almost every area of intellectual work. Many school districts in the United States expect that all of their students will have learned how to use these tools by the end of elementary or middle school. AppleWorks, formerly ClarisWorks, consists of a collection of generic tools that many students learn to use before finishing middle school.

Subject-specific tools. These tools are designed for a particular academic discipline. Hardware and software to aid in musical composition and performance is one example. Software for mechanical drawing (computer-assisted design) is another widely used example. Many different disciplines have developed hardware and software specifically designed to meet the needs of professionals within their disciplines.

Learner-centered tools. Some tools require programming skills but focus on learning to learn as well as on learning subjects besides programming. Most hypermedia or multimedia authoring systems are examples of such tools. In addition, many of the generic tools include a built-in "macro" feature that adds learner-centered options.

Progress in developing more and better applications packages, as well as better human-machine interfaces, has caused the tool use of computers to grow rapidly. In addition, computer scientists working in the field of artificial intelligence are producing application packages to solve a variety of difficult problems that require a substantial amount of human knowledge and skill. Such application packages will eventually change the content of a variety of school subjects.

What students should learn to do mentally versus what they should learn with assistance from simple aids (books, pencils, paper) versus what they should learn assisted by more sophisticated aids (calculators, computers, other IT) remains a key educational issue. Given the constantly changing state of IT, it is not an easy issue to answer with a single solution. The slow acceptance of the hand-held calculator into the curriculum suggests that more sophisticated aids to problem solving will encounter substantial resistance. The gap between what tools are available and what tools are used in education likely will increase.

The computer can also be a tool to increase teacher productivity. Computerized grade books, data banks of exam questions, computerized assistance in preparing individual education programs for students with learning disabilities, and word-processed lesson plans and class handouts are all good examples. These aids increase the teachers' productivity by improving overall efficiency of effort and saving valuable time. This benefit is particularly true if networks allow teachers to share successful materials easily.

Many teachers now use a desktop-presentation system to interact with a group or whole class of students. This format is a projector system attached to a computer that displays pre-prepared materials, graphs, and other materials generated during the interaction between students and the teacher. For example, in a math class, the computer and projection system can be used to create and project a graph of data or a function being explored.

IT-Assisted Learning and Research

IT offers tremendous classroom opportunities. IT-assisted learning and research combines three important uses of IT in education:

(1) Computer-assisted learning (CAL) is the interaction between a student and a computer system designed to help the student learn.

(2) Computer-assisted research is the use of IT as an aid to doing library and empirical research.

(3) Distance learning is the use of telecommunications to facilitate student learning.

Over the past 40 years, CAL has been given many different names, such as "computer-based instruction" and "computer-assisted instruction." In recent years, the field has come to include distance learning, e-mail-based instruction, and Web-based instruction. The CAL name is intended to emphasize "learning" rather than just "instruction." CAL includes drill and practice, tutorials, simulation, and a variety of virtual-reality environments designed to help students learn.

The computer can be used for instructional delivery to students of every age, in every subject area, and with all types of students. Evidence is mounting that CAL is especially useful in special education and in basic-skills instruction (Kulik 1994). In addition, CAL and distance education can provide students access to courses not available in their schools.

There are two major categories of computer-assisted research at the K–12 level. First, there is the use of computers to read CD-ROM materials and to search electronic databases (for example, using the Web). Students of all ages learn to make use of some of the knowledge and skills of the research librarian. Second, there is use of computerized instrumentation to gather data and the use of computers to help process data. Many middle school and secondary school students are learning to use microcomputer-based laboratory tools and statistical packages.

Distance learning is rapidly growing in use and importance (International Society for Technology in Education [ISTE] 1999). Through the use of telecommunications, students and instructors can be connected in a two-way audio and a one-way or a two-way video network that allows real-time interaction. The Web is increasingly being used to provide the needed connectivity. Oftentimes, such instruction is asynchronous (not real-time), making use of videotapes or materials stored on a computer. This dimension adds convenience for the student. In the typical Web-based course, students interact with one another and the instructors on group projects, even though they may be located at different places around the world.

IT AND PROBLEM SOLVING

Perkins (1995) has provided an excellent overview of education and the wide variety of attempts to improve it. He analyzed attempted improvements in terms of how well they contribute to accomplishing the following general goals of education: (1) acquisition and retention of knowledge and skills; (2) understanding of one's acquired knowledge and skills; and (3) active use of one's acquired knowledge and skills (ability to apply one's learning to new settings and ability to analyze and solve novel problems).

The third goal is the focus here. Various stakeholder groups differ significantly in what they believe should be the major goals of education. However, most agree that higher-order thinking skills—the ability to solve complex, novel problems and accomplish complex, novel tasks—is an important goal of education. Thus, higher-order thinking skills and problem solving are an implicit or an explicit component of almost all courses.

The term "problem solving," which in this instance includes both solving problems and accomplishing tasks, has been researched extensively (Pólya 1957; Frederiksen 1984; Frensch and Funke 1995; Moursund 1996). Many writers use a somewhat common set of vocabulary as they talk about problem solving. In essence, problem solving consists of moving from a given initial situation to a desired goal. That is, problem solving is the process of designing and carrying out a set of steps to reach a goal. Many writers also include provisos that, in a problem, it is not obvious how to reach the goal and there may be strict rules, constraints, and limitations of resources. If it is relatively obvious how to get from A to B, then the situation is called an exercise. Of course, the same situation can be a problem for one person and an exercise for another person.

Here is a formal definition of the term "problem." You (personally) have a problem if the following four conditions are satisfied: (1) you have a clearly defined given initial situation; (2) you have a clearly defined goal—a desired end situation; (3) you have a clearly defined set of resources that may be applicable in helping you move from the given initial situation to the desired goal situation (there may be specified limitations on resources, such as rules, regulations, and guidelines for what you are allowed to do in attempting to solve a particular problem); (4) you have some type of ownership—that is, you are committed to using some of your own resources, such as your knowledge, skills, and energies, to achieve the desired final goal. These four components of a well-defined problem are summarized by the four words: givens, goal, resources, and ownership.

People often get confused by the resources part of the definition of a formal problem. Resources do not tell you how to solve a problem; they merely tell you what you are allowed to do and/or use in solving the problem. Increasingly, IT is a readily available resource in problem solving. For example, you want to create an advertising campaign to increase the sales of a set of products that your company produces. The campaign is to be nationwide, to be completed in three months, and must not exceed $40,000 in cost. You have a computer available, and you know how to use a spreadsheet. You are not to make illegal agreements with your competitors or to violate the high ethical standards of your company. All of these givens fit under resources. You still have to figure out how to create the ad campaign.

This definition of a formal problem emphasizes that problems do not exist in the abstract. They exist only when there is ownership. The owner might be a person, an organization, or a country. One of the difficulties that teachers face is that they have textbooks that contain so-called "problems" (exercises and activities for students), yet the students often have no ownership of these exercises and activities. Project-based learning tends to allow students to define the problems that they will solve (the tasks that they will accomplish). Research indicates that this input increases student motivation, because the students have ownership of "their" problem (Blumenfeld, Soloway, Marx, Krajcik, Guzdial, and Palincsar 1991; Moursund 1999).

Over the years, humans have developed many important mental aids, including reading, writing, arithmetic, and computers. They have developed many important physical aids, including the plow, car, airplane, telecommunications, and automated machinery. They have developed a number of aids to formal and informal learning, such as schools, places of worship, playgrounds, and parks. Collectively and cumulatively, these three categories of aids allow people to solve problems routinely and accomplish tasks that were beyond what anybody could do a century ago.

In addition, over the years, humans have learned a great deal about problem solving. To illustrate some roles of IT in problem solving, we will focus on the single most important idea in problem solving: the idea of building on the previous work of yourself and others. In other words, do not reinvent the wheel! This idea means it is helpful to learn to conceptualize and to represent problems using the vocabulary and notation that people have developed over the millennia. This process of representing (modeling) problems is an idea that cuts across problem solving in many different disciplines. In addition, it is helpful to have the knowledge and skills of a research librarian and to have access to a good library.

Reading, writing, arithmetic, science, and technology are excellent examples of the previous work of others. Millions of researchers and practitioners have worked individually and collectively over thousands of years to develop our current knowledge base. Remember the story of Saundri in 2012? She will ask her PEA to find some data and organize it into a database that would be suitable for carrying out various statistical tests. Saundri did not invent computers, databases, and the various statistical tests she will use. Saundri and her Statistical Consultant will know what statistical tests will be appropriate to her study and how the data must be organized to allow the computer to carry out the tests.

Humans store their collected knowledge and skills in their minds, in books, in artifacts they build, and so on. A car represents a huge amount of knowledge, as does the infrastructure that supports automobile transportation. It is relatively easy for a person to learn to drive a car. It will be even easier in the future as people develop automated car-driving systems akin to automatic pilots in airplanes.

To a large extent, a book represents a static way of storing information and knowledge, while an artifact such as a car represents a more dynamic way of storing information and knowledge. In essence, a book can tell a person what he or she must learn and inform him or her how to solve a certain type of problem or accomplish a certain type of task. The person both needs to do the learning and follow the instructions. A car, however, can "just do it."

This explanation is an oversimplification; however, the point to be made is actually rather simple: People build artifacts that incorporate a great deal of knowledge and skill. Other people learn to use these artifacts—often quite quickly and easily. In essence, by doing so, they gain knowledge and skill from the previous work of others.

It is inevitable that the steadily increasing "just do it" capability of computer systems will eventually lead to major changes in the school curriculum and in assessment.

IT can be thought of as an artifact or a collection of artifacts that people have developed. What problems can a computer system solve? An answer is that computer systems can already do a lot, and every year the collection of computer-solvable problems is increasing substantially. A computer system is a way of storing information (databases) along with sets of directions on how to use the information—and the ability to "just do it."

The term "computer system" as used in the preceding paragraph includes everything from a hand-held calculator to a microcomputer to a fully automated factory. Consider the inexpensive, hand-held, solar-battery-powered calculator. In 1997, students could purchase a new calculator at an office supply store for $4.99. In addition to the usual four arithmetic functions, its capabilities include sine, cosine, tangent, logarithm, exponential, factorial, parentheses, and some internal storage. In high schools of yesteryear, square roots were calculated by hand, math tables were used to look up values of trigonometric functions, and learning to use a table of logarithms was necessary to carry out various calculations. Now, all of that instructional time as well as the math tables have been replaced by a reliable, easily portable, inexpensive, hand-held calculator.

Yet that is only a small piece of the story. Many high school students now use a calculator that also includes a key labeled "Solve" and one labeled "Graph." The calculator can solve equations and graph functions. Even that is only a small piece of the story. Microcomputer software can solve a wide range of problems covered in the traditional math curriculum up through the first two years of college. Indeed, this software is also available on a hand-held calculator.

Such calculators and microcomputer software have had impact on the math curriculum. It would be a far stretch to suggest that math education has been transformed, though. It has not been. Remember, our educational system is highly resistant to change.

The above examples focused on calculators and computers in math. However, each area of human intellectual activity can be analyzed from the point of view of the problems it addresses, and the current and potential roles of IT in helping solve these problems. IT is a powerful aid to problem solving in every academic discipline—the educational implications are profound!

Saundri will talk to her PEA. Should students spend time developing good keyboarding skills when voice input is available? Computers can graph functions and data. Should students spend time learning to do this by hand? Computers can decide who is an acceptable risk for a home loan, and they are a powerful aid to doing one's income taxes. A good Web search engine can do many of the things that a skilled research librarian can do. The mechanical drawing course has disappeared from the high school curriculum—replaced by a computer-aided design or graphic arts course.

Because a computer system is a "just do it" tool, it has become an everyday tool for many workers. For white-collar workers in the United States, the ratio of computers per employee is now in excess of 1:1. It is inevitable that the steadily increasing "just do it" capability of computer systems will eventually lead to major changes in the school curriculum and in assessment.

Assessment is a particularly interesting challenge as we try to reconcile authentic assessment with the capabilities of a PEA. How would you test Saundri and her PEA working together? An "open computer" test? How much weight should be given to spelling and grammar in writing? Even today's word processors detect and correct errors in spelling and grammar.

Current Goals for IT in Education

In very simple terms, there are two major goals for IT in education: One goal is to use IT as an effective aid in accomplishing the "traditional" (non-IT-related) goals of education. The second goal is to learn IT and its uses to solve problems and accomplish tasks—especially for situations in which use of IT conveys distinct advantages over nonuse of the technology.

As an example of the first goal, we all want students to learn how to read. We know a great deal about how to help children learn to read. We can capture part of the theory and practice of teaching reading into a CAL system. For most students, CAL is not nearly as effective as one-on-one tutoring by a highly skilled human teacher; however, for many students, CAL systems are more effective than large-group (whole-class) instruction for some components of learning to read. A number of CAL research-and-development efforts are being directed toward creating better CAL-based systems to help students learn to read.

There are many examples of the second goal, when IT is learned and used to solve problems. For example, a computer system can be used to simulate an airplane design. It can be used for computer-assisted design that ties in with computer-assisted manufacturing. A computer system can simulate the exploding of a nuclear weapon or conduct long-range weather forecasting. The World Wide Web is a new form of information storage and retrieval. One can think of the Web as a global digital library. The development of such a huge library, as well as providing lots of people access to it, was not possible before current technologies emerged. Many people find it is highly useful to have good skills in searching the Web as well as making use of the resources it provides.

The IT education goals outlined previously are quite general. More specific goals are needed to help guide the development of curriculum, instruction, and assessment. In recent years, ISTE has been developing standards for students and for preservice and in-service teachers. ISTE is a nonprofit professional society that publishes a variety of journals and books, participates in conferences, runs workshops, conducts research, and maintains a high-quality Web site. ISTE has worked with the National Council for Accreditation of Teacher Education to develop IT standards for preservice teachers. These ISTE standards are periodically revised to fit the continuing and rapid changes in IT and uses of IT for K–12 education. Several U.S. states have adapted these preservice standards to fit their needs for in-service teacher standards. These standards must be high enough so that teachers are well prepared to work with students trying to meet the student standards.

The following materials are from the ISTE National Educational Technology Standards (NETS) for pre-K–12 students (ISTE Standards). A number of states are making use of NETS as they develop their state standards and assessment. Teachers should check their own levels of IT knowledge and skill against the performance indicators for the various grade levels. Very few preservice and in-service teachers currently meet the suggested standards for students completing grades 9–12.

Six Broad Categories of Technology Standards

The technology foundation standards for students are divided into six broad categories. Standards within each category are to be introduced, reinforced, and mastered by students. These categories provide a framework for linking performance indicators for various grade levels given in the next section. Teachers can use these standards and profiles as guidelines for planning technology-based activities in which students achieve success in learning, communication, and life skills.

1. Basic operations and concepts: Students demonstrate a sound understanding of the nature and operation of technology systems. Students are proficient in the use of technology.

2. Social, ethical, and human issues: Students understand the ethical, cultural, and societal issues related to technology. Students practice responsible use of technology systems, information, and software. Students develop positive attitudes toward technology uses that support lifelong learning, collaboration, personal pursuits, and productivity.

3. Technology-productivity tools: Students use technology tools to enhance learn-

ing, increase productivity, and promote creativity. Students use productivity tools to collaborate in constructing technology-enhanced models, preparing publications, and producing other creative works.

4. Technology-communications tools: Students use telecommunications to collaborate, publish, and interact with peers, experts, and other audiences. Students use a variety of media and formats to communicate information and ideas effectively to multiple audiences.

5. Technology-research tools: Students use technology to locate, evaluate, and collect information from a variety of sources. Students use technology tools to process data and report results. Students evaluate and select new information resources and technological innovations based on the appropriateness to specific tasks.

6. Technology-problem-solving and decision-making tools: Students use technology resources to solve problems and make informed decisions. Students employ technology to develop strategies for solving problems in the real world.

Profiles Describing Technology-Literate Students

A major component of the NETS project is the development of a general set of profiles describing technology-literate students at key developmental points in their pre-college education. These profiles reflect the underlying assumption that all students should have the opportunity to develop technology skills that support learning, personal productivity, decision making, and daily life. These profiles and associated standards provide a framework for preparing students to be lifelong learners who make informed decisions about the role of technology in their lives.

The profiles for technology-literate students provide performance indicators describing the technology competence students should exhibit upon completion of the various grade ranges. In each profile list, the numbers in parentheses at the end of the items correspond to the six overarching technology standards for students given previously.

Prior to completion of Grade 2, students will:

1. use input devices (mouse, keyboard, remote control, and so forth) and output devices (monitor, printer, etc.) to operate computers, VCRs, audio tapes, and other technologies successfully (1);

2. use a variety of media and technology resources for directed and independent-learning activities (1, 3);

3. communicate about technology using developmentally appropriate and accurate terminology (1);

4. use developmentally appropriate multimedia resources (interactive books, educational software, elementary multimedia encyclopedias, etc.) to support learning (1);

5. work cooperatively and collaboratively with peers, family members, and others when using technology in the classroom (2);

6. demonstrate positive social and ethical behaviors when using technology (2);

7. practice responsible use of technology systems and software (2);

8. create developmentally appropriate multimedia products with support from teachers, family members, or student partners (3);

9. use technology resources (puzzles, logical-thinking programs, writing tools, digital cameras, drawing tools, etc.) for problem solving, communication, and illustration of thoughts, ideas, and stories (3, 4, 5, 6); and

10. gather information and communicate with others using telecommunications with support from teachers, family members, or student partners (4).

Prior to completion of Grade 5, students will:

1. use keyboards and other common input and output devices (including adaptive devices when necessary) efficiently and effectively (1);

2. discuss common uses of technology in daily life and the advantages and disadvantages those uses provide (1, 2);

3. discuss basic issues related to responsible use of technology and information and describe personal consequences of inappropriate use (2);

4. use general-purpose productivity tools and peripherals to support personal productivity, remediate skill deficits, and facilitate learning throughout the curriculum (3);

5. use technology tools (multimedia authoring, presentation, Web tools, digital cameras, scanners, etc.) for individual and collaborative writing, communication, and publishing activities to create knowledge products for audiences inside and outside the classroom (3, 4);

6. use telecommunications efficiently and effectively to access remote information, communicate with others in support of direct and independent learning, and pursue personal interests (4);

7. use telecommunications and on-line resources (e-mail, on-line discussions, Web environments, etc.) to participate in collaborative problem-solving activities for the purpose of developing solutions or products for audiences inside and outside the classroom (4, 5);

8. use technology resources (calculators, data-collection probes, videos, educational software, etc.) for problem solving, self-directed learning, and extended-learning activities (5, 6);

9. determine when technology is useful and select the appropriate tool(s) and technology resources to address a variety of tasks and problems (5, 6); and

10. evaluate the accuracy, relevance, appropriateness, comprehensiveness, and bias of electronic-information sources (6).

Prior to completion of Grade 8, students will:

1. apply strategies for identifying and solving routine hardware and software problems that occur during everyday use (1);

2. demonstrate knowledge of current changes in information technologies and the effect those changes have on the workplace and society (2);

3. exhibit legal and ethical behaviors when using information and technology, and discuss consequences of misuse (2);

4. use content-specific tools, software, and simulations (environmental probes, graphing calculators, exploratory environments, Web tools, etc.) to support learning and research (3, 5);

5. apply productivity/multimedia tools and peripherals to support personal productivity, group collaboration, and learning throughout the curriculum (3, 6);

6. design, develop, publish, and present products (Web pages, videotapes, etc.) using technology resources that demonstrate and communicate curriculum concepts to audiences inside and outside the classroom (4, 5, 6);

7. collaborate with peers, experts, and others using telecommunications and collaborative tools to investigate curriculum-related problems, issues, and information, and develop solutions or products for audiences inside and outside the classroom (4, 5);

8. select and use appropriate tools and technology resources to accomplish a variety of tasks and solve problems (5, 6);

9. demonstrate an understanding of concepts underlying hardware, software, and connectivity, and of practical applications to learning and problem solving (1, 6); and

10. research and evaluate the accuracy, relevance, appropriateness, comprehensiveness, and bias of electronic-information sources concerning real-world problems (2, 5, 6).

Prior to completion of Grade 12, students will:

1. identify capabilities and limitations of contemporary and emerging technology resources and assess the potential of these systems and services to address personal, workplace, and lifelong learning needs (2);

2. make informed choices among technology systems, resources, and services (1, 2);

3. analyze advantages and disadvantages of widespread use and reliance of technology in the workplace and in society as a whole (2);

4. demonstrate and advocate for legal and ethical behaviors among peers, family, and community regarding the use of technology and information (2);

5. use technology tools and resources for managing and communicating personal/professional information (finances, schedules, addresses, purchases, correspondence, etc.) (3, 4);

6. evaluate technology-based options, including distance and distributed education, for lifelong learning (5);

7. routinely and efficiently use on-line information resources to meet needs for collaboration, research, publications, communications, and productivity (4, 5, 6);

8. select and apply technology tools for research, information analysis, problem solving, and decision making in content learning (4, 5);

9. investigate and apply expert systems, intelligent agents, and simulations in real-world situations (3, 5, 6); and

10. collaborate with peers, experts, and others to contribute to a content-related knowledge base by using technology to compile, synthesize, produce, and disseminate information, models, and other creative works (4, 5, 6).

INFORMATION TECHNOLOGY NOW AND IN THE FUTURE

IT has changed markedly over the past 15 years. Moreover, this pace of change is likely to continue unabated—indeed, it may accelerate—for the next 15 years. Compare the following two advertisements taken from a local newspaper in 1984 and 1999, respectively:

Spring Special: New microcomputer, only $900! One megahertz speed, 8-bit, 64K memory, 5.25-inch floppy disk drive, printer, and monochrome monitor.

Spring Special: New microcomputer, only $750! 300 megahertz speed, 32-bit, 48M memory, 3.5-inch floppy drive, 5-gigabyte hard drive, 24X CD-ROM, 15-inch color monitor, color printer, and 56k modem.

Several of the 15-year changes are especially noteworthy:

• The change in speed from 1 MHz 8-bit to 300 MHz 32-bit is incredible. Depending on the types of operations being performed, the 1999 microcomputer is approximately 1,200 to 19,200 times as fast as the 1984 microcomputer.

• Internal memory in the 1999 microcomputer is about 1,300 times that of the 1984 machine.

• A 3.5-inch floppy disk holds about ten times as much as a 5.25-inch floppy disk.

• The 5-gigabyte hard drive and the 24X CD-ROM were not available for microcomputers in 1984. In those days, a 5-megabyte (one-thousandth as much storage) hard drive cost about $5,000, and the CD-ROM had not yet been invented.

• Though the Internet had been invented, telephone modems were relatively slow (300 bits per second, or about 180 times slower than the 56k modem), and relatively few microcomputer users had modems.

• The 1999 microcomputer costs less than the 1984 microcomputer. If one takes inflation into consideration, it costs significantly less than half as much.

It is more difficult to provide an analysis of changes in software, databases, networking, and other resources between 1984 and 1999. The advent of the Macintosh in 1984 introduced the general public to the graphical user interface, the laser printer, and powerful word-processing and graphics tools. Now, all of these facilities are commonplace. The World Wide Web has been developed, and use of the Internet has become commonplace. Interactive hypermedia, a huge range of CD-ROMs, and, now, DVD, along with streaming audio and video on the Web, are beginning to be taken for granted.

What does the future hold? Perhaps the most often quoted basis for predicting the future of computer hardware is Moore's Law. Gordon Moore was one of the founders of Intel. In the mid-1960s, he noted that the number of components (chips, resistors, capacitors) that could be manufactured on a single chip had been increasing at a steady and somewhat predictable pace. Eventually, Moore (Kurzweil 1999) made the statement that the density of components on a chip was doubling every 18 months, and this has come to be known as Moore's Law.

Moore's Law has proven to be relatively accurate for more than 30 years, and experts predict that it will continue to hold for about another 12 to 15 years. After that, no further doublings will be possible without a complete change in the technology, so the farther future is harder to predict (Kalianos 1997). Researchers are currently working on developing new forms of transistors and other related electronic components that will be much smaller than those expected to be manufactured 12 to 15 years from now. However, it is difficult to predict whether laboratory-produced discoveries will ever "scale up" to mass production at a reasonable cost.

What does this periodic doubling really mean? It means that, if a 1-million-component chip is state of the art, then 18 months later a 2-million-component chip will be state of the art—and 18 months later a 4-million-component chip will be state of the art. Over a 15-year period, there are 10 doubling periods of 18 months. Note that 2 x 2 x 2 x 2 x 2 x 2 x 2 x 2 x 2 x 2 is 1,024. Very roughly speaking, this progression tends to mean that the speed and memory of a state-of-the-art microcomputer will improve by a factor of 1,024 over a period of 15 years.

The PEA that Saundri will use will not be state of the art. Indeed, it will be a three-year-old model that will cost in the mid-price range in the year 2012. Saundri's PEA will be 100 times as fast, have 100 times the hard-disk capacity, and cost less than half as much as today's modest-priced microcomputers. Her PEA will have a speed of 35 gigahertz (35 billion operations per second), about five gigabytes of primary memory, and about 500 gigabytes of disk storage.

Such numbers are so large as to be meaningless to most people. A 300-page textbook with a reasonable number of diagrams and small low-resolution photographs requires approximately 2.5 megabytes of storage. This reference point means that the hard drive on Saundri's computer will be able to store approximately 200,000 such books. That is perhaps ten times the number of volumes in a typical secondary school library.

Of course, it would be silly to fill all of this disk memory space with books. With an Internet connection running at one megabyte per second, Saundri will be able to download a book in less than three seconds. So much of the PEA's disk storage will be used for video materials. It requires many billions of bytes (many gigabytes) of storage for a full-length, high-resolution movie.

Saundri's wireless connectivity to the Internet seems quite fast by today's telephone-modem standards. However, such speeds are possible with today's technology, and so they will be inexpensive and commonplace 15 years from now. Saundri will live in a poor, rural African village that lacks the infrastructure found in many wealthier parts of the world. Fiber-optic cabling has already been installed in many nations' businesses and schools, and it is beginning to be used to connect homes. If Saundri had a fiber-optic connection, it might be a thousand times as fast as her wireless connection.

What good is all of that computer speed—the 35 gigahertz? Recall that Saundri will talk to her computer. Voice input to computer is now in widespread use. Yet today's "voice input" simply means that the computer can input the stream of sounds, translate it into words, store the words in its memory, and display them on the screen. A 350-megahertz computer can do this almost in real time, and with an accuracy rate of perhaps 95 percent.

Today's voice-input systems do not understand the meaning of what they are hearing. Sure, a computer can be programmed to carry out specific tasks when it receives specific voice commands. For quite a few years, we have had computer systems that respond correctly to commands such as, "Computer, open the word processor" or "Computer, save the file." That is a very limited form of "understanding."

In recent years, however, computer translation of natural languages has made considerable progress. The next 15 years will bring still more progress in the theory and practice of voice input, language translation, and understanding of natural language. The gains to be expected in computer speed and memory capacity will also help. In 15 years, we will have relatively good simultaneous (real-time) translation (voice input, voice output) of natural languages. Such systems will still not be nearly as good as a highly qualified human translator, but they will be quite adequate for many communication tasks.

Voice input and natural-language translation are not the only problems being addressed by researchers in artificial intelligence and other aspects of the field of computer and information science. Films such as the 1999 *Star Wars* movie, *Episode 1: The Phantom Menace*, required many thousands of hours laboring on state-of-the-art microcomputers. In the movie, can you tell the difference between creatures animated by human actors inside costumes and creatures fully created by computer animation? Progress in the field of computer animation, along with faster computers, will narrow this gap even more. The increased speed of computers will make it possible for people like Saundri to do very high-quality animation work on their personal computers.

What difference does this progress make in education? Saundri will make use of Intelligent Computer-Assisted Learning (ICAL). This program will cover a range of learning aids, such as drill-and-practice, tutorials, simulations, and virtual realities. Simulators are so good that they have become a routine aid to training airplane and spaceship pilots. In such computer simulations, it is necessary to generate video images very rapidly—a pilot turns the airplane, changes altitude, or looks out a side window; new images have to be produced in real time.

> *Saundri's ICAL system, however, will include virtual reality that allows her to meet and talk with key historical figures, "be they alive or be they dead."*

Saundri's ICAL system, however, will include virtual reality that allows her to meet and talk with key historical figures, "be they alive or be they dead," explore the cities of the current and ancient worlds, and carry out scientific experiments too dangerous and costly to "actually" do. The PEA will give her access to original sources of information from the great libraries of the world. Although her Personal Tutor will not really be very smart from a human point of view, it will provide a lot of help as Saundri explores these virtual-reality worlds and makes use of other learning tools.

Saundri's PEA will get better year after year, due to continued progress in development of software, teaching theory, learning theory, and so on. Her PEA will be fast enough and have enough storage capacity to accommodate a great deal of continued progress in the non-hardware areas.

In a recent issue of the *New York Times*, this quote appeared: "Researchers from Hewlett-Packard and the University of California at Los Angeles have developed a way to create molecular-sized computing components using chemical processes (rather than light beams) to make integrated circuits. Although their accomplishment is just a first step for the new field of molecular electronics—moletronics—it leads in the direction of a new world in which computers will be 100 billion times as fast as a Pentium processor and a space no bigger than a grain of salt will hold the power of 100 workstations" (Markoff 1999). This type of "far out" research suggests that there may well be major technological breakthroughs in the future that will lead to still faster, smaller computers. Current technologies will make Saundri's PEA quite possible by the year 2012. Future technologies may produce a far more powerful PEA of wristwatch size!

POTENTIALS FOR IMPROVING LEARNING

Saundri's use of her PEA illustrates some ways that information technology will improve learning. In addition to having good access to people and information, her use of automatic language translation will open up still more library and people resources. The Internet will provide her access to human teachers, fellow students, and a wide range of formal coursework. Distance learning will allow her to pursue a curriculum appropriate to her abilities, current interests, and long-term goals. The PEA's ICAL system will allow Saundri to study almost any topic she can think of—at any time she wants. The instructional materials presented will be appropriate to her current levels of knowledge, skills, and learning styles. Her Personal Tutor will have knowledge of subjects Saundri has studied, general theories of teaching and learning, and how to provide help in her studies. Finally, the PEA will provide Saundri with learning opportunities that would not otherwise be available to her.

The potentials for improving learning can be grouped into three areas: (1) computer-assisted learning, distance learning, and improving learning; (2) computer-as-tool and improving learning; (3) improving learning through IT-based changes in curriculum content.

Computer-Assisted Learning, Distance Learning, and Improving Learning

CAL can be thought of as attempts to use IT to implement teaching theory, learning theory, brain research, and so on. This process has been going on for more than 40 years, and significant progress has occurred. Kulik's (1994) meta-metastudy of computer-assisted learning suggested that, over a huge range of studies, students learn about 30 percent faster and somewhat better, as compared to the various control groups that were used in the studies. This is impressive.

Mann, Shakeshaft, Becker, and Kottkamp (1999) have reported a large-scale, multiyear use of CAL in West Virginia. The results are consistent with the Kulik (1994) study. In addition, the overall project suggested that such wide-scale implementation is economically and politically possible, even in a state that has economic problems (West Virginia does not spend nearly as much money per student as a number of other states).

At some point, CAL will inevitably become a routine component of our educational system. Some CAL will be delivered through the Internet, and some will be delivered from local sources, such as CD-ROM, DVD, and local-area networks. This integration will lead to improved learning over a broad range of subject-matter areas for most students. Another aspect of CAL, and all types of distance learning, is that it makes available courses of instruction otherwise inaccessible to students. If a student gets an opportunity to take a physics course—when the student's school does not offer such a course—do we call this improved learning? Certainly.

Computer-as-Tool and Improving Learning

There have been innumerable small studies (for example, doctoral dissertations) on use of individual tools such as word processors or databases in a wide range of schools and grade levels. Collectively, such studies provide some evidence that an individual computer tool may lead to small improvements in learning.

An interesting parallel exists with business computer use. Over the past 40 years, business has invested hugely in IT. Initially, the investment was for isolated applications. Businesses did not detect much in the way of overall improvements in their efficiency, levels of productivity, and profitability due to these initial investments. In recent years, many more, and more powerful, computers have been acquired, and networking has been implemented. Substantial amounts of money have been spent on staff development. Businesses have come to understand use of IT as an integral part of their overall system, and this realization has made a major difference in productivity and profitability. In recent years, the United States has had a very long period of increasing prosperity and productivity, coupled with low inflation. Research suggests that much of this economic success is due to IT (Moursund 1998). That same scenario will likely occur in education.

Until recently, IT has neither been readily available to students nor networked. Even now, U.S. schools have only about one microcomputer per five students (Becker and Anderson 1998). Many of these microcomputers are quite old, and the majority of them are not networked. Research literature suggests that making IT regularly available to each student, along with providing supportive professional development, improves learning. For example, Sandholtz, Ringstaff, and Dwyer (1997) presented results from ten years of research on high-density computer sites. Each student had a computer at school and a computer at home. Initially, these computers were not networked. Many different measures were used to explore potential improvements in education, such as student performance on tests, student attendance, student drop-out rates, and students going on to post-secondary education. The results were quite positive. The Sandholtz et al. (1997) study also included a considerable amount of discussion about project-based learning and how this improved learning.

A report by the President's Committee of Advisors on Science and Technology (1997) summarized research on IT in education, with evidence that it improves learning. The report placed special emphasis on project-based learning and constructivism. It also noted that insufficient funds are being used for educational-technology research. IT is changing education, the committee agreed, and the United States should be spending more money doing research on IT uses to produce positive changes.

Rockman Et Al. (1998) studied school settings in which whole classes of students have laptops and Internet connectivity to use at school and home. As with the Sandholtz et al. (1997) study, there were multiple measures and a large number of participants. At the time, the laptop program had only been in progress for two years, and improved learning was occurring. Such laptop projects began in Australia in the early 1990s. Increased learning was noted in these earlier Australian projects as well.

The Web is a tool beginning to have an impact on student learning, but we lack definitive research on the nature of this impact. One of the arguments for providing students and teachers Web access is its rich source of information. Students and teachers can easily access current information from varied sources. If you have not spent much time looking at educational resources on the Web, you might want to look, for example, at the Federal Resources for Educational Excellence (1999) site—*www.ed.gov/free*. The U.S. Government has made available a huge amount of current materials and continues to add to these resources. Perhaps you will want to check out the Central Intelligence Agency site; it includes detailed information on about 250 countries.

Schools in the United States and a number of other countries will continue to increase their numbers of computers and to improve their connectivity. Some school systems take a CAL approach, while others focus on computer-as-tool. In both cases, improved learning is a likely outcome if the implementation is done well. In both cases, professional development is important, though it appears to be more critical in the computer-as-tool approach.

IT-Based Changes in Curriculum Content

Earlier, the issue was raised about what we want students to learn in situations when a computer can solve or greatly contribute to solving a problem in a school assignment. For example, should students learn to calculate square roots using paper-and-pencil techniques when the least expensive hand-held calculators have a square root key? Should students learn to do graphic-artist and mechanical-drawing work by hand when computer-assisted design tools are a powerful aid to accomplishing such tasks? In some cases, the answer has already been made.

Changes have occurred in the math curriculum. Mechanical-drawing courses have disappeared from the curriculum. Paper-and-pencil bookkeeping courses have been replaced by courses in which students learn to use spreadsheet and accounting software. One can argue that these changes represent improvements in learning. What sense is there in spending learning time to develop skills that will never equal those of a computer? The time is better spent in learning to work with a computer, with the human doing problem posing, reality checks, and other activities that computers do not do very well. Students in architecture schools study a wide range of topics, including design as well as structural soundness and energy use. Many students are especially interested in the creative aspect of architecture. Yet creativity seems unimportant if buildings are not structurally sound or energy efficient. In recent years, software has been developed for structural engineering and energy-use analysis of proposed buildings. These complex problems are well suited to the capabilities of a modern computer. Such software will gradually have an impact on the curriculum content in architecture programs.

Over time, the IT-based changes in curriculum content will have a major impact on student learning. The overall learning of students will be improved substantially by providing students with better tools and teaching them to use these tools.

POTENTIALS FOR TRANSFORMING OUR EDUCATIONAL SYSTEM

Nowadays, school reform, school restructuring, and school renewal are in vogue. The first two terms suggest that our educational system is in some sense "broken" and that major changes are needed. The third term suggests that perhaps less drastic action is required.

There are many possible definitions of what it might mean to "transform" our educational system. Among the possible goals related to technological issues are these three:

Goal 1: Provide every student with lifelong opportunities to obtain a good education. Substantially narrow the gap between the "haves" and the "have-nots." Do this by significantly improving the opportunities available to the have-nots—not by lessening opportunities available to the haves.

Goal 2: Implement the best theory-based and practitioner-based ideas that have been developed for improving education.

Goal 3: Help students gain effective levels of expertise over a wide range of disciplines that society deems important as well as over disciplines students deem important. For example, our society considers math an important discipline. We require students to study this subject for many years. Indeed, many students are required to take at least one year of math in college.

If we could accomplish all three of these goals, education would be transformed. Of course, many items could be added to this list, and, undoubtedly, many individuals will consider their additions more important. Yet these particular goals focus on the potential of IT.

We are used to the idea of providing all students with textbooks; it is not a far stretch of the imagination to think of providing all students with a PEA. Saundri's PEA will be mass-produced and mass-distributed—a considerable economy of scale. We might well come to consider a PEA and its connectivity as a birthright—something made available to everybody throughout his or her lifetime, even in the poorer nations of the world. That would be a significant step toward meeting the first goal of transforming education.

In terms of the second goal, our current educational system struggles with translating theory and best practices into widespread use. When a well-proven new idea becomes available, how does it get implemented in several million classrooms? Professional development is always listed as an important part of the answer. Yet this approach cannot possibly succeed. The pace of progress in research in all knowledge—including all aspects of education—far overwhelms the ability of educators to keep up with everything relevant to their professional work. Many researchers estimate that the totality of human knowledge is doubling every so many years—three, five, ten?

Improvements in curriculum, instruction, assessment, and educational materials have long been part of the answer: Provide the teacher with new, better textbooks and lesson plans. Many school districts manage to do this on a six-year cycle (time for four doublings in areas covered by Moore's Law; perhaps the time for one doubling of the totality of human knowledge). Clearly, these two traditional approaches are doomed to failure when faced by exponential rates of change.

Does Saundri's PEA provide a solution to the second goal? Yes—at least partly. The electronic availability of content and learning materials means they can be updated easily and frequently. Updates can occur automatically every time Saundri accesses the Internet. The PEA will certainly change the role of a teacher to a learning facilitator, not a primary source of information and of delivering instruction. The skills of being a learning facilitator (what many of us would currently call a "good teacher") tend to be long lasting, growing with experience and maturity. Professional development remains important, but it is a less overwhelming challenge.

The third goal focuses on students gaining a useful level of expertise in many disciplines that society deems necessary. Yet the meaning of "useful" changes over time. Education levels needed for factory jobs serve as a very general example. At the end of World War II, the typical industrial manufacturing job in the United States required a fourth-grade education. Now, less than one-third as many of these jobs are available, and new employees typically need at least a high school diploma.

Bereiter and Scardamalia (1993) presented an excellent overview of the research and practice on expertise. It takes a long period of study and practice for persons to achieve their full potential in a particular field. If a person has the potential to achieve world-class ranking in a field such as gymnastics, chess, or mathematics, it takes 10 years or more of hard work to reach this potential. Thus, a person does not have enough years to achieve a really high level of expertise in many fields. However, few of us aspire to being world class in multiple disciplines. A more practical view is to consider how long it takes to achieve a functional level of expertise in various disciplines important to our lives.

For a specific example, consider the level of knowledge and skill it takes to fill out a federal income tax form correctly. Not only is this task complex, the tax laws change somewhat every year. Consequently, many tax preparers make a living by maintaining a level of tax expertise adequate to complete the task successfully. Some people hire a professional to do their income tax returns. Others use software (a computer-based expert system) to help do the task. Indeed, a computer system can provide most people the knowledge and skills to complete the task. Yearly updates to the software and a modest amount of yearly learning can maintain the expertise of an income tax preparer.

As a final example, consider arithmetic and mathematics. Everyone learns to perform paper-and-pencil long division. Most educated people can still perform this task as adults. Yet how many can figure monthly payments for a house or a car loan? How many make appropriate fiscal plans for retirement? These problems relate to math, and they are beyond the capabilities of most people who have studied only a year or two of college mathematics. Our current system of math education does not provide an adequate level of math expertise for most people.

Similar examples can be found in any area of academic expertise. Increasingly, a PEA can be part of a solution to the problems that the third goal addresses. Together with his or her PEA, and appropriate education and training on using it, a student can achieve a level of expertise appropriate to address many problems and tasks. Unaided by a PEA, and/or with inappropriate education, the student does not have much of a chance.

SAUNDRI'S OUTCOMES

By now, you probably have made up your mind about the extent to which you believe the Saundri scenario set in the year 2012. Set at the secondary school level, this scenario portrays an anywhere-anytime educational system that makes use of computer agents, ICAL, distance learning, the Internet, the Web, and local opportunities for face-to-face participation in sports, music lessons, and so on. The worldwide demand for such educational opportunities, which includes considerable demand from rural areas in wealthy countries like the United States, is driving the creation of this type of educational system. Development of facilities like those Saundri will use is inevitable.

How soon Saundri's facilities become available will be determined mainly by funding. Various components of the PEA system have already been built, and they are gradually improving. Bringing these components together could be carried out by an enterprising company or through large grants from governmental agencies or very large foundations. Progress on developing each of the needed components is ongoing. Thus, the cost of pulling it all together will gradually decline over time; 15 years seems far enough into the future for a reasonably good version of Saundri's PEA to be available.

Clearly, the PEA will have an impact on education. Even in quite traditional schools, we will see the PEA becoming a routine tool. Students will come together in classrooms, and the teacher will provide face-to-face facilitation as students work in a combination of traditional and PEA-assisted learning. Students in rural settings, home-schooled students, and students in less affluent locations throughout the world will gradually come to use the PEA as a major component of their educational system. Even students in affluent traditional school systems will begin to receive a significant portion of their formal instruction via the PEA.

The PEA and the facilities Saundri will use constitute a type of competition for our current educational system. As Norman (1998) noted, the PEA is a disruptive technology—that is, a type of technological change that can completely transform an industry. Our educational system is a large and complex industry. It may be able to accommodate the PEA, or it may be severely disrupted. An example of severe disruption would be privatization of much of the current public educational system, perhaps with a majority of schools being run by for-profit companies. A different type of disruption would be a huge growth in home schooling or very small private schools run by groups of parents and a few paid staff—made possible by the PEA. A third type of disruption would be major changes in secondary education, perhaps with a large number of secondary school students engaged in a work-study situation run by the companies in which they work.

Create your own scenarios, including "business as usual." Will IT transform education? The answer is inevitable: many goals of education no longer can be met without appropriate use of IT. Because so many people believe these goals are important—both to themselves as individuals and to our society or nation—IT will and must be used. Such use will transform education. Whatever the scenario, the future holds interesting times for our educational system.

References

Becker, H., and R. Anderson. 1998. Teaching, learning and computing: 1998—A national survey of schools and teachers. Irvine, Calif.: Center for Research on Information Technology and Organizations. Available at: *http://www.crito uci.edu/tlc/html/tlc_home.html.*

Bereiter, C., and M. Scardamalia. 1993. *Surpassing ourselves: An inquiry into the nature and implications of expertise.* Chicago: Open Court.

Blumenfeld, P. C., E. Soloway, R. W. Marx, J. S. Krajcik, M. Guzdial, and A. Palincsar. 1991. Motivating project-based learning: Sustaining the doing, supporting the learning. *Educational Psychologist* 26(3–4): 369–98.

Federal Resources for Educational Excellence. 1999. Federal resources for educational excellence. Available at: *http://www.ed.gov/free.*

Frederiksen, N. 1984. Implications of cognitive theory for instruction in problem solving. *Review of Educational Research* 54(3): 363–407.

Frensch, P. A., and J. Funke, eds. 1995. *Complex problem solving: The European perspective.* Hillsdale, N.J: L. Erlbaum Associates.

International Society for Technology in Education. 1999. An ISTE distance education summit: A dialogue about online teaching and learning. Available at: *http://www.iste.org/ProfDev/Events/DistanceEdPaper.*

Kalianos, M. 1997. Moore says Moore's Law to hit wall. *CNET News,* 30 September. Available at: *http://news.cnet.com/news/0-1003-202-322592.html.*

Kulik, J. A. 1994. Meta-analytic studies of findings on computer-based instruction. In *Technology assessment in education and training,* ed. E. L. Baker and H. F. O'Neill Jr., 9–34. Hillsdale, N.J.: L. Erlbaum Associates.

Kurzweil, R. 1999. *The age of spiritual machines: When computers exceed human intelligence.* New York: Penguin Group.

Mann, D., C. Shakeshaft, J. Becker, and R. Kottkamp. 1999. West Virginia story: Achievement gains from a state-wide comprehensive instructional technology program. CD-ROM: 59-103 (on the Milken Exchange).

Markoff, J. 1999. Tiniest circuits hold prospect of explosive computer speeds. *New York Times,* 16 July.

Moursund, D. 1996. Increasing your expertise as a problem solver: Some roles of computers, 2d ed. Eugene, Ore.: International Society for Technology in Education.

Moursund, D. 1998. Is information technology improving education? *Learning and Leading with Technology* 26(4): 4–5.

Moursund, D. 1999. *Project-based learning using information technology.* Eugene, Ore.: International Society for Technology in Education.

Norman, D. A. 1998. *The invisible computer: Why good products can fail, the personal computer is so complex, and information appliances are the solution.* Cambridge: MIT Press.

Perkins, D. N. 1995. *Smart schools: Better thinking and learning for every child.* New York: Free Press.

Pólya, G. 1957. *How to solve it: A new aspect of mathematical method,* 2d ed. Princeton, N.J.: Princeton University Press.

President's Committee of Advisors on Science and Technology. 1997. Report to the president on the use of technology to strengthen K–12 education in the United States. Washington, D.C.: PCAST. ERIC ED 410 950.

Rockman Et Al. 1998. Powerful tools for schooling: Second year study of the laptop program. Available at: *http://microsoft.com/education/k12/aal/resource/research2.doc.*

Sandholtz, J. H., C. Ringstaff, and D. C. Dwyer. 1997. *Teaching with technology: Creating student-centered classrooms.* New York: Teachers College Press.

Epilogue

By *Barbara D. Day*

As the chapters in this book illustrate, teaching and learning in the 21st century certainly will be different than they are today. The goal of public education, however, will forever remain the same: to prepare our children to succeed in the world of tomorrow as good global citizens. To meet this primary goal, we must stay on the cutting edge of technology and hone our skills. As educators, we must excel in our own quest for learning so we can truly shape the leaders of tomorrow. We must forge new and better partnerships to strengthen our schools and reinforce the importance of public education for our communities. We must think ahead to prepare students today for what they will face tomorrow.

Each of the contributors to *Teaching and Learning in the New Millennium* offers crucial advice and insight to reach the seemingly fantastic view of education in the 21st century. In Chapter 12, Dave Moursund paints a picture we all can see clearly: We must simultaneously shed what is no longer useful from "traditional" education and hold onto what is still applicable. We must constantly examine trends in society and reevaluate our teaching techniques and educational institutions. To make wise decisions, we must thoroughly research our options and develop better assessment instruments to evaluate current instructional techniques. In this process, technology can either be our greatest ally or our worst enemy. To succeed, we must reach out to new technology and be willing to experiment with new techniques. Yet we must avoid the pitfall of viewing technology as a panacea. Technology without proper application is worse than useless—it is a dangerous waste of our energy.

As with any movement toward a goal, we must find consensus on a shared vision of what education in the 21st century should look like. Most of us have made a lifelong commitment to ensuring that students receive the best education possible. Though there is a general feeling that our schools need improvement, as Tracie Y. Hargrove notes in Chapter 7, most parents report that the schools in their own communities are doing a good job. This inclination toward a call for improvement, even while our schools are seen as satisfactory, points to the need for continuous improvement. As the world changes at an ever-increasing pace, we must improve and reform our schools and the education system (both nationally and globally) at a faster pace—just to maintain today's level.

Success tomorrow requires teamwork today. We must encourage teamwork among educators, administrators, parents, students, policy makers, corporate leaders, and elected officials. As emphasized by all of our contributors, we need the entire community working together for our children and our future. We must remember the words from the Kappa Delta Pi Motto:

> *So to teach that our words inspire a will to learn; so to serve that each day may enhance the growth of exploring minds; so to live that we may guide young and old to know the truth and love the right.*

This motto is our call to arms in working for the best education possible for our children. In the midst of our work, we must remember to live humanely, take part in artistic endeavors, and enjoy the diversity of a richly multicultural world. As we strive to help our students learn, they may benefit most from our example.

About the Authors

Barbara D. Day, Ph.D., is Professor and Chair of Curriculum and Instruction at the University of North Carolina at Chapel Hill. She has authored four textbooks and numerous articles on early childhood education, her specialization. In addition, Dr. Day is an international lecturer and traveler who has served on many national and international panels, including President of the Delta Kappa Gamma Society International, International President of the Association for Supervision and Curriculum Development (ASCD), and chair of the ASCD Policy Commission in Early Childhood Education. Currently the President of Kappa Delta Pi, International Honor Society in Education, and Counselor for the Society's Pi Theta Chapter, she has previously served as chair of KDP's Publications Committee. Dr. Day also serves on the ATE/KDP Commission on Professional Support and Development for Novice Teachers.

Michael Fullan, Ph.D., is Dean of the newly formed Ontario Institute for Studies in Education at the University of Toronto. He researches, consults, trains, and acts as a policy advisor in a wide range of educational-change projects, working with school systems, teacher federations, research-and-development institutes, and government agencies internationally. Dr. Fullan is considered an innovator and leader in teacher education who designs school improvement and educational reform practices. He has published widely on the subject of educational change. In 1998, he was named a member of Kappa Delta Pi's Laureate Chapter and in July 1999 was granted an Honorary Doctor of Education Degree from the University of Edinburgh.

Bettye Caldwell, Ph.D., has worked in the development of early childhood programs in the United States for more than three decades. She launched and guided the Kramer project, a "school for the future" in Little Rock, Arkansas, that provided all-day, year-round childcare and education for children six months to 12 years of age. In addition, her work with famed pediatrician Dr. Julius B. Richmond in Syracuse, New York, often is cited as having helped provide the foundation for Head Start. Environmental influence on the development of young children has long been her research specialty and the impetus for her HOME Inventory—Home Observation for Measurement of the Environment—an educational instrument. Dr. Caldwell became a member of the Kappa Delta Pi Laureate Chapter in 1978.

Charles R. Coble, Ph.D., is Vice President for University–School Programs at the University of North Carolina General Administration, where he serves as liaison with the 15 UNC schools of education, coordinating all the outreach programs of the university that support public schools. He serves on key state and national committees related to teacher preparation and development, as well as science education. The network, University–School Teacher Education Partnerships, was advanced through several grants received by Dr. Coble. He is also moderator of a biweekly live television program, "Parents and Schools," produced by the North Carolina Agency for Public Telecommunications.

James A. Banks, Ph.D., is Professor and Director of the Center for Multicultural Education at the University of Washington, Seattle. Well known in the field of multicultural education, he has written or edited more than 15 books and 100 articles on multicultural and social studies education. Professor Banks is the editor of the *Handbook of Research on Multicultural Education*, and a member of the Board of Children, Youth and Families of the National Research Council and the Institute of Medicine of the National Academy of Sciences. His research focuses on the relationship between the lives and community cultures of researchers and the knowledge they construct. Dr. Banks is Past President of the American Educational Research Association and a past president of the National Council for the Social Studies. He became a member of the Kappa Delta Pi Laureate Chapter in 1997.

R. Freeman Butts, Ph.D., is the first William F. Russell Professor Emeritus in the Foundations of Education at Teachers College, Columbia University, where he taught courses and wrote about the historical, social, and philosophical foundations for 40 years. He was director of international studies for 20 years. Since his retirement in 1975, he has devoted most of his research and writing to the reform of civic education in the United States and abroad. He has been a Rockefeller Foundation Fellow in the Humanities, Visiting Professor at the University of Wisconsin at Madison and San Jose State University, Visiting Scholar at the School of Education and Hoover Institution of Stanford University, Senior Fellow at the Kettering Foundation, and member of the Board of Directors of the Center for Civic Education. Dr. Butts was elected a Kappa Delta Pi Laureate member in 1960.

Tracie Y. Hargrove, Ph.D., works in the Duplin County, North Carolina, school district as a Technology Coordinator, following eight years as a fourth- and fifth-grade teacher. She received her doctorate in Curriculum and Instruction from the University of North Carolina at Chapel Hill. Her dissertation is entitled "Teacher Perceptions of the North Carolina ABC Program and Its Relationship to Classroom Practice."

William S. Palmer, Ph.D., is Professor of English Education at the University of North Carolina at Chapel Hill. He has written and published more than 80 articles concerned with improving teaching of English/Language Arts. His scholarship focuses upon methodological strategies that enhance the integration of communication skills, particularly reading and writing, and primarily at the secondary level. He is a member of the National Commission of Teacher Education in English and the North Carolina English Teachers Association, for which he serves as chair of the Committee for Classroom Projects Grants.

David K. Pugalee, Ph.D., is Assistant Professor in the Department of Middle, Secondary, and K–12 Education of the University of North Carolina at Charlotte. He received his doctorate from the University of North Carolina at Chapel Hill. His research focuses on mathematical literacy, especially the role of written and spoken discourse in facilitating mathematical understanding. He has authored numerous publications related to the role of technology, writing, reading, and communication in constructing classroom environments that foster a conceptual development of mathematics.

David Elkind, Ph.D., is Professor of Child Development at Tufts University in Medford, Massachusetts. A former National Science Foundation Senior Postdoctoral Fellow at Piaget's Institut d'Epistemologie Genetique in Geneva, Dr. Elkind's research in perceptual, cognitive, and social development builds upon the research and theory of Jean Piaget. He is a prolific writer whose bibliography lists more than 400 publications, and he lectures extensively around the world. In addition, he is a past president of the National Association for the Education of Young Children and is a consultant to state education departments, clinics, mental health centers, government agencies, and private foundations.

Hunter Ballew, Ph.D., is Professor of Education at the University of North Carolina at Chapel Hill, and Coordinator of the MAT Program for liberal arts graduates preparing to teach in high schools. He received his Bachelors, Masters, and Doctor of Philosophy degrees in Mathematics Education at the University of North Carolina, where for the past 37 years he has taught mathematics education courses. Previously, he taught mathematics at the high school level. Dr. Ballew also has been editor of the *High School Journal*, Chair of the Division of Curriculum and Instruction, and Director of the Mathematics and Science Education Center at UNC.

Xue Lan Rong, Ed.D., is Associate Professor in the School of Education, University of North Carolina at Chapel Hill. Her writings concentrate on social and cultural foundations of social studies, immigration and education, and comparative education. She has been published in various professional journals and has presented her works at annual meetings of many national professional organizations, such as National Council of Social Studies, American Educational Research Association, and American Sociological Association.

David Moursund, Ph.D., is Professor of Education at the University of Oregon, and has been teaching and writing in the field of information technology in education since 1963. From 1969 to 1975, he served as the first chairman of the Department of Computer Science at the University of Oregon and has been either the major professor or on the dissertation committees of more than 75 computer education doctoral students. Dr. Moursund founded the International Council for Computers in Education in 1979, which became the International Society for Technology in Education (ISTE) in 1989. He now serves as its Executive Officer for Research, Development, and Evaluation.

KAPPA DELTA PI, International Honor Society in Education, was founded in 1911. Dedicated to scholarship and excellence in education, the Society promotes among its intergenerational  membership of educators the development and dissemination of worthy educational ideas and practices, enhances the continuous growth and leadership of its diverse membership, fosters inquiry and reflection of significant educational issues, and maintains a high degree of professional fellowship. Key to the fulfillment of the mission is the Society's publications program. Kappa Delta Pi's journals, newsletters, books, and booklets address a wide range of issues of interest to educators at all stages of the profession.

Other titles available from KAPPA DELTA PI Publications

Life Cycle of the Career Teacher, by Betty E. Steffy, Michael P. Wolfe, Suzanne H. Pasch, and Billie J. Enz (1999)—$15.00 M; $22.95 NM

Star Principals Serving Children in Poverty, by Martin Haberman (1999)—$12.00 M; $18 NM

Star Teachers of Children in Poverty, by Martin Haberman (1995)—$8.00 M; $15 NM

Experience and Education: The 60th Anniversary Edition, by John Dewey (1998)—$20.00 M; $26 NM (cloth) / $12.00 M; $18 NM (paper)

Teacher Leaders: Making a Difference in Schools, by Nathalie Gehrke and Nancy Sue Romerdahl (1997)—$13.00 M; $20 NM

Substitute Teaching: Planning for Success, edited by Elizabeth S. Manera (1996)—$15.00 M; $20 NM

A.C.T.: All Can Thrive—Supporting Mainstreamed Students, by Marjorie Goldstein and Susan Kuveke (1996)—$8.00 M; $15 NM

At the Essence of Learning: Multicultural Education, by Geneva Gay (1994)—$8.00 M; $15 NM

On Being a Teacher, by Nathalie Gehrke (1987)—$8.00 M; $9.75 NM

To place an order, call 1-800-284-3167, or visit KDP On-line at *www.kdp.org*. Quantity discounts are available, and shipping and handling charges will be applied.

M = KDP Member price
NM = Nonmember price

Have You Heard What They're Saying?

"In small-town America, the illusion of a safe haven is gone forever. It is time to stop standing around assigning blame or waxing existential. These are the behaviors of impotence and passive aggression. We can do more."
—*Vicky Schreiber Dill*

"We cannot have a free society without an enlightened citizenry. People must be able to judge the issues so they can vote intelligently, participate intelligently, and help change the nature of society."
—*Deborah Cannon Partridge Wolfe*

"When the arts are absent from schools, students whose aptitudes or interests lie in the arts are denied the opportunity to find their place in the education sun. The ultimate deprivation is a reduction of the variety and depth of meaning that youngsters can have."
—*Elliot W. Eisner*

"The call for legitimating both curriculum-as-planned and curriculum-as-lived is a call to recognize the living experiences of teachers. Teaching in a live situation is midst the planned and unplanned, between the plannable and the unplannable."
—*Ted Aoki*

"The time has come for educators to join with parents, their schools, and community leaders to say 'no' to money that does not advance the mission of local schools. We must insist that a much larger percentage be made available for plans that address local needs."
—*John Goodlad*

Have you read the *Kappa Delta Pi Record* lately?

If you haven't, you have missed great interviews like these, as well as stimulating articles on Classroom Management and Discipline, Alternative Certification, Conflict Resolution, and Parental Involvement in Learning and Curriculum.

Don't miss out! Call 1-800-284-3167 to order back issues or subscribe to this award-winning publication.

The Educational Forum offers a true forum for the discussion and debate of critical educational issues and practices in the United States and other nations of the world. In this scholarly quarterly, authors with ideologically and culturally diverse viewpoints present educational theories, research, analyses, and criticism of general interest to educators at all levels. Each issue provides readers a thorough study of the specified topic.

Volume 64 1999–2000

Winter 2000 • Unthemed
Spring 2000 • Literacy and Integrated
   Studies
Summer 2000 • Unthemed

Volume 65 2000–2001

Fall 2000 • The Most Important Educational
   Developments of the 20th Century
Winter 2001 • Unthemed

Published by
KAPPA DELTA PI
International Honor
Society in Education